NATURE AND LANDSCAPE

Nature and Landscape: An Introduction to Environmental Aesthetics

ALLEN CARLSON

Columbia University Press   *New York*

Columbia University Press
Publishers Since 1893
New York   Chichester, West Sussex

Copyright © 2009 Columbia University Press
All rights reserved

Library of Congress Cataloging-in-Publication Data
Carlson, Allen.
Nature and landscape : an introduction to environmental
aesthetics / Allen Carlson.
p. cm.
Includes bibliographical references and index.
ISBN 978-0-231-14040-9 (cloth : alk. paper)
ISBN 978-0-231-14041-6 (pbk. : alk. paper)
ISBN 978-0-231-51855-0 (e-book)
1. Environment (Aesthetics)   2. Nature (Aesthetics)
3. Landscape assessment.   I. Title.

BH301.E58C38   2009
111'.85—dc22   2008023538

Columbia University Press books are printed on permanent and durable acid-
free paper.
Printed in the United States of America

c 10 9 8 7 6 5 4 3 2
p 10 9 8 7 6 5 4 3 2

CONTENTS

ILLUSTRATIONS

PREFACE

This book is designed as an introduction to the emerging discipline of environmental aesthetics. It is intended to accompany and complement *Nature, Aesthetics, and Environmentalism: From Beauty to Duty* (New York: Columbia University Press, 2008), edited by Sheila Lintott and me. It also supplements and expands on some of the ideas that are developed in my *Aesthetics and the Environment: The Appreciation of Nature, Art and Architecture* (London: Routledge, 2000).

Some of the chapters were initially conceived as independent pieces investigating particular themes in environmental aesthetics. However, the material has been revised such that it comes together to constitute a unified line of thought. The opening chapter is an overview of environmental aesthetics that presents a clear picture of the discipline. The notes for this chapter extensively reference the current literature in the field and are intended to be a useful resource for those who wish to pursue different topics and read the work of other scholars beyond the discussion that I present. The concluding chapter is also an overview, but of a different kind. It brings together several aspects of my own work in environmental aesthetics and presents them as one point of view. The other five chapters explore specific topics concerning the aesthetic appreciation of both natural and human environments.

I thank Wendy Lochner of Columbia University Press and its editorial board for suggesting that I prepare this volume to complement *Nature, Aesthetics, and Environmentalism*, as well as Columbia's editorial, design, and production staff for their assistance and advice during its preparation for publication.

I also express my appreciation to the Social Sciences and Humanities Research Council of Canada and the University of Alberta for teaching release and financial support for the writing of some of the material in this book. I am especially grateful for a University of Alberta Faculty of Arts McCalla Research Professorship, which allowed me to devote my time fully to research during the 2006/2007 academic year.

Moreover, I thank several individuals and publishers for the use of the material and illustrations that are included in this book. They are listed in the acknowledgments or cited in the captions.

And I am grateful for the comments and suggestions of a number of individuals who attended presentations of the material in these chapters or read earlier versions of them, especially Emily Brady, Baird Callicott, Renee Conroy, Denis Dumas, Marcia Eaton, John Fisher, Stan Godlovitch, Ned Hettinger, Thom Heyd, Andrew Kania, Arlene Kwasniak, Andrew Light, Ron Moore, Joan Nassauer, Alex Neill, Ira Newman, Glenn Parsons, Christopher Preston, Yuriko Saito, Yrjö Sepänmaa, Bob Stecker, Ted Toadvine, Alison Wylie, and Nick Zangwill. They are recognized in the notes of the relevant chapters.

Above all, I express my appreciation to my friends and acquaintances in the discipline of philosophy, to my colleagues in the Department of Philosophy at the University of Alberta, and to the members of my family for their support and encouragement.

Allen Carlson

ACKNOWLEDGMENTS

Although all the material in this book has been revised to constitute a unified study of environmental aesthetics, much of it has been published in other forms and in other places. The following sources are acknowledged:

Chapter 1 is an expanded version of "Environmental Aesthetics," in Edward N. Zalta, ed., *The Stanford Encyclopedia of Philosophy* (Stanford, Calif.: Metaphysics Research Lab, Center for the Study of Language and Information, 2007) (available at http://plato.stanford.edu/entries/environmental-aesthetics/), on which the author holds the copyright. In part, the chapter is expanded with material from "Environmental Aesthetics," in Berys Gaut and Dominic McIver Lopes, eds., *The Routledge Companion to Aesthetics*, 2nd ed. (London: Routledge, 2005), 541–555. It is used with the permission of Taylor & Francis, Ltd.

Chapter 2 is a substantially modified and updated version of "Appreciation and the Natural Environment," *Journal of Aesthetics and Art Criticism* 37 (1979): 267–276. This version, on which the author holds the copyright, initially appeared as "Aesthetic Appreciation of the Natural Environment," in Richard G. Botzler and Susan J. Armstrong, eds., *Environmental Ethics: Divergence and Convergence*, 2nd ed. (Boston: McGraw-Hill, 1998), 108–114.

Chapter 3 is a revised version of "The Requirements for an Adequate Aesthetics of Nature," in Seppo Knuuttila, Erkki Sevänen, and Risto Turunen, eds., *Aesthetic Culture: Essays in Honour of Yrjö Sepänmaa on His Sixtieth Birthday, 12 December 2005* (Helsinki: Maahenki, 2005), 15–34. It is printed with the consent of the editors and the publisher of *Aesthetic Culture*.

Chapter 4 originally appeared as "On Aesthetically Appreciating Human Environments," *Philosophy and Geography* 4 (2001): 9–24. It is reprinted with the permission of Taylor & Francis, Ltd.

Chapter 5 is an extensively revised version of "The Aesthetic Appreciation of Architecture Under Different Conceptions of the Environment," *Journal of Aesthetic Education* 40 (2006): 77–88. It is copyright (2005) by the Board of Trustees of the University of Illinois Press and is used with the permission of the University of Illinois Press.

Chapter 6 originally appeared as "Viljelysmaisemien Esteettinen Arvo Ja Touttavuus" [Productivity and the Aesthetic Value of Agricultural Landscapes], in Yrjö Sepänmaa and Liisa Heikkilä-Palo, eds., *Pellossa Perihopeat* [*Fields: The Family Silver*] (Helsinki: Maahenki, 2005), 52–61. It is printed here for the first time in English and is used with the permission of the editors and the publisher of *Pellossa Perihopeat*.

Chapter 7 is an extensively revised version of "Education for Appreciation: What Is the Correct Curriculum for the Appreciation of Landscapes?" *Journal of Aesthetic Education* 35 (2001): 97–112. It is copyright (2001) by the Board of Trustees of the University of Illinois Press and is used with the permission of the University of Illinois Press.

Different versions of some of this material have also been reprinted in other places: "Aesthetic Appreciation of the Natural Environment," in Susan L. Feagin and Patrick Maynard, eds., *Aesthetics* (Oxford: Oxford University Press, 1997), 30–40; in Alex Neill and Aaron Ridley, eds., *Arguing About Art: Contemporary Philosophical Debates*, 3rd ed. (London: Routledge, 2007), 155–166; and in Allen Carlson and Sheila Lintott, eds., *Nature, Aesthetics, and Environmentalism: From Beauty to Duty* (New York: Columbia University Press, 2008), 119–132; "The Requirements for an Adequate Aesthetics of Nature," *Environmental Philosophy* 4 (2007): 1–12; "On Aesthetically Appreciating Human Environments," in Arnold Berleant and Allen Carlson, eds., *The Aesthetics of Human Environments* (Peterborough, Ont.: Broadview Press, 2007), 47–65; and "Education for Appreciation: What Is the Correct Curriculum for Landscape?" in Andrew Light and Jonathan M. Smith, eds., *The Aesthetics of Everyday Life* (New York: Columbia University Press, 2005), 92–108, and as "Tarkasteluum Kasvattaminen: Mikä on Olennaista Maisemassa?" [Aesthetic Experience: What Is Relevant to Landscape?], in

Yrjö Sepänmaa, Liisa Heikkilä-Palo, and Virpi Kaukio, eds., *Maiseman Kanssa Kasvokkain* [*Face to Face with the Landscape*] (Helsinki: Maahenki, 2007), 92–107. In addition, some of the material has been translated into Chinese by Li-bo Chen and published as *Nature and Landscape* (Changsha: Hunan Publishing House, 2005).

NATURE AND LANDSCAPE

1 / THE DEVELOPMENT AND NATURE
OF ENVIRONMENTAL AESTHETICS

In this chapter, I present an overview of environmental aesthetics.[1] It includes a sketch of the historical background to the field and an account of the more recent circumstances that have contributed to its development. I also summarize different contemporary positions on both the natural and the human environment as well as discuss the relationship between environmental aesthetics and environmentalism. Finally, I present the current nature and scope of the field. The overview is designed to introduce the subject matter of environmental aesthetics and to clarify the essential issues that will be addressed in the chapters that follow. This chapter has a very extensive set of notes, which will facilitate following up the themes and positions that are introduced throughout the chapter.

Environmental aesthetics is one of the two or three major areas of aesthetics to have emerged in the second half of the twentieth century. Before the emergence of the field, aesthetics within analytic philosophy was concerned largely with the philosophy of art. Environmental aesthetics originated as a reaction to this emphasis, pursuing instead the investigation of the aesthetic appreciation of natural environments. The scope of environmental aesthetics has since broadened to include not simply natural environments but also human-influenced and human-constructed ones. At the same time, the discipline has also come to include the examination of that which falls within such environments, giving rise to what is called the aesthetics of everyday life. This area involves the aesthetics of not only more common objects and environments, but also a range of everyday activities. Thus in the early twenty-first century, environmental aesthetics embraces the study of the aesthetic significance of almost everything other than art.

Although the field has come into its own only recently and now treats human as well as natural environments, it has historical roots in earlier philosophical work on the aesthetic experience of nature. In the eighteenth and nineteenth centuries, there were important advances in the aesthetics of nature. They included the development of the idea of nature as an ideal object of aesthetic experience, the emergence of concepts such as the picturesque, and the introduction of the notion of positive aesthetics. These ideas continue to play a role in contemporary work in environmental aesthetics, especially in the context of its relationship to environmentalism, which I consider later in this chapter. Thus to understand the current nature of the field, it is useful to briefly examine its historical background and the developments that followed from it.

AESTHETICS OF NATURE IN THE EIGHTEENTH CENTURY

The first major philosophical developments in the aesthetics of nature occurred in the eighteenth century, when the founders of modern aesthetics began to take nature rather than art as the paradigmatic object of aesthetic experience. At the same time, they also developed the concept of disinterestedness as the mark of such experience. Over the century, this concept was elaborated by various thinkers, who employed it to purge from aesthetic appreciation an ever-increasing range of interests and associations. According to one standard account, the concept originated primarily with the third Earl of Shaftesbury (Anthony Ashley Cooper), who introduced it as a way to characterize the notion of the aesthetic as distinct from that of personal interest or concern. Later it was embellished by Francis Hutcheson, who expanded it to exclude from aesthetic experience not simply personal and utilitarian interests, but also more general kinds of associations. Toward the end of the century, it was further developed by Archibald Alison, who took it to refer to a particular state of mind, which he famously described as "vacant and unemployed."[2] The concept of disinterestedness finally was given its classic formulation in Immanuel Kant's *Critique of the Power of Judgment*, in which nature is taken as an exemplary object of aesthetic experience.[3] Kant argued that the beauty of nature is superior to that of art and that it complements the best habits of mind. It is no accident that the development of the concept of disinterestedness and the acceptance of nature as an ideal object of aesthetic appreciation went hand in hand. The clarification of the notion of the aesthetic in terms of the concept of disinterestedness dissociated the aesthetic appreciation of nature from the appreciator's particular personal, religious, economic, or utilitarian interests, any of which could impede aesthetic experience.

The theory of disinterestedness also provided groundwork for understanding the aesthetic dimensions of nature in terms of three distinct conceptualizations. The first involved the idea of the *beautiful*, which readily applies to tamed and cultivated European gardens and landscapes. The second centered on the concept of the *sublime*. In the experience of the sublime, the more threatening and terrifying of nature's manifestations, such as mountains and wilderness, when viewed with disinterestedness, can be aesthetically appreciated, rather than simply feared or despised. These two notions were importantly elaborated by Edmund Burke and Kant.[4] However, concerning the appreciation of nature, a third concept was to become more significant than either the beautiful or the sublime: the notion of the *picturesque*. Thus by the end of the eighteenth century, each of three clearly different ideas about the aesthetics of nature was focusing on distinct aspects of nature's diverse and often contrasting moods. One historian of the picturesque summarizes the differences: beautiful objects tend to be small and smooth, but subtly varied, delicate, and fair in color, while sublime things, by contrast, are powerful, vast, intense, and terrifying. Picturesque items are typically in the middle ground between those that are beautiful and those that are sublime, being complex and eccentric, varied and irregular, rich and forceful, and vibrant with energy.[5]

It is not surprising that of these three notions, the picturesque, rather than the beautiful or the sublime, achieved the greatest prominence in regard to the aesthetic experience of nature.[6] Not only does it occupy the extensive middle ground of the complex, irregular, forceful, and vibrant—all of which abound in the natural world—but it reinforces various long-standing connections between the aesthetic appreciation of nature and the treatment of nature in art. The term "picturesque" literally means "picture-like," and the theory of the picturesque advocates aesthetic appreciation in which the natural world is experienced as though divided into art-like scenes, which ideally resemble works of art, especially landscape painting, in both subject matter and composition. Thus since the concept of disinterestedness mandated appreciation of nature stripped of the appreciator's own personal interests and associations, it helped to clear the ground for experience of nature governed by the idea of the picturesque, by which the appreciator is encouraged to see nature in terms of a new set of artistic images and associations. In this way, the idea of the picturesque relates to earlier conceptions of the natural world as composed of what were called the works of nature, which, although considered proper and important objects of aesthetic experience, were thought to be more appealing when they resembled works of art. The idea also resonates with other artistic traditions, such as that of viewing art as the mirror of nature.

The theory of the picturesque received its fullest treatment in the late eighteenth century, when it was popularized in the writings of William Gilpin, Uvedale Price, and Richard Payne Knight.[7] At that time, it provided an aesthetic ideal for English tourists, who pursued picturesque scenery in the English Lake District, the Scottish Highlands, and the Swiss Alps. Following its articulation in the eighteenth century, the idea of the picturesque remained a dominant influence on popular aesthetic experience of nature throughout the nineteenth and well into the twentieth century. Indeed, the picturesque is still an important component of the kind of aesthetic experience commonly associated with ordinary tourism, which involves seeing and appreciating the natural world as it is represented in the depictions found in travel brochures, calendar photos, and picture postcards. In short, the idea of the picturesque has been and continues to be an important factor in our aesthetic experience. (I return to the influence of the picturesque later in this chapter, in chapter 2, and especially in chapter 6, where I investigate its significance for the aesthetic appreciation of particular kinds of human environments.)

AESTHETICS OF NATURE IN THE NINETEENTH CENTURY

In the nineteenth century, the aesthetics of nature took a new direction. Although the idea of the picturesque continued to guide popular aesthetic appreciation of nature, the philosophical study of the aesthetics of nature, after flowering in the eighteenth century, went into steady decline. Many of the main themes—such as the concept of the sublime, the notion of disinterestedness, and the theoretical centrality of nature rather than art—culminated with Kant, who had given some of them such exhaustive treatment that a kind of philosophical closure was seemingly achieved. Following Kant, a new world order was initiated by G. W. F. Hegel. In his philosophy, art is the highest expression of "Absolute Spirit," and it, rather than nature, was destined to become the favored subject of philosophical aesthetics.[8] Thus in the wake of Hegel, the theoretical study of the aesthetics of nature almost came to an end. In the nineteenth century, both on the Continent and in Great Britain, only a few philosophers and a scattering of thinkers of the Romantic movement seriously treated the aesthetic experience of nature. There was no theoretical work comparable to that of the eighteenth century.

As the philosophical study of the aesthetics of nature languished in Europe, however, a new way of understanding the aesthetic appreciation of the natural world was developing in North America. This conception of nature appreciation had its roots in the American tradition of nature writing, as exemplified in the essays of Henry David Thoreau.[9] It was initially influenced by the idea of the picturesque, especially in its artistic manifestations, such as the paintings of Thomas Cole and his pupil Frederick Church. As nature writing became its more dominant form of expression, though, the conception of nature appreciation was increasingly shaped by developments in the natural sciences. In the middle of the nineteenth century, it was further influenced by the geographical work of George Perkins Marsh, who argued that humanity was increasingly causing the destruction of the beauty of nature. He regarded humanity as "the great disturber of nature's harmonies," claiming that of all of nature's blessings, natural beauty alone is only disrupted, not ennobled, by humans—for "unaided nature," even in a "degraded state, enchant[s] every eye."[10] Marsh's contentions helped to shift the focus of the appreciation of nature away from the human-centered idea of the picturesque and toward a more naturalistic approach, thereby foreshadowing many of the ideas of contemporary environmentalism. His writings have been described as "the fountain-head of the conservation movement."[11]

This new approach to the aesthetics of nature was most forcefully presented toward the end of the century in the work of American naturalist John Muir, who explicitly distinguished this kind of understanding of aesthetic appreciation from that governed by the idea of the picturesque. In a well-known essay, "A Near View of the High Sierra," Muir described two of his artist companions, who focused exclusively on mountain *scenery*, as exemplifying aesthetic experience of nature as guided by the idea of the picturesque.[12] This is contrasted with Muir's own aesthetic experience, which involved an interest in and appreciation of the mountain environment akin to that of a geologist. This sort of approach to experiencing nature eventually brought Muir to see the whole of the natural environment, especially wild nature, as aesthetically beautiful and to find ugliness only where nature was subject to human intrusion. The range of things that he regarded as aesthetically appreciable seemed to encompass the entire natural world, from creatures considered hideous in his day, such as snakes and alligators, to natural disasters thought to ruin the environment, such as floods and earthquakes. For example, about the alligator, he said: "[D]oubtless these creatures are happy and fill the place assigned to them by the great Creator of us all. Fierce and cruel they appear to us, but beautiful in the eyes of God."[13] And his response to the Inyo earthquake, which struck Yosemite Valley in 1872, was: "A noble earthquake! . . . a terrible sublime and beautiful spectacle."[14]

The kind of nature appreciation that was practiced by Muir has become associated with the contemporary point of view called positive aesthetics, which is the contention that untouched, pristine nature has only or primarily positive aesthetic qualities. I return to positive aesthetics later is this chapter. Here it is significant to note that insofar as such appreciation eschews humanity's marks on the natural environment, it is somewhat the converse of aesthetic appreciation influenced by the idea of the picturesque, which finds interest and delight in evidence of human presence.

ENVIRONMENTAL AESTHETICS IN THE TWENTIETH CENTURY

The ideas developed in the nineteenth century about the appreciation of nature continued to flourish in the first half of the twentieth century. Nonetheless, during that time, philosophers largely ignored the aesthetics of nature. There were some noteworthy exceptions. In North America, for example, George Santayana investigated the topic as well as the concept of nature itself.[15] Somewhat later, John Dewey contributed to the understanding of the aesthetic experience of both nature and everyday life, and Curt Ducasse discussed the beauty of nature as well as that of the human form.[16] In England, R. G. Collingwood worked on both the philosophy of art and the idea of nature, but the two topics did not significantly come together in his thought.[17] Other exceptions included Arthur Lovejoy and Harold Osborne.[18] Aside from a few such individuals, however, as far as aesthetics was pursued in the first half of the twentieth century, no philosophers seriously considered the aesthetics of nature.

On the contrary, the discipline was completely dominated by an interest in art. Throughout the first part of the century, the two major aesthetic theories were the formalist theory and the expressionist theory, both of which were concerned almost exclusively with the nature of art.[19] Likewise, as far as the idea of disinterestedness was defended, as in the psychical distance theory of psychologist Edward Bullough and the aesthetic attitude theory of aesthetician Jerome Stolnitz, it was mainly in regard to the aesthetic appreciation of art.[20] Moreover, even later developments in twentieth-century aesthetics, such as the rejection of disinterestedness as the central concept of aesthetic theory, did little to change the situation.[21] They helped to supplant the earlier formalist and expressionist theories and cleared the way for cultural theories of art, such as the institutional theory of philosopher George Dickie. Yet even these newer theories only reinforced the exclusive interest in art by placing it in what become known as the "artworld."[22] The artworld is essentially the cultural context of art making, art criticism, and art appreciation, a context that is separate from those of both the everyday world and the natural world.[23]

Thus throughout much of the twentieth century, the theoretical marginalization of the aesthetic appreciation of anything other than art was ubiquitous. At mid-century, within analytic philosophy, the principal philosophical school in the English-speaking world at that time, the discipline of aesthetics was virtually equated with the philosophy of art. The leading textbook in the field was *Aesthetics: Problems in the Philosophy of Criticism*, and the two major aesthetics anthologies were *Philosophy Looks at the Arts* and *Art and Philosophy*.[24] With a total of 1,527 pages among them, none of these volumes, each a classic of its kind, even mentions the aesthetics of nature. Indeed, the textbook opens with the assertion: "There would be no problems of aesthetics, in the sense in which I propose to mark out this field of study, if no one ever talked about works of art."[25] This comment was meant to emphasize the importance of the analysis of language, but it also reveals the art-dominated construal of aesthetics at that time. Moreover, if and when the aesthetic appreciation of nature was discussed, it was treated—unlike that of art—as a messy, subjective business of less philosophical interest. Some of the major aestheticians of the second half of the twentieth century have argued that aesthetic judgments beyond the artworld must remain relative to conditions of appreciation and unfettered by the kind of constraints that govern the appreciation of art.[26]

The domination of the discipline of aesthetics by an interest in art has had two ramifications. On the one hand, it helps to motivate a controversial philosophical position that denies the possibility of any aesthetic experience of nature. The view contends that aesthetic appreciation necessarily involves aesthetic judgments, which entail considering the object of appreciation as the achievement of a designing intellect. However, since nature is not the product of a designing intellect, its appreciation is not aesthetic.[27] On the other hand, the art-dominated construal of aesthetics also gives support to approaches that stand within the many different historical traditions that conceptualize the natural world as essentially art-like—for instance, as a set of "works of nature," as the "handiwork" of a creator, or as picturesque scenery. For example, the tradition of the picturesque gives rise to what might be called a landscape model of nature appreciation, which proposes that we should aesthetically experience nature as we appreciate landscape paintings. This requires seeing nature to some extent as though it were a series of two-dimensional scenes and focusing on artistic and formal aesthetic qualities. Such art-based models of the aesthetic appreciation of nature are supported by powerful and long-standing traditions of thought.[28] Moreover, they are defended in some recent work in environmental aesthetics.[29] Likewise, the defense of the appreciation of nature in terms of formal aesthetic qualities has recently been renewed.[30]

Although both the nonaesthetic position and the art-oriented approaches to nature appreciation find some grounding in analytic aesthetics' reduction of aesthetics to philosophy of art, they are thought by some philosophers to be deeply counterintuitive. Concerning the former, many of our fundamental paradigms of aesthetic experience seem to be instances of appreciation of nature, such as our delight in a sunset or a bird in flight. Moreover, the Western tradition in aesthetics, as well as other traditions, such as the Japanese, has long been committed to a doctrine that explicitly contradicts the nonaesthetic conception of nature appreciation: the conviction that, as one philosopher expresses it, anything that can be viewed can be viewed aesthetically.[31] Concerning the art-based approaches, it is argued that they do not fully realize the serious, appropriate appreciation of nature, but distort the true character of natural environments; for example, the landscape model recommends framing and flattening environments into scenery. The problem, in short, is that they do not acknowledge the importance of aesthetically appreciating nature, as a leading aesthetician puts it, "as nature."[32] (I return to these and related problems with both approaches in chapters 2 and 3.)

In the last third of the twentieth century, a renewed interest in the aesthetics of nature emerged. This revival was the result of several factors. In part, it was a response to the growing public concern about the apparent degeneration of the environment, aesthetic and otherwise.[33] It was also a result of the academic world's becoming aware of the significance of the environmental movement—at the level of both theoretical discussion and practical action. Some of the earlier work in environmental aesthetics focused on empirical research that was conducted in response to the newly developing public apprehension about the aesthetic state of the environment.[34] Critics argued that the landscape-assessment and -planning techniques used in environmental management were inadequate because they stressed mainly formal features, but overlooked expressive and other kinds of aesthetic qualities.[35] Empirical approaches were also faulted for being fixated on "scenic beauty" and unduly influenced by ideas such as the picturesque.[36] These and other problems were attributed to the lack of an adequate theoretical framework; research was said to be conducted in a "theoretical vacuum."[37] Attempts to fill this theoretical vacuum prompted the idea of sociobiological underpinnings for the aesthetic appreciation of nature, such as "prospect-refuge theory" and other evolution-related approaches.[38] In addition, the concerns of this period motivated the development of a variety of theoretical models of aesthetic response grounded in, for example, developmental and environmental psychology.[39] There are several overviews and collections of this and related kinds of more empirically oriented research.[40] Moreover, a number of philosophers more recently have addressed various theoretical issues related to this research.[41]

Within philosophical aesthetics itself, however, the renewed interested in the aesthetics of nature was also fueled by another development: the publication of Ronald Hepburn's seminal article, "Contemporary Aesthetics and the Neglect of Natural Beauty."[42] Hepburn's essay helped to set the agenda for the aesthetics of nature in the late twentieth century. After noting that by essentially reducing all of aesthetics to the philosophy of art, analytic aesthetics had virtually ignored the natural world, Hepburn argued that the appreciation of art frequently provides misleading models for the appreciation of nature. However, he also observed that there is in the aesthetic appreciation of nature, as in that of art, a distinction between appreciation that is only trivial and superficial and that which is serious and deep.[43] He furthermore suggested that for nature, such serious appreciation may require new and different approaches that can accommodate not only nature's indeterminate and varying character, but also both our multisensory experience and our diverse understanding of it. By focusing attention on natural beauty, Hepburn demonstrated that there can be significant philosophical investigation of the aesthetic experience of the world beyond the artworld. He thereby not only generated renewed interest in the aesthetics of nature, but also laid foundations for environmental aesthetics in general as well as for the aesthetics of everyday life.

CONTEMPORARY POSITIONS IN ENVIRONMENTAL AESTHETICS

Following in the wake of earlier critical work in environmental aesthetics and influenced by Hepburn's groundbreaking article, several kinds of approaches to the appreciation of environments developed toward the end of the twentieth century. These initial contemporary positions involve different points of view about the aesthetic appreciation of nature. They are frequently divided into two camps, alternatively labeled "cognitive" and "noncognitive," "conceptual" and "nonconceptual," or "narrative" and "ambient."[44] Within each camp, a number of distinct positions have emerged.

The cognitive (conceptual or narrative) positions in environmental aesthetics are united by the idea that knowledge about the nature of an object of appreciation is central to its aesthetic appreciation. Thus they champion the notion that nature must be appreciated, as one author puts it, "on its own terms."[45] These positions tend to reject aesthetic approaches to environments, such as that governed by the idea of the picturesque, that draw heavily on the aesthetic experience of art for modeling the appreciation of nature. Yet they affirm that art appreciation can show some of what is required in an adequate account of nature appreciation. For example, in the serious, appropriate aesthetic appreciation of art, it is taken to be essential that we experience works as what they in fact are and in light of knowledge of their real natures. Thus, for instance, the appropriate appreciation of a work such as Picasso's *Guernica* (1937) requires that we experience it as a painting and, moreover, as a Cubist painting, and therefore that we appreciate it in light of our knowledge of paintings in general and of Cubist paintings in particular.[46]

Following this general line of thought, one cognitive approach holds that nature appreciation should be analogous in this respect to art appreciation. The position is labeled the Natural Environmental Model, or scientific cognitivism.[47] It argues that just as the serious, appropriate aesthetic appreciation of art requires knowledge of art history and art criticism, the aesthetic appreciation of nature requires knowledge of natural history—that provided by the natural sciences, especially geology, biology, and ecology. The idea is that scientific knowledge about nature can reveal the actual aesthetic qualities of natural objects and environments in the way that knowledge about art history and art criticism can for works of art. In short, to appropriately aesthetically appreciate nature "on its own terms" is to appreciate it as it is characterized by natural science.[48] (I discuss the Natural Environmental Model in chapter 2 and further defend it in chapter 3.)

Other cognitive or quasi-cognitive approaches to the aesthetic appreciation of environments differ from scientific cognitivism in regard to either the kind of cognitive resources taken to be relevant to such appreciation or the degree to which these resources are considered relevant. On the one hand, several cognitive models emphasize different kinds of information, claiming that appreciating nature "on its own terms" may well involve experiencing it in light of various cultural and historical traditions. Thus in appropriate aesthetic appreciation, local and regional narratives, folklore, and even mythological stories about nature are endorsed either as complementary to or as alternative to scientific knowledge.[49] On the other hand, another at least quasi-cognitive approach strongly supports the idea that nature must be appreciated "as nature." The justification for accepting the "as nature" restriction is that the aesthetic experience of nature should be true to what nature actually is. This, however, is the extent of the position's cognitivism. It rejects the idea that scientific knowledge about nature can reveal the actual aesthetic qualities of natural objects and environments in the way that knowledge about art history and art criticism can for works of art. Moreover, it holds that, unlike the case with art, many of the most significant aesthetic dimensions of natural objects and environments are relative to conditions of observation. Thus the aesthetic appreciation of nature is taken to allow a degree of freedom that is denied to the aesthetic appreciation of art.[50] (I consider this "freedom approach" as well as other cognitive and quasi-cognitive accounts more fully in chapter 3.)

Standing in contrast to the cognitive positions in environmental aesthetics are several noncognitive (nonconceptual or ambient) approaches. The word "noncognitive" should not be taken in its older philosophical sense, as meaning primarily or only "emotive." Rather, it indicates simply that these views hold that something other than a cognitive component, such as scientific knowledge or cultural tradition, is the central feature of the aesthetic appreciation of environments.

The leading noncognitive approach, called the Aesthetics of Engagement, rejects many of the traditional ideas about aesthetic appreciation not only for nature, but also for art. It argues that the theory of disinterestedness involves a mistaken analysis of the concept of the aesthetic and that this is most evident in the aesthetic experience of natural environments. According to the engagement approach, disinterested appreciation—with its isolating, distancing, and objectifying gaze—is out of place in the aesthetic experience of nature, for it wrongly abstracts both natural objects and appreciators from the environments in which they properly belong and in which appropriate appreciation is achieved. Thus the Aesthetics of Engagement stresses the contextual dimensions of nature and our multisensory experience of it. Viewing the environment as a seamless unity of places, organisms, and perceptions, it challenges the importance of traditional dichotomies, such as that between subject and object. It beckons appreciators to immerse themselves in the natural environment and to reduce to as small a degree as possible the distance between themselves and the natural world. In short, appropriate aesthetic experience is held to involve the total immersion of the appreciator in the object of appreciation.[51] (I return to the Aesthetics of Engagement in chapters 2 and 3.)

Other noncognitive positions in environmental aesthetics contend that dimensions other than engagement are central to aesthetic experience. What is known as the arousal model holds that we may appreciate nature simply by opening ourselves to it and being emotionally aroused by it. On this view, a less intellectual, more visceral experience of nature constitutes a legitimate way of aesthetically appreciating it that does not require any knowledge gained from science or elsewhere.[52] Another alternative similarly argues that neither scientific nor any other kind of knowledge facilitates real, appropriate appreciation of nature—not because such appreciation need involve only emotional arousal, but because nature itself is essentially alien, aloof, distant, and unknowable. This position, which may be called the mystery model, contends that an appropriate experience of nature incorporates a sense of being separate from it and not belonging to it—a sense of mystery that involves a state of appreciative incomprehension.[53]

A fourth noncognitive approach brings together several features thought to be relevant to nature appreciation. It attempts to balance the notion of engagement and the traditional idea of disinterestedness, while giving center stage to imagination. This position distinguishes a number of kinds of imagination—associative, metaphorical, exploratory, projective, ampliative, and revelatory. It also responds to concerns that imagination introduces subjectivity, by appealing to factors such as guidance by the object of appreciation, the constraining role of disinterestedness, and the notion of "imagining well."[54] A related point of view, which stresses the metaphysical dimensions of imagination, may also be placed in the noncognitive camp, although doing so requires making certain assumptions about the cognitive content of metaphysical speculation. According to this account, the imagination interprets nature as revealing metaphysical insights about such things as the meaning of life, the human condition, or our place in the cosmos. Thus this position includes within appropriate aesthetic experience of nature those abstract meditations and ruminations about ultimate reality that our encounters with nature sometimes engender.[55] (I have considered some of these noncognitive approaches elsewhere and discuss them in more detail in chapter 3.)[56]

AESTHETICS OF HUMAN ENVIRONMENTS

The current positions in environmental aesthetics have been developed, by and large, in regard to the aesthetic appreciation of natural environments. More recently, however, the various approaches in environmental aesthetics have expanded from this initial focus to consider human and human-influenced environments and to include an aesthetic investigation of everyday life in general. Each of the cognitive and noncognitive camps in environmental aesthetics has resources that may be brought to bear on the aesthetic investigation of human and human-influenced environments as well as everyday life.

The cognitive accounts hold that the appropriate aesthetic appreciation of human environments, like that of natural environments, depends on knowledge of what something is, what it is like, and why it is as it is. Thus for human and human-influenced environments, both rural and urban—such as the landscapes of agriculture, mining, and industry—what is relevant to appropriate appreciation is information about their histories, their functions, and their roles in our lives.[57] Thus the cognitive approaches contend, parallel to the Natural Environment Model, that the aesthetic appreciation of human environments should be informed by, in addition to the natural sciences, the social sciences: history, geography, anthropology, and sociology. One version of this view draws an analogy between the functioning of the human environment and that of the natural environment, arguing for what is called an ecological approach to the aesthetics of human environments.[58] (I develop these ideas in chapters 4–6.)

Some cognitively oriented accounts also stress, as they do in the case of natural environments, the aesthetic potential of cultural traditions in the aesthetic experience of human environments. Such traditions seem especially relevant to the appreciation of what might be termed cultural landscapes—environments that constitute important places in the cultures and histories of particular groups of people. What is often called a sense of place, together with ideas and images from folklore and mythology, frequently plays a significant role in individuals' aesthetic experience of their home environments.[59] Similarly, the aesthetic significance of religion—for example, Christianity in the West and Buddhism in the East—has not been overlooked.[60] Granting the aesthetic relevance of all such information may provide grounds for a rather pluralistic or even relativistic theory of the aesthetic appreciation of landscapes. (I return to the idea of a sense of place in chapter 5 and to landscape relativism, landscape pluralism, and the aesthetic relevance of folklore, mythology, and religion in chapter 7.)

The noncognitive approaches to environmental aesthetics also provide several channels for exploring the aesthetics of human and human-influenced environments and, especially, for pursuing the aesthetics of everyday life. The Aesthetics of Engagement is presented as a model for the aesthetic appreciation of not simply both nature and art, but also just about everything else. It studies the aesthetic dimensions of small towns, large cities, theme parks, museums, and the like.[61] Moreover, under the name social aesthetics, it even investigates the aesthetics of human relationships, delving into the idea of "getting along beautifully."[62] Likewise, accounts that emphasize imagination help us to understand our responses, aesthetic and otherwise, to everything from our exploiting of environments to our smelling and tasting of them.[63]

Fruitful approaches to the aesthetic appreciation of human environments and other aspects of everyday life can also be found in views that draw on features of both the cognitive and the noncognitive camp. Several attempts have been made to forge connections between the two orientations, with respect to both the natural and the human environment.[64] Moreover, numerous studies, without being totally either cognitive or noncognitive, inform our understanding of the aesthetic appreciation of commonplace human environments, such as rural countrysides and urban cityscapes, as well as more specialized environments, such as shopping centers.[65] Beyond the consideration of these large, public environments, the aesthetics of everyday life becomes especially relevant.[66] It investigates not only the aesthetic qualities of smaller, more personal environments, such as individual living spaces—for example, yards and houses—but also the aesthetic dimensions of normal day-to-day experiences.[67] In addition, it considers such everyday activities as playing sports and dining.[68] Several recent collections focus on the aesthetics of human environments and of everyday objects, activities, and events.[69]

With the aesthetic investigation of, say, sports and food, the aesthetics of everyday life begins to come full circle, connecting environmental aesthetics with the edges of more traditional aesthetics. At this point, environmental aesthetics makes contact with the philosophy of borderline art forms, not only the "arts" of sport and cuisine, but also the art of gardening.[70] Moreover, the arts of landscaping, planning, and architecture are addressed.[71] With the consideration of landscaping and related activities, environmental aesthetics also touches base with more traditional fields of environmental investigation, such as landscape ecology and cultural geography.[72] In addition, it connects to the tradition of what may be called, for lack of a better phrase, landscape criticism.[73]

And finally, but now in the context of environmental aesthetics, there is a return to the consideration of the traditional art forms. Poetry, painting, sculpture, dance, and music are explored and reexplored— both as aesthetically significant dimensions of our everyday experiences and for their roles in shaping the aesthetic appreciation of both the natural and human worlds.[74] Newer art forms, such as film and environmental art, are likewise pursued.[75] Many of these more recent investigations of the arts seem to avoid the old pitfalls (noted earlier and discussed more fully in chapters 2, 4, and 6) of imposing restrictive artistic models on the appreciation of either natural or human environments. (I consider the relevance of art and literature to the appreciation of landscapes in chapters 6 and 7.)

ENVIRONMENTAL AESTHETICS AND ENVIRONMENTALISM

In addition to the focus on the aesthetics of human environments and everyday life, a recent development in environmental aesthetics involves the investigation of the relationship between environmental aesthetics and environmentalism. On the one hand, this has resulted in extensive criticism of earlier work in the aesthetics of nature as well as detailed assessments of the current positions.[76] On the other, it has spawned an increasing number of attempts to utilize environmental aesthetics to promote an environmental agenda. Concerning the latter development, as in the case of the growth of the aesthetics of human environments, approaches that combine the resources of both cognitive and noncognitive points of view seem especially fruitful.

Some of the discussion of the relationship between environmentalism and the positions and ideas of environmental aesthetics stems from the aesthetics of nature developed in the eighteenth and nineteenth centuries. As noted earlier, in the nineteenth and early twentieth centuries, appreciation of and concern for the environment in both Europe and North America were fostered by picturesque-influenced tourism that was grounded in eighteenth-century aesthetics of nature.[77] Moreover, the early environmental movements, especially in North America, were largely fueled by a mode of aesthetic appreciation shaped not only by the notion of the picturesque but also by the ideas developed by thinkers such as Muir.[78] The latter ideas are exemplified in positive aesthetics, which, given its commitment to the positive aesthetic value of nature, seemingly constitutes a firm foundation for environmentalism.

In other ways, though, the relationship between environmental aesthetics and environmentalism is less congenial. Individuals interested in the conservation and protection of both natural and human heritage environments have not always found in the traditional aesthetics of nature the resources that they believe they need in order to carry out an environmental agenda. The problem is especially acute with environments, such as wetlands, that do not fit conventional conceptions of scenic beauty.[79] In line with the criticisms that much of the empirical work in landscape assessment and planning is fixated on "scenic beauty" and unduly influenced by ideas such as the picturesque, much of the historical tradition of the aesthetic appreciation of nature has come under attack. Various themes in the aesthetics of nature, such as appreciation grounded in the idea of the picturesque, have been criticized in a number of ways: as anthropocentric, scenery-obsessed, trivial, subjective, and/or morally vacuous.[80] Similarly, in agreement with the critique by the Aesthetics of Engagement of the theory of disinterestedness, some find that concept to be questionable from an environmental standpoint.

There are a variety of responses to these kinds of criticisms of the traditional aesthetics of nature and the notions of disinterestedness and the picturesque. Some philosophers argue that although the idea of the picturesque may indeed be questionable, the theory of disinterestedness is yet essential, since without it the notion of the aesthetic itself lacks conceptual grounding.[81] Moreover, others claim that an analysis of aesthetic experience in terms of the concept of disinterestedness helps to meet the charge that traditional aesthetics is anthropocentric and subjective, since such an analysis supports the objectivity of aesthetic judgments.[82] The allegation of anthropocentricity is explicitly addressed by the mystery model, which attempts to give the aesthetic appreciation of nature what is called an acentric basis—that is, a basis that does not presuppose a view from any particular perspective, human or otherwise.[83] Similarly, the resources of other noncognitive positions, especially the Aesthetics of Engagement, are taken to counter the criticism that, due to the influence of ideas such as the picturesque, the aesthetic experience of nature must be both anthropocentric and scenery-obsessed.[84]

The cognitive accounts also furnish replies to some of these charges. Scientific cognitivism in particular, with its focus on scientific knowledge, which is a paradigm of objectivity, is said to help meet the concern that the aesthetic appreciation of environments is of little significance in environmental conservation and protection, since it is subjective.[85] Moreover, the accusation of triviality is addressed in that this kind of view is interpreted as an "ecological aesthetic" in the tradition of Aldo Leopold, who linked the beauty of nature to ecological integrity and stability.[86] Thus it is endorsed by environmental philosophers who are concerned to bring our aesthetic appreciation of environments, both natural and human, in line with our environmental and moral responsibilities to maintain ecological health.[87] In this sense, it also speaks to the charge that traditional aesthetic appreciation is morally vacuous.

Unlike that of the picturesque, the historical tradition that connects the aesthetic appreciation of nature with positive aesthetics has been embraced by some environmental philosophers.[88] Moreover, the contention that untouched, pristine nature has only or primarily positive aesthetic qualities has been related to scientific cognitivism. Some suggest that linking the appreciation of nature to scientific knowledge explains how positive aesthetic appreciation is nurtured by a scientific worldview that increasingly interprets the natural world as having such positive aesthetic qualities as order, balance, unity, and harmony.[89] Others regard the relationship between scientific cognitivism and positive aesthetics somewhat conversely, arguing that the latter should simply be assumed, in which case it provides support for the former.[90] Nonetheless, several aestheticians and environmental philosophers think that positive aesthetics is problematic, since it appears to undercut the possibility of the kind of comparative assessments of the aesthetic value of nature that seem necessary for environmental planning and protection.[91] Other philosophers find the perspective of positive aesthetics to be unintuitive, obscure, and/or inadequately justified.[92]

In light of this kind of uncertainty and debate, at least from the point of view of environmentalism, perhaps the proposals most useful for supporting conservation and protection of all kinds of environments are those that do not depend on any one particular model of aesthetic appreciation, but attempt to constructively bring together the resources of several approaches.[93] For example, there are efforts by some philosophers to combine elements of cognitive perspectives with noncognitive points of view, such as imagination-based models.[94] Others combine a cognitive approach with aspects of the Aesthetics of

Engagement.[95] Such research points the way toward innovative, eclectic approaches in environmental aesthetics that may be the most successful in furthering a wide range of environmentalist goals and practices.[96] (I return to some of these issues in chapter 5 and develop a somewhat eclectic approach in chapter 7.)

THE NATURE OF ENVIRONMENTAL AESTHETICS

What, then, is the nature of the emerging field of environmental aesthetics? In concluding this introductory chapter, I want to emphasize three points that will become more evident in the following chapters.

The first is that, as noted in conjunction with the relationship between environmental aesthetics and environmentalism, there is some movement toward a convergence of the cognitive and noncognitive lines of thought. This potential consolidation of the field provides a viable alternative to some of the older ideas about the appreciation of environments, such as appreciation influenced by the notion of the picturesque or as primarily distanced contemplation of artistic and formal qualities. Moreover, insofar as this point of view parallels contemporary theories about the aesthetic experience of art, it offers a new path toward reinstating the traditional symmetry between the appreciation of art and that of the rest of the world. In this new approach, instead of the appreciation of the latter simply being modeled on that of the former, both realms are aesthetically experienced *as* what they are.

The second point concerns the scope of environmental aesthetics. Given the richness and diversity of the field, its scope is almost limitless. It extends from pristine nature to the borders of traditional art. It ranges from wilderness; through rural landscapes and countrysides; to cityscapes, neighborhoods, amusement parks, shopping centers, and beyond. It stretches from large environments that can completely surround us—dense forests, fields of grain, and downtowns of cities—to smaller and more intimate ones—backyards, offices, and living spaces. Moreover, it reaches into all these kinds of environments to consider the everyday objects, events, and activities that occupy them. In addition, it treats the ordinary and the mundane as well as the extraordinary and the exotic. Just as environmental aesthetics is not limited to the large, it is not limited to the spectacular. Ordinary scenery, commonplace sights, and day-to-day activities and experiences are proper objects of aesthetic appreciation. Environmental aesthetics is developing into the aesthetics of everyday life.

The third point is that, in light of the current approaches to the aesthetic appreciation of environments and in line with the limitless scope of the field, environmental aesthetics embodies the view that every environment—natural, rural, or urban; large or small; ordinary or extraordinary—offers much to aesthetically appreciate. Our different environments and their objects, events, and activities can be as aesthetically rich and rewarding as are the very best of our works of art. In the chapters that follow, I investigate exactly how and why this is so.

2 / AESTHETIC APPRECIATION
AND THE NATURAL ENVIRONMENT

Having outlined several approaches to understanding the aesthetic appreciation of nature, I now examine five of them more closely, developing and defending one of them, in part by comparison with and in contrast to the other four, two of which are traditional and two contemporary. All five approaches are similar in that they address what might be called the central problem of the aesthetics of nature.

THE CENTRAL PROBLEM OF THE AESTHETICS OF NATURE

One version of the central problem of the aesthetics of nature is posed by aesthetician, philosopher, and poet George Santayana. In his classic work *The Sense of Beauty*, he observes:

> The natural landscape is an indeterminate object; it almost always contains enough diversity to allow . . . great liberty in selecting, emphasizing, and grouping its elements, and it is furthermore rich in suggestion and in vague emotional stimulus. A landscape to be seen has to be composed. . . . [T]hen we feel that the landscape is beautiful. . . . The promiscuous natural landscape cannot be enjoyed in any other way.[1]

The natural landscape, Santayana says, is "indeterminate" and "promiscuous." To be appreciated, it must be composed. Yet, it is so rich in diversity, suggestion, and emotional stimulus that it allows "great liberty in selecting, emphasizing, and grouping." Thus the problem is *what* and *how* to select, emphasize, and group—what and how to compose—in order to achieve appropriate aesthetic appreciation.

It is significant that there is no parallel problem in regard to the appreciation of art. With traditional works of art, we typically know both the what and the how of appropriate aesthetic appreciation. We know *what* to appreciate because we know the difference between a work and that which is not it or a part of it and between its aesthetically relevant and irrelevant qualities. We know that we are to appreciate the sound of a piano in the concert hall, but not the coughing that interrupts it; we know that we are to appreciate the delicacy and balance of a painting, but not the wall on which it happens to hang. Similarly, we know *how* to appreciate works of art because we know the modes of appreciation that are appropriate for different kinds of works. We know that we are to listen to the sound of the piano and look at the surface of the painting. Moreover, we know that for different types of paintings, for instance, we must use different approaches. Philosopher Paul Ziff introduces the notion of "acts of aspection," pointing out that different acts of aspection are appropriate for works of different types and therefore that "to contemplate a painting is to perform one act of aspection; to scan it is to perform another; to study, observe, survey, inspect, examine, scrutinize, are still other acts of aspection. . . . I survey a Tintoretto, while I scan an H. Bosch. . . . Do you drink brandy in the way you drink beer?"[2]

With art, our knowledge of what and how to appreciate is grounded in the fact that works of art are our creations. We know what are and are not parts of works, which of their qualities are aesthetically relevant, and how to appreciate them because we have made them for the purpose of aesthetic appreciation—and to fulfill that purpose, this knowledge must be accessible. In making an object, we know what we make, and thus we know its parts, its purposes, and what to do with it. With a painting, we know that it ends at the frame, that its colors and lines are aesthetically important, and that we are to look at it rather than listen to it. Moreover, works of different types have different kinds of boundaries and different foci of aesthetic significance, and they demand different acts of aspection. Thus in knowing the classification, we know what and how to appropriately appreciate. According to Ziff:

Generally speaking, a different act of aspection is performed in connection with works belonging to different schools of art, which is why the classification of style is of the essence. Venetian paintings lend themselves to an act of aspection involving attention to balanced masses; contours are of no importance. . . . The Florentine school demands attention to contours, the linear style predominates. Look for light in a Claude, for color in a Bonnard, for contoured volumes in a Signorelli.[3]

Although we know what and how to appreciate in regard to art, since we have created it, this knowledge does not solve the central problem of the aesthetic appreciation of nature. Nature is not art, and it is not our creation. Rather, it is our whole natural environment, our natural world. It surrounds us and confronts us, in Santayana's words, indeterminately and promiscuously, rich in diversity, suggestion, and emotional stimulus. But *what* are we to appreciate in all this richness? What are the limits and the proper foci of appreciation? And *how* are we to appreciate? What are the appropriate modes of appreciation and acts of aspection? Moreover, what are the grounds on which we can justifiably base answers to such questions?

SOME ARTISTIC APPROACHES TO APPRECIATING NATURE

Given that we know how to answer the questions of what and how to appreciate in regard to art, it seems reasonable to model the aesthetic appreciation of nature on the aesthetic appreciation of works of art. Indeed, various art-based models of appreciation often have been accepted as the grounds on which to base answers to the questions of what and how to aesthetically appreciate with respect to the natural environment.

One such approach may be called the Object Model. Consider our appreciation of a nonrepresentational sculpture—for example, Constantin Brancusi's *Bird in Space* (1919). We appreciate the actual physical object; the aesthetically relevant features are its sensuous, design, and abstract expressive qualities. Such a sculpture need not relate to anything external to itself; it is a self-contained aesthetic unit. *Bird in Space* has no direct representational ties to the rest of reality and no relational connections with its immediate surroundings. Yet it has significant aesthetic qualities: it glistens, has balance and grace, and expresses flight itself. Clearly, we can aesthetically appreciate objects of nature in accord with the Object Model. We can appreciate a rock or a piece of driftwood as we appreciate a sculpture by Brancusi; we may actually or imaginatively remove the object from its surroundings and dwell on its sensuous and possible expressive qualities. Natural objects are often appreciated in precisely this way: mantelpieces are littered with rocks and pieces of driftwood. Moreover, the model fits the fact that natural objects, like nonrepresentational sculpture, have no representational ties to the rest of reality.

Nonetheless, the Object Model is in many ways inappropriate for the aesthetic appreciation of nature. Santayana notes that the natural environment is indeterminate. He also observes that nature contains objects that have determinate forms, but suggests that when our appreciation is directed specifically to them, we no longer have genuine aesthetic appreciation of nature.[4] Santayana's observation marks a distinction between appreciating nature and simply appreciating the objects of nature. In fact, on one understanding of the Object Model, natural objects when so appreciated become "ready-mades" or "found art." They are granted what is called artistic enfranchisement and, like such artifacts as Marcel Duchamp's urinal, which he enfranchised as a work called *Fountain* (1917), become works of art.[5] The questions of what and how to aesthetically appreciate are answered, but for art rather than for nature; the appreciation of nature is lost in the shuffle. Appreciating a sculpture that was once driftwood is no closer to appreciating nature than is appreciating a purse that was once a sow's ear.

The Object Model does not have to turn natural objects into art objects, however. It may treat the objects of nature only by actually or imaginatively removing them from their surroundings. We can appreciate the rock on the mantelpiece not as a ready-made sculpture, but simply as an aesthetically pleasing object. Our appreciation focuses on the sensuous and a few expressive qualities of the physical object: the rock has a wonderfully smooth and gracefully curved surface and expresses solidity. Nonetheless, the Object Model remains problematic because it involves the removal of natural objects from their surroundings. The model is appropriate for art objects that are self-contained aesthetic units, for which neither their environments of creation nor their environments of display are aesthetically relevant. However, natural objects are part of their environments of creation, having been formed there by the natural forces at work within them. Thus, for natural objects, their environments of creation are aesthetically relevant and, because of this, their environments of display are equally relevant in being either the same as or different from their environments of creation.

To understand the extent of the Object Model's problem, again consider the rock: on the mantelpiece, it seems gracefully curved and expressive of solidity, but in its environment of creation it has more and different aesthetic qualities—qualities resulting from the connections between it and its environment. It is expressive of the forces that shaped and continue to shape it and displays for aesthetic appreciation its place in and relationship to its environment. Moreover, it may not express those qualities, such as solidity, that it appears to express on the mantelpiece. The problem for the Object Model is a dilemma: either we remove the object from its environment, or we leave it where it is. If the object is removed, the model answers the questions of what and how to appreciate, but its removal results in the appreciation of a limited and questionable set of aesthetic qualities. If the object is left in place, however, the model does not constitute an adequate basis for much of the appreciation that is possible. And it makes little headway with the questions of what and how. In either case, the Object Model is a poor paradigm for the appreciation of nature.

A second art-based approach to aesthetic appreciation of nature is the Landscape Model (chap. 1). In one of its senses, the word "landscape" means "prospect"—usually an imposing prospect—seen from a specific standpoint and distance.[6] Landscape painting frequently represents such prospects, and the Landscape Model is closely tied to this genre. In appreciating landscape painting, the focus is typically not the actual object (the painting) or the represented object (the prospect), but the representation of the object and its represented features. Thus the appreciative emphasis is on visual qualities that play an essential role in depicting a prospect: line, color, and overall design. Such features are central to landscape painting and are the focus of the Landscape Model. The model encourages perceiving and appreciating nature as though it were a landscape painting, as an imposing prospect to be viewed from a specific position and distance. It directs appreciation to formal, artistic qualities of line, color, and shape.

There can be no doubt that the Landscape Model has been historically significant in the aesthetic appreciation of nature.[7] It is the direct descendent of the eighteenth-century concept of the picturesque. As noted in chapter 1, the term "picturesque" means "picture-like" and suggests a mode of appreciation by which the natural world is experienced as though it were divided into scenes, each of which aims at an ideal dictated by art, especially landscape painting. The concept guided the aesthetic appreciation of tourists in the eighteenth and nineteenth centuries as they pursued picturesque scenery with the help of the "Claude-glass." Named for the famous landscape painter Claude Lorrain, this small, tinted, convex mirror was designed for viewing the landscape as it would appear in a painting. Thomas West's popular *Guide to the Lakes* (1778), a guidebook to the Lake District in northern England, says of the glass that "where the objects are great and near, it removes them to a due distance, and shews them in the soft colours of nature, and most regular perspective the eye can perceive, art teach, or science demonstrate . . . to the glass is reserved the finished picture, in highest colouring, and just perspectives."[8]

In a similar fashion, modern tourists frequently show a preference for the Landscape Model by visiting "scenic viewpoints," where the actual space between tourist and prescribed "view" constitutes "a due distance" that aids the impression of "the soft colours of nature, and most regular perspective the eye can perceive." And the regularity of the perspective is enhanced by the position of the viewpoint itself. Moreover, modern tourists also desire "the finished picture, in highest colouring, and just perspectives"—whether in the form of the "scene" framed and balanced in a camera viewfinder; a color print of the framed "scene"; or "artistically" composed postcard and calendar reproductions of the "scene," which often receive more appreciation than the actual landscape they "reproduce." Geographer Ronald Rees points out that "the taste has been for a view, for scenery, not . . . our ordinary, everyday surroundings. The average modern sightseer . . . is interested not in natural forms and processes, but in a prospect."[9]

The answers of the Landscape Model to the questions of what and how to appreciate cause some uneasiness in a number of thinkers. The model dictates the appreciation of the natural environment as though it were a series of landscape paintings. Following in the footsteps of the picturesque, it requires dividing nature into scenes, each to be viewed from a specific position by a viewer separated by appropriate spatial (and emotional?) distance. It reduces a walk in the natural environment to something like a stroll through an art gallery. In light of this, some thinkers, such as human ecologist Paul Shepard, find the Landscape Model so misguided that they doubt the wisdom of any aesthetic approach to nature.[10] Others also consider such an approach to be ethically and environmentally worrisome. For example, after contending that modern tourists are interested only in prospects, Rees concludes that the picturesque "simply confirmed our anthropocentrism by suggesting that nature exists to please as well as to serve us. Our ethics . . . have lagged behind our aesthetics. It is an unfortunate lapse which allows us to abuse our local environments and venerate the Alps and the Rockies."[11]

The Landscape Model is also questionable on aesthetic grounds. It construes the environment as though it were a static, essentially "two-dimensional" representation, reducing it to a scene or view. But the natural environment is not a scene, not a representation, not static, and not two dimensional. In short, the model requires that the environment be appreciated not as what it is and with the qualities it has, but as what it is not and with qualities it does not have. The model is unsuited to the actual nature of the object of appreciation. Consequently, the Landscape Model, like the Object Model, not only unduly limits appreciation—in this case, to certain artistic and formal qualities—but also misleads it. Philosopher Ronald Hepburn, who was instrumental in initiating the contemporary interest in the aesthetics of nature, puts the point in general terms:

> Supposing that a person's aesthetic education . . . instills in him the attitudes, the tactics of approach, the expectations proper to the appreciation of art works only, such a person will either pay very little aesthetic heed to natural objects or else heed them in the wrong way. He will look—and of course look in vain—for what can be found and enjoyed only in art.[12]

SOME ALTERNATIVE APPROACHES TO APPRECIATING NATURE

If traditional art-based approaches to the aesthetic appreciation of nature, such as the Object Model and the Landscape Model, both unduly limit and mislead appreciation, how are we to deal with Santayana's indeterminate natural environment? How are we to correctly answer the questions of what and how to aesthetically appreciate? Perhaps we can learn from the failures of the art-based approaches, which limit and mislead appreciation largely because they do not adequately acknowledge the true nature of the object of appreciation. It is the natural environment, but the Object Model, in focusing on particular natural objects, overlooks the environmental dimension, while the Landscape Model, in focusing on artistic and formal qualities, downplays the natural dimension. Awareness of these failures has inspired the development of some alternative approaches to the appreciation of nature that share the conviction that such appreciation requires full recognition of the true character of its object and cannot simply be assimilated into the aesthetic appreciation of art.

One alternative, alive to the problems of appreciation influenced by the idea of the picturesque and by the Landscape Model, is seemingly skeptical about aesthetic approaches to nature in general. Indeed, this nonaesthetic position simply denies the possibility of aesthetic appreciation of nature (chap. 1). This position accepts the traditional account of the aesthetic appreciation of art, but emphasizes that nature is natural, neither art nor our creation. It argues that aesthetic appreciation necessarily involves aesthetic evaluation, which entails judging the object of appreciation as the achievement of its creator. Since nature, unlike art, is not our creation—indeed, is not the product of any designing intellect—the appreciation of it is not aesthetic.[13] One version of this position is called the Human Chauvinistic Aesthetic. Environmental philosopher Robert Elliot elaborates on this view, claiming that our appreciative responses to nature do not "count as aesthetic responses." He holds that the "judgemental element in aesthetic evaluation serves to differentiate it from environmental evaluation. . . . Evaluating works of art involves explaining them, and judging them, in terms of their author's intentions; . . . locating them in some tradition and in some special *milieu*. . . . [But] nature is not a work of art."[14]

A second alternative to the art-based approaches to the appreciation of nature is more troubled by the limitations of the Object Model and focuses on the environmental dimension of the natural environment. It argues that traditional art-based approaches, as exemplified by the Object Model and to a lesser extent by the Landscape Model, presuppose a subject/object dichotomy that involves an isolating, distancing, and objectifying stance, which is inappropriate for aesthetic appreciation not only of nature but of art as well. It suggests that this stance wrongly abstracts both natural objects and their appreciators from the environments in which they properly belong and in which appropriate appreciation is achieved. Thus this position proposes to replace abstraction with engagement, distance with immersion, and objectivity with subjectivity, calling for a participatory aesthetics of nature. A version of this view, the Aesthetics of Engagement, was introduced in chapter 1. It is developed by philosopher Arnold Berleant:

> The boundlessness of the natural world does not just surround us; it assimilates us. Not only are we unable to sense absolute limits in nature; we cannot distance the natural world from ourselves. . . . [When we perceive] environments from within, as it were, looking not *at* it but being *in* it, nature . . . is transformed into a realm in which we live as participants, not observers. . . . The aesthetic mark of all such times is . . . total engagement, a sensory immersion in the natural world.[15]

By highlighting the natural and environmental dimensions of the natural environment, the Human Chauvinistic Aesthetic and the Aesthetics of Engagement address many of the shortcomings of the traditional art-based models. However, they have problems of their own. The Human Chauvinistic Aesthetic runs counter to both the orthodox view that everything is open to aesthetic appreciation and the commonsense idea that at least some instances of appreciation of natural phenomena, such as fiery sunsets and soaring birds, constitute paradigmatic cases of aesthetic appreciation.[16] The Aesthetics of Engagement is also problematic. First, since at least some degree of the subject/object dichotomy seems to be integral to the very nature of aesthetic appreciation, its total rejection may necessitate a rejection of the aesthetic itself, reducing the Aesthetics of Engagement to a version of the Human

Chauvinistic Aesthetic. Second, the Aesthetics of Engagement appears to embrace an unacceptable degree of subjectivity in the aesthetic appreciation of both nature and art.[17] However, the main problem with both positions is that, in the last analysis, they do not provide adequate answers to the questions of what and how to aesthetically appreciate in nature. Concerning the what question, the answer of the Human Chauvinistic Aesthetic is simply "nothing," while that of the Aesthetics of Engagement is seemingly "everything." And, therefore, concerning the how question, the former view has nothing more to say, while the latter apparently recommends "total immersion," an answer that offers little guidance for the aesthetic appreciation of nature.

A NATURAL ENVIRONMENTAL MODEL FOR APPRECIATING NATURE

In spite of the problems inherent in the Human Chauvinistic Aesthetic and the Aesthetics of Engagement, both positions, in their respective emphases on the natural and the environmental, point toward a certain kind of paradigm for the appreciation of nature. This paradigm is exemplified in a description of appreciation by geographer Yi-Fu Tuan:

> An adult must learn to be yielding and careless like a child if he were to enjoy nature polymorphously. He needs to slip into old clothes so that he could feel free to stretch out on the hay beside the brook and bathe in a meld of physical sensations: the smell of the hay and of horse dung; the warmth of the ground, its hard and soft contours; the warmth of the sun tempered by breeze; the tickling of an ant making its way up the calf of his leg; the play of shifting leaf shadows on his face; the sound of water over the pebbles and boulders, the sound of cicadas and distant traffic. Such an environment might break all the formal rules of euphony and aesthetics, substituting confusion for order, and yet be wholly satisfying.[18]

Tuan's characterization of nature appreciation accords with the answer of the Aesthetics of Engagement to the question of what to appreciate—that is, everything. This answer, of course, will not do. We cannot appreciate everything; there must be limits and emphases in the appreciation of nature, as there are in the appreciation of art. Without such limits and emphases, our experience of the natural environment would be only "a meld of physical sensations" without any meaning or significance, what philosopher William James characterized as a "blooming buzzing confusion."[19] Such an experience would indeed substitute "confusion for order" and, contrary to both Tuan and the Aesthetics of Engagement, would be neither "wholly satisfying" nor aesthetic. It would be too far removed from the aesthetic appreciation of art to merit the label "aesthetic" or even the label "appreciation." Consider again the case of art; the boundaries and foci of aesthetic significance for works of art are functions of the type of art that they are: paintings end at their frames, and their lines and colors are significant. Our knowledge of the conventions of art is a result of our being the creators of works of art. But here we run up against the point emphasized by the Human Chauvinistic Aesthetic: the natural environment is natural, not a work of art or our creation. Consequently, no boundaries or foci of aesthetic significance for the natural environment are given, nor do we have knowledge of what and how to appreciate in it due to any involvement on our part in its creation. Indeed, nature itself seemingly has no such boundaries or foci.[20] Must the what and how questions therefore remain unanswered? Must nature remain indeterminate, promiscuous, and ultimately beyond aesthetic appreciation?

We need not accept such a conclusion. That the natural environment is natural—not our creation—does not mean, of course, that we must be without knowledge of it. We have discovered much about nature independent of any involvement in its creation. This knowledge, essentially common sense and science, is a plausible candidate for playing the role in the appreciation of nature that our knowledge of art forms, types of works, and artistic traditions plays in the appreciation of art. Consider again Tuan's example: we experience a "meld of physical sensations"—the smell of hay and of horse dung, the feel of the ant, the sound of cicadas and of distant traffic. If our response to these sensations is to be aesthetic appreciation rather than just raw experience, however, the meld cannot remain a "blooming buzzing confusion." Rather, it must become what philosopher John Dewey called a consummatory experience: one in which knowledge and intelligence transform raw experience by making it determinate, harmonious, and meaningful.[21] For example, we must recognize the smell of hay and that of horse dung and perhaps distinguish between them; we must feel the ant as an insect rather than as, say, a twitch. Such recognizing and distinguishing generate foci of aesthetic significance, natural foci appropriate to a particular natural environment. Likewise, knowledge of the environment may yield appropriate boundaries and limits; the sound of cicadas may be appreciated as a proper component of the environment, but that of distant traffic may be excluded, much as we ignore coughing in the concert hall.

Moreover, common sense and scientific knowledge of natural environments are relevant not only to the question of what to appreciate, but also to that of how to appreciate. Tuan's case may be taken as exemplifying a paradigm of nature appreciation, rather like a general environmental act of aspection. But since natural environments differ in type, as do works of art, they require different acts of aspection. As with the question of what to appreciate, knowledge of particular environments indicates how to appreciate, indicates the appropriate act or acts of aspection. Ziff tells us to look for contours in paintings of the Florentine school, for "light in a Claude," and for "color in a Bonnard"; to "survey a Tintoretto"; and to "scan" a Bosch. Likewise, we must survey a prairie, looking at the subtle contours of the land, feeling the wind blowing across the open space, and smelling the mix of grasses and flowers. But such acts of aspection have little place in a dense forest, where we must examine and scrutinize, inspecting the detail of the forest floor, listening carefully for the sounds of birds, and smelling intently for the scent of spruce and pine. Similarly, Tuan's description, in addition to characterizing environmental acts of aspection in general, indicates the act of aspection that is appropriate for a particular type of environment—perhaps best classified as pastoral. In the appropriate aesthetic appreciation of nature, as in that of art, classification is, as Ziff says, "of the essence."[22]

Thus the questions of what and how to aesthetically appreciate with respect to the natural environment may be answered in the same way as the parallel questions about art. The difference is that with natural environments, the relevant knowledge is our common sense and the scientific discoveries that we have made about those environments. Such information yields appropriate boundaries of appreciation, particular foci of aesthetic significance, and relevant acts of aspection. If to appropriately aesthetically appreciate art we must have knowledge of art forms, classifications of works, and artistic traditions, then to appropriately aesthetically appreciate nature we must have knowledge of diverse natural environments and their different systems and their components. As the knowledge provided by art critics and art historians equips us to aesthetically appreciate art, that provided by naturalists, ecologists, and geologists equips us to aesthetically appreciate nature.[23] Thus the natural and environmental sciences are central to the appropriate aesthetic appreciation of nature.[24]

This position, which takes natural and environmental science to be the key to the aesthetic appreciation of the natural environment, is the Natural Environmental Model. Like the Human Chauvinistic Aesthetic and the Aesthetics of Engagement, it recognizes that the natural environment is both natural and an environment, and, unlike the Object Model and the Landscape Model, it does not assimilate natural objects into art objects or natural environments into scenery. Yet, unlike the Human Chauvinistic Aesthetic and the Aesthetics of Engagement, the Natural Environmental Model does not reject the general and traditional structure of the aesthetic appreciation of art as a model for the aesthetic appreciation of the natural world. Indeed, it applies that structure rather directly to nature, making only such adjustments as are necessary in light of the character of the natural environment. In doing so, it avoids the absurdity of deeming the appreciation of nature nonaesthetic, while promoting the aesthetic appreciation of nature for what it is and for the qualities it has. Thus it helps us *not* to, as Hepburn puts it, "either pay very little aesthetic heed to natural objects or else heed them in the wrong way," *not* to "look—and of course look in vain—for what can be found and enjoyed only in art."

THE RAMIFICATIONS OF A NATURAL ENVIRONMENTAL APPROACH

The Natural Environmental Model acknowledges Santayana's assessment of the natural environment as indeterminate and promiscuous, so rich in diversity, suggestion, and emotional stimulus that it must be composed to be appreciated. Moreover, it suggests that to achieve appropriate aesthetic appreciation, or, as Santayana says, to find nature beautiful, the composition must be in terms of common sense and scientific knowledge. In addition to answering the central problem of the aesthetics of nature, this suggestion has a number of other ramifications.

Some of them concern what is called applied aesthetics, specifically the popular appreciation of nature, as practiced not only by tourists but also by each of us in our daily pursuits. As explained earlier, such appreciation is frequently based on art-appreciation models, especially the Landscape Model. The idea of the picturesque does not have a monopoly on applied aesthetic appreciation, however, but is in competition with a somewhat different approach. As noted in chapter 1, this other mode of appreciation began with thinkers such as Henry David Thoreau and had its paradigmatic realization in John Muir. For Muir, everything in the natural world, all nature and especially all wild nature, is aesthetically beautiful, and ugliness exists only where nature is despoiled by human intrusion.[25] This conception, akin to the contemporary view called positive aesthetics, is closely tied to the idea of wilderness preservation and to the appreciation of nature often associated with environmentalism. The Natural Environmental Model is relevant to positive aesthetics because it provides theoretical underpinnings for this mode of appreciation. When nature is aesthetically appreciated in terms of knowledge offered by the natural and environmental sciences, positive aesthetic appreciation is singularly appropriate. On the one hand, pristine nature—nature in its natural state—is an aesthetic ideal. On the other, nature as revealed by science—which appears to find in it unity, order, and harmony—seems more fully beautiful.[26]

Other ramifications of the Natural Environmental Model are more clearly environmental and ethical. The traditional art-based models, and by implication other aesthetic approaches, are frequently condemned as totally anthropocentric, not only antinatural but also arrogantly disdainful of environments that do not conform to artistic ideals. The root source of these environmental and ethical concerns is that art-based approaches do not encourage the appreciation of nature for what it is and for the qualities it has. However, the Natural Environmental Model bases aesthetic appreciation on a scientific view of nature and its qualities. It thereby endows the aesthetic appreciation of nature with a degree of objectivity that helps to dispel environmental and moral criticisms, such as that of anthropocentrism. Moreover, the possibility of an objective basis for the aesthetic appreciation of nature also holds out promise of some direct practical relevance in a world increasingly engaged in environmental assessment.[27] Individuals who make such judgments, although typically not worried about anthropocentrism, are frequently reluctant to acknowledge the relevance and importance of aesthetic considerations, regarding them as (at worst) completely subjective whims or (at best) relativistic, transient, and soft-headed cultural and artistic ideals. Recognizing that the aesthetic appreciation of nature has scientific underpinnings helps to alleviate such doubts.

Another consequence concerns the discipline of aesthetics itself. The Natural Environmental Model, in rejecting art-based approaches in favor of a dependence on common sense and scientific knowledge of nature, provides a blueprint for aesthetic appreciation in general. The model suggests that the aesthetic appreciation of anything—people or pets, farmyards or neighborhoods, shoes or shopping malls—must be centered on and driven by the object of appreciation itself.[28] What is appropriate is not the imposition of artistic ideals, but dependence on and guidance by knowledge, scientific or otherwise, that is relevant to the character of the thing in question.[29] This turn away from artistic preconceptions and toward the true nature of objects of appreciation points the way to a general aesthetics, an aesthetics that expands the traditional conception of the discipline, which has at times narrowly identified aesthetics with the philosophy of art. The upshot is a more universal aesthetics—the kind of environmental aesthetics that is the subject of this book.

Finally, in initiating a more universal and object-centered aesthetics, the Natural Environmental Model aids in the alignment of aesthetics with other areas of philosophy—such as ethics, epistemology, and philosophy of mind—that are increasingly rejecting archaic, inappropriate models and embracing knowledge relevant to their particular areas of concern. For example, environmental aesthetics parallels environmental ethics in the latter's rejection of anthropocentric models for the moral assessment of the natural world and replacement of such models with paradigms drawn from the environmental and natural sciences.

In light of these various ramifications, it becomes clear that the challenge implicit in Santayana's remarks—that *we* confront a natural world that allows great liberty in selecting, emphasizing, and grouping, and that *we* must therefore compose it in order to appropriately aesthetically experience it—holds out an invitation not simply to find the natural world beautiful, but also to appreciate its true nature.

3 / THE REQUIREMENTS FOR AN ADEQUATE AESTHETICS OF NATURE

Having compared the Natural Environmental Model, or scientific cognitivism, with both the traditional Object Model and Landscape Model and the modern Human Chauvinist Aesthetic and Aesthetics of Engagement, I now present a methodological framework with which to further assess the three contemporary positions as well as a number of other current ideas concerning the aesthetic appreciation of nature.

A METHODOLOGICAL FRAMEWORK

The methodological framework is based on a number of requirements for an adequate aesthetics of nature. By "requirements," I mean a set of intuitions, constraints, desiderata, and the like that must be met by any satisfactory account of the aesthetic appreciation of nature. I recommend five such requirements, each of which is exceedingly plausible and has been suggested and defended by one or more philosophers other than me. Thus each requirement is named for a philosopher whom I think has clearly and forcefully articulated it. The combination of the five has not been previously examined, as far as I know, and although each requirement by itself has significant ramifications for the aesthetics of nature, it is the consideration of the complete set of five that is revealing, especially in regard to the Natural Environmental Model.

ZIFF'S ANYTHING VIEWED DOCTRINE

The first requirement, which is by far the most basic, is *Ziff's Anything Viewed Doctrine*. This label is apt, since the requirement is vigorously defended by Paul Ziff, the philosopher whose views on the aesthetic appreciation of art are part of the basis for the Natural Environmental Model. This requirement, essentially that anything whatsoever is open to aesthetic appreciation, is so deeply entrenched in the Western tradition of aesthetics that it deserves to be characterized as a doctrine. It has been accepted since at least the eighteenth century, when it developed in conjunction with the concept of disinterestedness, which began with Shaftesbury (Anthony Ashley Cooper) and culminated with Immanuel Kant (chap. 1). Moreover, it is forcefully reaffirmed by the twentieth century's best-known articulation of that tradition, aesthetician Jerome Stolnitz's aesthetic attitude theory, which holds that aesthetic appreciation is appropriate for "any object of awareness whatever."[1] And it is worth noting that the doctrine is also accepted by the most zealous critics of the disinterestedness tradition, such as philosopher George Dickie, who argues that "it is unlikely that any object would lack some quality which is apreciatable."[2] A spirited statement of the Anything Viewed Doctrine is offered by Ziff:

> Unless one has a compelling narcissistic obsession with the marks of men's endeavors one can view things in the world aesthetically without being concerned with or inhibited by their lack of status as artifacts. . . . [A]nything that can be viewed can fill the bill of an object fit for aesthetic attention and none does it better than any other.[3]

Ziff's way of putting the doctrine, with the suggestion that the aesthetic appreciation of objects might be thought to be "inhibited by their lack of status as artifacts," is especially relevant to the aesthetics of nature. This is because at least one of the views on the appreciation of nature that the doctrine calls into question suggests that such appreciation is not aesthetic precisely because nature lacks the status of being an artifact. This nonaesthetic approach to the appreciation of nature, as noted in chapter 2, is exemplified by what philosopher Don Mannison calls the Human Chauvinistic Aesthetic, which has been endorsed by not only Mannison but also environmental philosopher Robert Elliot.[4] The view is characterized by Mannison:

> The conceptual structure of an aesthetic judgement includes a reference to a creator; i.e. an artist. It follows . . . that only artifacts which have been fashioned with the intention of being, at least, in part, objects of aesthetic judgment can be objects of aesthetic judgement. . . . Nature cannot be the object of aesthetic appreciation.[5]

The idea that "nature cannot be the object of aesthetic appreciation" is, I think, wildly implausible, and the way in which Ziff's Anything Viewed Doctrine completely undercuts its acceptability as an account of the appreciation of nature clearly demonstrates the relevance of the doctrine as a basic requirement for an adequate aesthetics of nature. However, the nonaesthetic approach to the appreciation of nature is not the only view that the doctrine calls into question. Those who hold the nonaesthetic approach explicitly claim that the appreciation of nature cannot be aesthetic, but some philosophers who would certainly not accept this blanket assertion seem to slip into a view not unlike that of the nonaesthetic approach. For example, Stan Godlovitch's mystery model of nature appreciation requires that our stance toward nature be governed by an overwhelming awareness of its mysterious, alien, aloof, distant, and unknowable character.[6] To the extent that this is so, perhaps no real aesthetic appreciation of nature is possible, but only something like religious veneration.[7] For a somewhat different reason, perhaps Arnold Berleant's Aesthetics of Engagement has a similar problem.[8] As noted in chapter 1, the Aesthetics of Engagement involves the total rejection of the disinterestedness tradition of the aesthetic, but, given this dismissal, Berleant is seemingly left without any theoretical resources by which to constitute any appreciation—whether of nature or of art—as aesthetic.[9]

BUDD'S AS NATURE CONSTRAINT

Ziff's Anything Viewed Doctrine claims that the appreciation of nature can be aesthetic, even though nature is not an artifact. The second requirement for an adequate aesthetics of nature insists that nature must not be appreciated as though it were an artifact. This requirement holds that nature must be appreciated *as nature*. I label it *Budd's As Nature Constraint* in light of philosopher Malcolm Budd's succinct statement of it:

> Just as the aesthetic appreciation of art is the appreciation of art *as art*, so the aesthetic appreciation of nature is the aesthetic appreciation of nature *as nature*. For, given that the natural world is not anyone's artifact, the aesthetic appreciation of nature as nature, if it is to be true to what nature actually is, must be the aesthetic appreciation of nature not as an intentionally produced object (and so not as art).[10]

Budd's As Nature Constraint is widely accepted and defended by philosophers who work on the aesthetics of nature.[11] Moreover, its acceptability is strongly supported by two arguments that are suggested in Budd's statement. The first is by analogy with the aesthetic appreciation of art, which is rightly assumed to be the aesthetic appreciation of art as art. The second is that the aesthetic appreciation of nature as nature is required in order "to be true to what nature actually is." I think that these two arguments conclusively establish the constraint as an essential requirement for an adequate aesthetics of nature.

The most significant ramification of the As Nature Constraint is also suggested in Budd's statement when he notes that the aesthetic appreciation of nature must not be "as an intentionally produced object (and so not as art)." In this way, the constraint challenges a venerable tradition of the appreciation of nature that has dominated the aesthetics of nature from at least the eighteenth century. This is the picturesque tradition, which was initially solidified by such thinkers as William Gilpin, Uvedale Price, and Richard Payne Knight; continues to have a great influence on the popular appreciation of nature; and is occasionally defended in the contemporary literature (chap. 1).[12] Insofar as this tradition recommends that nature be appreciated as art—for example, as landscape painting—it runs afoul of the As Nature Constraint and is consequently unacceptable in a number of ways as a model for the appropriate aesthetic appreciation of nature (chap. 2).

Moreover, not simply the grand tradition of the picturesque, but also the somewhat related views of several contemporary philosophers are challenged by the As Nature Constraint. Budd himself employs it to reject Anthony Savile's endorsement of the idea of appreciating nature as though it were art, which is motivated in part by Savile's attempt to offer a treatment of beauty that is unified and univocal across both nature and art.[13] In a similar way, Nick Zangwill tries to breathe life back into formalism as an account of much of the aesthetic appreciation of both nature and art. But the formalist contention that nature is to be appreciated in terms of formal qualities of line, shape, and color leads Zangwill to explicitly reject Budd's As Nature Constraint, which he refers to as the "weak Qua thesis" that nature is to be appreciated qua nature.[14] Thus he courts implausibly in his aesthetics of nature and, especially, in his aesthetics of inorganic nature, the appreciation of which he takes to be purely formalistic.[15] Likewise, Thomas Heyd connects art and nature by contending that diverse cultural stories drawn from the art, literature, and mythology of "people from a great variety of walks of life and cultures" should inform the aesthetic appreciation not just of works of art and various human environments, but also of the natural environment. Therefore, Heyd's position, like Savile's and Zangwill's, seems to violate Budd's As Nature Constraint, for it sometimes requires us to appreciate nature as something other than natural.[16]

BERLEANT'S UNIFIED AESTHETICS REQUIREMENT

Positions on the aesthetic appreciation of nature such as those of Savile, Zangwill, and Heyd are motivated, at least in part, by the desire to give an account of the aesthetic that spans both art and nature and does so without equivocation on its key concepts, such as "beauty" and "appreciation." Although these approaches are in conflict with Budd's As Nature Constraint, the reasoning behind them is admirable. Indeed, the idea of such a unified aesthetics is central not only to the aesthetics of nature, but to the discipline of aesthetics itself. In the context of the aesthetics of nature, the idea is clearly articulated by Arnold Berleant, who defends the Aesthetics of Engagement for both nature and art. Thus the third requirement is *Berleant's Unified Aesthetics Requirement*.

Berleant argues that what is needed is not an aesthetics that "harbors two dissimilar types of phenomena, one concerning art and another nature," but an aesthetics of art and nature in which "both actually involve a single all-embracing kind of experience, which requires a comprehensive theory to accommodate it."[17]

The centrality to aesthetic theory of Berleant's Unified Aesthetics Requirement is particularly well demonstrated by the case of formalism. As noted, Zangwill has endeavored to resuscitate formalism as an aesthetics of *both* art and nature. This is not surprising, for its attempt to be a unified theory constitutes much of the appeal of this kind of view, whether it is traditional formalism, such as that defended by British art critic Clive Bell in the early twentieth century, or the new version articulated by Zangwill.[18] Formalism can give *one simple account* of aesthetic appreciation—in terms of lines, shapes, and colors—that seemingly applies equally not only to both art and nature, but to everything else. Moreover, given formalism's other obvious weaknesses—not only its violation of Budd's As Nature Constraint, but also the misleading and superficial nature of formalist aesthetic appreciation—its continued appeal must be attributed largely to its success in meeting the Unified Aesthetics Requirement.

Unlike Bell's early-twentieth-century view and Zangwill's contemporary position, many of the aesthetic theories that stand historically between them have trouble meeting Berleant's Unified Aesthetic Requirement. In part for this reason, theories like the expressionist theory of art and "cultural" aesthetic theories to a greater or lesser extent problematize the aesthetics of nature. For example, the expressionist theory builds its entire account of art creation and aesthetic appreciation around the artist's expression of emotion. Clearly, such an artist-centered theory does not easily apply to the appreciation of nature. Likewise, cultural accounts as diverse as Dickie's institutional theory and Kendall Walton's categories-of-art approach, each in its own way, fail to meet the Unified Aesthetics Requirement. Dickie holds that none of the characteristics of natural objects "enjoy the conventionally engendered status which the aesthetic aspects of works of art possess," and thus in the appreciation of such objects, unlike that of art, "we can be content to appreciate whatever happens to fall together."[19] Walton widens the gap between the appreciation of art and that of nature even farther by suggesting that while our aesthetic judgments about art lend themselves to an objectivist account, those about nature remain relative to how we happen to perceive it.[20]

Philosophers such as Dickie and Walton make their observations about the aesthetic appreciation of nature only in passing. However, some philosophical accounts that are explicitly directed at understanding the appreciation of nature likewise fail to meet Berleant's Unified Aesthetics Requirement. Central to one such point of view, characterized in chapter 1 as the freedom approach, is the idea that the aesthetic appreciation of nature is marked by a degree of freedom not found in the appreciation of art. The idea is developed by Malcolm Budd and John Andrew Fisher. Budd argues that the aesthetic appreciation of nature, even though it must be the appreciation of nature as nature, is "endowed with a freedom denied to artistic appreciation."[21] This is because "in a section of the natural world we are free to frame elements as we please, to adopt any position or move in any way, at any time of the day or night, in any atmospheric conditions, and to use any sense modality," and, moreover, free to do so "without thereby incurring the charge of misunderstanding."[22] Fisher defends a position not dissimilar to Budd's, although he develops his version of the freedom approach for only the sounds of nature. He contends that the complexity of such sounds and the diversity of human "ways of hearing" combine to allow many appropriate ways to aesthetically appreciate them. Thus Fisher embraces a completely unrestrained freedom in our appreciation of natural sounds, which, as he puts it, "simply yields an even greater abundance to listen to."[23] Although Budd's and Fisher's positions have a kind of intuitive appeal, they split aesthetic experience into two separate realms and thus fail to satisfy the intuitions that are captured by Berleant's Unified Aesthetics Requirement.

HEPBURN'S SERIOUS BEAUTY INTUITION

If positions that attribute excessive freedom to our aesthetic appreciation of nature, such as those of Budd and Fisher, lack the support of the intuitions that lie behind Berleant's Unified Aesthetics Requirement, they have even more difficulty accommodating what is perhaps a deeper and certainly a more common intuition: that some instances of the aesthetic appreciation of nature are in some straightforward ways better—less superficial and more worth having—than others. For the paradigmatic expression of this idea, I return to Ronald Hepburn's seminal article, "Contemporary Aesthetics and the Neglect of Natural Beauty," and refer to the fourth requirement for an aesthetics of nature as *Hepburn's Serious Beauty Intuition*:

> Suppose the outline of a cumulo-nimbus cloud resembles that of a basket of washing, and we amuse ourselves in dwelling upon this resemblance. Suppose that on another occasion we . . . try instead to realize the inner turbulence of the cloud, the winds sweeping up within and around it, determining its structure and visible form. Should we not . . . say that this latter experience was less superficial . . . than the other, that it was truer to nature, and for that reason more worth having? . . . If there can be a passage, in art, from easy beauty to difficult and more serious beauty, there can also be such passage in aesthetic contemplation of nature.[24]

Hepburn's Serious Beauty Intuition stresses the contrast between "superficial . . . easy beauty" and "difficult and more serious beauty" and, more important, emphasizes the greater value of the latter in comparison with the former. Moreover, as Hepburn suggests, this view is supported by two arguments very similar to those that support Budd's As Nature Constraint. The first is by analogy with the aesthetic appreciation of art, which is rightly assumed to involve "a passage . . . from easy beauty to difficult and more serious beauty." The second, comparable to Budd's contention that the appreciation of nature as nature is required in order "to be true to what nature actually is," is that the aesthetic appreciation of the serious beauty of nature is "more worth having," since it is "truer to nature." As with Budd's As Nature Constraint, I think that these two arguments, together with our intuitions about the beauty of nature, conclusively establish Hepburn's Serious Beauty Intuition as a requirement that any adequate aesthetics of nature must satisfy.

The Serious Beauty Intuition calls into question theories, such as the freedom approaches, that seemingly allow for a wide range of "easy beauty." The freedom that Fisher and Budd find in the aesthetic appreciation of nature yields, in their words, "an even greater abundance" of aesthetic experience "without thereby incurring the charge of misunderstanding." However, there is a set of theories about the aesthetic appreciation of nature, which I introduced in chapter 1 as noncognitive approaches, that are much more deeply challenged by Hepburn's Serious Beauty Intuition than are the freedom accounts. These are positions that give pride of place in the aesthetic appreciation of nature to our less cognitive and more personal and emotional responses, for such reactions are paradigms of superficial, easy beauty.

Foremost among these theories is Berleant's Aesthetics of Engagement, which advocates transcending traditional dichotomies, such as subject/object, and diminishing the distance between the appreciator and the appreciated, aiming at a total, multisensory immersion of the former within the latter, be it nature or art (chap. 2). Thus while Berleant's Aesthetics of Engagement, not surprisingly, nicely meets Berleant's Unified Aesthetics Requirement, it has more difficulty with Hepburn's Serious Beauty Intuition. Another theory that also may be thought to put too little emphasis on serious beauty is Noël Carroll's arousal model, which stresses the "immediate," "directly elicited," and "more visceral" emotional responses that nature often arouses in us.[25] Similarly, Cheryl Foster relates the aesthetic appreciation of nature to a range of feelings that she terms the "ambient" dimension of aesthetic experience, characterizing it as involving the almost ineffable "feeling of being surrounded by or infused with an enveloping, engaging tactility."[26] Multisensory immersion in nature, emotional arousal by nature, and ambient feeling for nature are interesting aspects of human experience and without doubt constitute some dimensions of our aesthetic appreciation of nature. Each state is also at the easy end of the spectrum that runs from easy to serious beauty, however, and thus to make any of them the central core of the aesthetic appreciation of nature is to disregard Hepburn's Serious Beauty Intuition.

THOMPSON'S OBJECTIVITY DESIDERATUM

The last of the five requirements for an adequate aesthetics of nature is closely linked to Hepburn's Serious Beauty Intuition, since it seemingly can be met only if the aesthetic appreciation of nature involves a substantial component of serious rather than superficial beauty. It is the idea that our aesthetic appreciation of nature, and thus our aesthetic judgments about it, should possess a degree of objectivity. I name this requirement *Thompson's Objectivity Desideratum* after environmental philosopher Janna Thompson, who clearly articulates both the requirement and its more general significance:

> The link . . . between aesthetic judgment and ethical obligation fails unless there are objective grounds—grounds that rational, sensitive people can accept—for thinking that something has value. If beauty in nature . . . is merely in the eyes of the beholder, then no general moral obligation arises out of aesthetic judgments. A judgment of value that is merely personal and subjective gives us no way of arguing that everyone ought to learn to appreciate something, or at least to regard it as worthy of preservation.[27]

Thompson's Objectivity Desideratum is just that, a desideratum. As Thompson makes clear, however, objectivity secures the connection between our aesthetic judgments and our ethical obligations—between the aesthetic appreciation and the preservation of nature. Consequently, it is vital that it be accepted as a requirement for an adequate aesthetics of nature.[28] An aesthetics of nature that cannot support grounds for preserving that which we find beautiful is not worthy of consideration.

Nonetheless, many of the theories that have been found wanting in regard to the other four requirements for an adequate aesthetics of nature also fail to satisfy Thompson's Objectivity Desideratum. The freedom accounts are especially noteworthy in this respect. Budd seems to be unconcerned about the relativity that he embraces in the aesthetic appreciation of nature, referring to the "search for a model of the correct or appropriate aesthetic appreciation of nature" as "a chimerical quest" and welcoming the freedom that he attributes to the aesthetic appreciation of nature as "one aspect of nature's distinctive aesthetic appeal."[29] Fisher takes an even more extreme position on this issue, explicitly rejecting the "insistence that aesthetic responses to nature produce objective judgments," which he attributes to Thompson and me. His dismissal is based mainly on "the familiar fact that people differ greatly in their responses."[30] However, it is a philosophical truism that the *fact* of disagreement in responses does not establish the relativity of corresponding judgments.

Most of the positions that give center stage in the aesthetic appreciation of nature to our less cognitive and more personal and emotional responses to nature also have some difficulty with Thompson's Objectivity Desideratum. This is not surprising, for states such as Berleant's multisensory immersion in nature, Carroll's emotional arousal by nature, and Foster's ambient feeling for nature are notoriously subjective and by themselves do not seem to be adequate foundations for objective judgments of the aesthetic value of nature. However, the concerns expressed by the Objectivity Desideratum are greeted by those who defend such views in different ways. On the one hand, Berleant appears to welcome the subjectivity that is embodied in his Aesthetics of Engagement, while, on the other, Foster, although she thinks it "is a challenge to philosophers . . . to make a case for . . . [the ambient aesthetics'] . . . legitimacy as a form of aesthetic value," recognizes the importance of "more discursive modes of expression that might lend themselves usefully to the defense of objective judgements."[31]

Moreover, Carroll goes even further than Foster in acknowledging the significance of the Objectivity Desideratum. Although committed to the view that being emotionally moved by nature has "a genuine claim to be counted among the ways in which nature may be legitimately appreciated," he accepts what he calls "the claims of objectivist epistemology" and attributes to me. He argues that any "picture of nature appreciation, if it is to be taken seriously," must have a means "for solving the problem of the objectivity of nature appreciation."[32] Carroll's solution to the problem relies on what is often called the cognitive theory of emotions, which holds that an emotional response can be assessed as appropriate or inappropriate in light of our cognitive appraisal of the object of the emotion. For example, our fear of a snake is an appropriate emotional response just in case we cognitively appraise it as the very dangerous, highly poisonous coral snake. This approach to emotions does indeed allow for a degree of objectivity in our emotional responses, but it goes only halfway toward meeting Thompson's Objectivity Desideratum. This is because, although it accounts for how our emotional responses may be assessed as appropriate or inappropriate in light of our cognitive appraisals, it does not provide resources for establishing the objectivity of the appraisals themselves. The object of our fear may not be the coral snake, but the similarly red, yellow, and black–striped but completely harmless shovel-nosed snake.[33]

Another theory that explicitly attempts to meet the Objectivity Desideratum is the imagination approach, which is most fully developed by environmental philosopher and aesthetician Emily Brady.[34] Although Brady regards her account as akin to less cognitive approaches to the aesthetics of nature, she gives pride of place not to emotion, but to imagination, and directly speaks to the worry that imagination might open the door to subjectivity. Moreover, unlike several other philosophers discussed earlier, she is particularly concerned to establish the objectivity of aesthetic judgments about nature for preservationist and conservationist reasons similar to those articulated by Thompson. Her response to the concerns about the subjectivity of imagination appeals, in part, to the idea of "imagining well," which she characterizes as the ability to imagine more or less skillfully or appropriately. However, she categorically rejects suggestions by such philosophers as Marcia Eaton and Robert Fudge that knowledge is necessary in order to restrain and guide imagination in order to achieve objectivity.[35] Brady opts instead for "a flexible approach to truth."[36] But it is unclear how such a notion of truth, whatever it amounts to, rather than plain old-fashioned knowledge, could establish objectivity. Brady further attempts to base objectivity on the utilization of what well-known aesthetician Frank Sibley calls a "perceptual proof," a process of bringing appreciators to see for themselves the appropriateness of certain aesthetic judgments. But, as Brady herself observes, the foundation of a perceptual proof is "a straightforward non-aesthetic description."[37] So, once again, her rejection of an important role for knowledge in the aesthetic appreciation of nature hamstrings her attempt, for certainly knowledge is necessarily involved in the nonaesthetic description of any object of appreciation.[38] Thus although Brady's account is one of the more determined efforts to satisfy Thompson's Objectivity Desideratum, it seemingly does not succeed in doing so.

THE UPSHOT

I have argued that many of the current attempts to characterize the aesthetic appreciation of nature fail to meet one or more of the five requirements for an adequate aesthetics of nature. What, then, is the upshot of considering not just any one of the five requirements, but the whole set? What follows from the conjunction of Ziff's Anything Viewed Doctrine, Budd's As Nature Constraint, Berleant's Unified Aesthetics Requirement, Hepburn's Serious Beauty Intuition, and Thompson's Objectivity Desideratum?

I suggest, not surprisingly, that given this set of requirements for an adequate aesthetics of nature, the approach that best satisfies the conjunction of the five is the Natural Environmental Model,[39] the view that

> our appreciation of nature is aesthetic and is analogous to that of art in both its nature and its structure. The significant difference is that while in art appreciation . . . the knowledge given by art criticism and art history are relevant, in nature appreciation . . . the knowledge is that provided by natural history—by science. But this difference is not unexpected; nature is not art.[40]

The Natural Environmental Model satisfies all five requirements. It accommodates Ziff's Anything Viewed Doctrine by affirming, as the quotation emphasizes, that the appreciation of nature is aesthetic, while recognizing that since nature is not art, it must be appreciated as nature and not as art, thereby meeting Budd's As Nature Constraint. The aesthetic appreciation of nature as nature rather than as art is ensured by insisting that centrally relevant to such appreciation is knowledge—scientific knowledge—that informs us about the nature of nature. Moreover, since scientific knowledge plays in the aesthetic appreciation of nature a role similar to that played by art critical and art historical knowledge in the aesthetic appreciation of art, the aesthetic appreciation of nature is, again as the quotation points out, "analogous to that of art in both its nature and its structure." Thus the Natural Environmental Model satisfies Berleant's Unified Aesthetics Requirement. In addition, the placement of scientific knowledge as centrally relevant to—indeed, as essential to—the appropriate aesthetic appreciation of nature also ensures that such appreciation is serious rather than superficial, thereby meeting Hepburn's Serious Beauty Intuition. Finally, Thompson's Objectivity Desideratum is served in that the centrality of scientific knowledge, the paradigm of objectivity, in the aesthetic appreciation of nature endows our aesthetic judgments about nature with a reasonable degree of objectivity.

If the five requirements for an adequate aesthetics of nature demonstrate the importance of scientific knowledge in the aesthetic appreciation of the natural world, it is now appropriate, in light of this, to inquire about their relevance to the other great domain of environmental aesthetics: the environments that have been modified or constructed by humans. Considerations analogous to the five requirements also have a role to play in the aesthetics of human environments.

4 / AESTHETIC APPRECIATION AND
THE HUMAN ENVIRONMENT

Environmental aesthetics is centrally concerned with the aesthetics of nature and the natural environment. For many of us, however, the environments in which we spend most of our time are not natural, but those environments in which we work, play, and otherwise carry on our day-to-day lives. These environments are what I call human environments. Thus in addition to the issues addressed in the previous chapters, a major question of environmental aesthetics is how to aesthetically appreciate our human environments. What is the right approach to aesthetically appreciating the immediate world in which we live?

HUMAN ENVIRONMENTS AND DESIGNER LANDSCAPES

Addressing the question of how to aesthetically appreciate our human environments requires, of course, considering some assumptions about how we think about such environments. There is a long tradition, especially prominent in the discipline of landscape architecture, of thinking about human environments as designed environments. As an example, consider Geoffrey Jellicoe and Susan Jellicoe's classic study *The Landscape of Man*, which beautifully illustrates what it terms "the landscapes of man" from the Paleolithic period to the mid-twentieth century. It attempts to explain the development of such landscapes in terms of such factors as the geographic environment, social history, and economic, philosophical, and artistic ideas of the time. Nonetheless, in spite of the historical and explanatory scope of this undertaking, the authors declare that to "qualify as a 'landscape of man' an environ-ment must be deliberately shaped at a specific time," and they construe their study as "a concise global view of the designed landscape past and present, inclusive of all environments."[1] What is noteworthy in such an approach is that either human environments are simply construed as being in general "deliberately shaped" and "designed," or they are thought worthy of aesthetic consideration only insofar as they are so shaped and designed. Moreover, the emphasis ultimately falls on the second disjunct, since the first is so clearly an exaggeration, if not sim-ply false. I call this approach to human environments the designer landscape approach.

The immediate ramification of the designer landscape approach for the aesthetic appreciation of human environments is that the aesthetics of human environments becomes closely aligned with the aesthetics of art. Since human environments are conceived of as deliberately de-signed, they are regarded as importantly akin to works of art, and all the theories, conceptions, and assumptions about the philosophy of art are brought to the question of how to aesthetically appreciate such en-vironments. This approach appears to have the virtue of satisfying Ber-leant's Unified Aesthetics Requirement. Nonetheless, there are numer-ous problems with simply taking the aesthetics of art as the model for the aesthetics of human environments, some of which are analogous to those concerning art-based models for the aesthetics of natural envi-ronments (chap. 2).

PROBLEMS FOR THE DESIGNER LANDSCAPE APPROACH

To illustrate some of the specific aesthetic problems generated by the designer landscape approach, let us consider the approach as it applies to a particular component of human environments. This element is perhaps both the most central one in our human environments and the one for which the designer landscape approach has considerable plausibility: *buildings*.

The application of the designer landscape approach to buildings, in particular, results in the view that buildings either are simply con-strued as being deliberately designed or are thought worthy of aesthetic consideration only insofar as they are so designed. Of course, the designer landscape view is initially plausible in this case, since buildings are in general deliberately designed and their having been so is importantly relevant to their aesthetic appreciation. In the case of buildings, though, the designer landscape approach typically takes an extreme form that embraces two assumptions:

1. The relevant kind of design must be *artistic* in nature.
2. Buildings are worthy of aesthetic consideration only if and as far as they are the result of such artistic design.

This form of the view has been the most prominent and is of most interest here. In essence, it is the position that the aesthetics of buildings, insofar as it is of any aesthetic interest, is essentially the aesthetics of architecture.

The aesthetics of architecture thus stands as a species of the genus constituted by the designer landscape approach to human environments. A passing glance at the aesthetics of architecture illustrates some of the aesthetic problems generated by this approach.[2] Of course, the aesthetics of architecture has traditionally been thought of as a part of not environmental aesthetics, but the aesthetics of art. This causes some theoretical strain, as architecture itself has often been considered a lesser art form. The place of architecture in the philosophical theories of G. W. F. Hegel and Arthur Schopenhauer serves to illustrate this point. Schopenhauer, for example, put architecture at the lowest possible level in his hierarchy of the arts, holding that it expresses only "those ideas that are the lowest grades of the will's objectivity."[3] Nonetheless, in spite of such reservations about the purity of architecture as art, there has been almost universal agreement in the history of aesthetics that architecture must yet find a proper place in a unified artistic aesthetic. Consequently, even if the fit has not always been perfect, the aesthetic concepts and theories that serve in the analysis of the fine or pure arts have been pressed into service for architecture as well.[4]

The upshot has been that the aesthetics of architecture has concentrated on particular structures that can be viewed as "works of architecture" comparable to works of art and that have features comparable to those we find aesthetically interesting and pleasing in works of art. The attention has been on solitary, unique structures that have been carefully designed and created by the architect as artist. And if they are in certain ways artwork-like, especially sculpture-like, so much the better. The concentration on the unique, sculpture-like "works" of the architect as "artist" has been and continues to be ubiquitous. For example, Stephen Bungay claims of Hegel, who actually called one type of architecture *unorganische Skulptur*, that "most of the examples he considers are not works of architecture at all, but statues."[5] The trend is similar in contemporary philosophy. For instance, in the volume on aesthetics in the Foundations of Philosophy series, Virgil Aldrich discusses sculpture and architecture under a single heading, treating the architect as an artist comparable to the sculptor.[6] Works on criticism also emphasize the unique, individual creations of "artists." One typical study in contemporary architectural criticism is based entirely on only thirteen "key twentieth-century architectural monuments."[7] In short, the focus has been on individual, magnificent, sculpture-like structures—the works of artists.

At the heart of the difficulties with the aesthetics of architecture is the fact that, even more so than the concept "work of art," the concept "work of architecture" is a curious abstraction, and the class of works of architecture is highly gerrymandered. Even so-called paradigmatic works of architecture are unlike typical works of art in a number of ways. For example, since they are buildings, they have functions, and thus are intrinsically connected to the peoples and cultures that use them. As buildings, they are also related to other buildings—not only functionally related to those with similar uses, but structurally related to those similarly designed and constructed, and even physically related to those adjacent to them. Moreover, as buildings, they are erected in places and thus are intimately tied not only to physically adjacent buildings, but also to the human environments within which they exist. Given this web of interrelationships, it is difficult to securely ground the abstraction "work of architecture," and picking out particular works of architecture begins to look like a rather arbitrary process. In short, once we start looking at and thinking about buildings, we realize that they do not easily fit into a concept analogous to the favored concept of a work of art, which is that of a unique, functionless, and typically portable object of aesthetic appreciation.[8]

This consideration of the aesthetics of architecture and its difficulties helps to highlight the problems of the designer landscape approach for the aesthetic appreciation of human environments in general. When the aesthetics of human environments is closely aligned with the philosophy of art and all the theories, conceptions, and assumptions of the aesthetics of art are brought to the question of how to aesthetically appreciate such environments, problems similar to those evident in the aesthetics of architecture also confront the aesthetics of human environments. In the latter case, however, the problems are much more extreme, for, as noted, the designer landscape approach has the most plausibility in regard to buildings. Thus if in the guise of the aesthetics of architecture it generates numerous theoretical and appreciation-related problems, it should be obvious that when applied to human environments as a whole, which are in general much less the products of deliberate design than are buildings, the approach is at best very limited and at worst deeply flawed. Indeed, when applied to human environments, the designer landscape approach dramatically fails to satisfy the analogue for human environments of Budd's As Nature Constraint. In short, the designer landscape approach to human environments is not "true to" what the human environment "actually is."

AN ECOLOGICAL APPROACH AND FUNCTIONAL FIT

If we abandon the designer landscape approach and the idea that the aesthetics of human environments is closely aligned with the philosophy of art, what are we to put in their place? My answer so far is to replace the aesthetics of art with environmental aesthetics. But what does this entail? A clue is given by the field called landscape ecology. Landscape architect Joan Nassauer describes this area of research: "From its beginnings in Europe, landscape ecology was conceived as an approach to understanding landscapes that drew upon both cultural and ecological knowledge."[9] She notes that one of the central tenets of landscape ecology is that human beings and the environments they create are significant parts of our ecosystems. The implication is clear. If we are to appropriately aesthetically appreciate human environments, we cannot look only to culture, as the designer landscape approach and the traditional aesthetics of architecture have done. We must also look to ecology. This points to what may be called an ecological approach to the aesthetics of human environments. Such an approach would stress ecological factors as a basis for appreciating human environments not as analogous to works of art, but as integral human ecosystems comparable to the ecosystems that make up natural environments.

Before it can be put to use, an ecological approach to the aesthetics of human environments must address a pressing methodological question. The question is similar to what may be regarded as a central issue of the field of landscape ecology, which strives to see culture and nature as working together. But nature has an inherent necessity revealed by the natural sciences and especially by ecology, whereas culture appears not to have a parallel necessity. Without some such necessity, culture seemingly works more or less at random and thus not in conjunction with, or even parallel to, ecological systems. Thus a key question faces the landscape ecologist: Where can we find some form of cultural necessity that will enable culture to be regarded as working in tandem with nature to produce human environments? Nassauer provides an answer to one version of this question. She turns to aesthetics, arguing that we can "take advantage of the ready-made cultural necessities of scenic beauty and landscape care" by attaching "ecological health to these lawlike aesthetic conventions."[10] Since she is concerned about not only appreciating but also preserving and protecting desirable human environments, Nassauer works out the required links between aesthetic and ecological goodness, arriving at a refined concept of "intelligent and vivid care."[11] Her goal is human environments that are "culturally sustainable" because they are both ecologically sound and, in evoking human enjoyment and approval, "more likely to be sustained by appropriate human care over the long term."[12]

Nassauer's approach is interesting and original, and it speaks directly to the question that faces landscape ecology. As it stands, however, it is not an ideal way to address the slightly different question that confronts an ecological approach to the aesthetically appreciation of human environments. This is because of a slight difference in focus between landscape ecology and an ecological approach to the aesthetics of human environments. Landscape ecology strives to make culture and nature work together by finding in culture some kind of necessity parallel to that revealed by ecology. By contrast, an ecological approach to the aesthetics of human environments seeks to bring culture and nature in line with each other by identifying a kind of ecological necessity that has application to culture, particularly to human environments. Although different kinds of ecological necessity may be applicable to culture, one that seems especially relevant to the aesthetic appreciation of human environments is what may be called functional fit.[13] To clarify this concept, we must first examine its role in our understanding and appreciation of the natural world. Then we may turn to the question of its application to the appreciation of human environments.

Concerning the natural world, the concept of functional fit is meant to roughly capture the way in which the natural environment is composed of many-layered, interlocking ecosystems. Each ecosystem must fit with various other systems, and the constituents of any system must likewise fit within it. At the level of the individual organism, this amounts to having an ecological niche. The importance of such niches, and of functional fit in general, has to do with survival. They are means by which organisms and systems survive. This involves an ecological interpretation of the biological principle of the survival of the fittest: without a fit, neither individual organisms nor ecosystems long survive. It is in this sense that the fit is functional. Ecosystems and their components do not fit together as the pieces of a puzzle, but as, to use a traditional image, the parts of a machine. Each has a function, the performance of which helps to maintain not only the part itself, but also the other components of the system, the system itself, and ultimately the whole natural environment.

As a backdrop to the application of the notion of functional fit to the appreciation of human environments, it is useful to note how functional fit finds a significant place in the aesthetic appreciation of the natural world. What this concept makes clear is that no "components" of an ecosystem can be fully appreciated in isolation, but each must be perceived in terms of its fit within larger wholes. Moreover, since the fit is functional, functional descriptions take on a new significance. Landscapes become habitats, ranges, and territories—that is, the dwelling, feeding, and surviving spaces and places of organisms—and organisms themselves become players in a unified drama of life. Thus, when aesthetically appreciated in light of this concept, nature can no longer be perceived simply in the way that more traditional, art-based notions such as the picturesque have ordained. It cannot be appreciated simply as either a collection of individual, disjointed natural objects or as a series of static scenes or landscape views. Consequently, the recognition of functional fit supplements the argument that was directed against the Object Model and the Landscape Model of appreciation of nature (chap. 2). In this sense, the application of the ecological notion of functional fit to the aesthetic appreciation of the natural world is one dimension of the Natural Environmental Model of the appreciation of nature.

It may be thought at this point that although an ecological notion such as functional fit appears to enhance the appreciation of the natural world, it is not clear that the resulting appreciation is actually aesthetic. This worry may be met to some extent by noting that the ecological concept of functional fit is analogous to the traditional and paradigmatic aesthetic notion of organic unity. This notion, not unlike that of functional fit, is imported from the natural world and the appreciation of nature, but traditionally it has been utilized as a fundamental concept in the aesthetic appreciation of works of art. Indeed, in his historical treatment of aesthetics, Harold Osborne traces this tradition back to Plato and Aristotle, particularly to a passage in the *Phaedrus*.[14] However, he adds that the passage "may not warrant the burden of significance which in later ages been read into it."[15] Be that as it may, what is important to note is that in later ages this "burden of significance" has indeed been placed on it, thereby helping to make organic unity an essential aesthetic concept. Aesthetician John Hospers spells out the significance of organic unity in the appreciation of modern art and makes clear its connection to the natural world, summarizing the concept as indicating "the kind of unity that is present in a living organism."[16] Thus if organic unity can function as a key concept in aesthetic appreciation without jeopardizing the aesthetic nature of that appreciation, then so can functional fit.

THE ECOLOGICAL APPROACH AND THE HUMAN ENVIRONMENT

An ecological approach is relevant to the aesthetic appreciation of human environments in a number of ways. First and foremost, it means perceiving human environments as constituted of components analogous to interlocking ecosystems, with the notion of functional fit as the key to appreciating their creation, development, and continued survival. When so perceived, human environments can display the kind of organic unity that we aesthetically appreciate in both nature and art. Many human environments, landscapes or cityscapes or even particular buildings, have developed, as it were, "naturally" over time— have grown "organically"—in response to human needs, interests, and concerns and in line with various cultural factors. Such an environment thus has a fit that is the result primarily not of the deliberate design valorized by the designer landscape approach and by the traditional aesthetics of architecture, but of those forces that have so shaped it that a fit of its components has come into being. Such fits are explicitly functional in that they accommodate the fulfillment of various interrelated functions. Indeed, the fact that these functions are fulfilled is frequently the essence of the fit. As in the natural world, the success or failure of the functional fit may well ultimately determine the fate— whether or not they survive—of various human environments.

Examples of this kind of functional fit and the buildings, cityscapes, and landscapes that it creates and preserves are everywhere in our everyday human environments. We perhaps see them most clearly or recognize them most quickly in what may be called the working world, for it constitutes a human environment that we readily accept and easily regard as functional. For example, many of us are familiar with such functional fits in rural and agricultural landscapes, where certain kinds of buildings, together with farms and rural communities, fit functionally together and into the environment they occupy and help to shape (chap. 6).[17] Likewise, the fit can be clearly seen in those parts of cities that are dedicated to industry and commerce. A human environment of factories or refineries makes its functional fit especially clear. Perhaps two of the best examples are rail yards and harbors, where industry and commerce are facilitated by traditional forms of transportation. However, functional fit can also be observed in the more residential parts of a city, especially in older neighborhoods, ethnic districts, and local market areas. When a functional fit is achieved in all such places, there is an ambience of everything being and looking right or appropriate, an ambience of the environments looking as they should. It appears as though the whole were the result of "natural" processes akin to the ecological and evolutionary forces that shape natural environments.

These examples bring out a second way in which an ecological approach is relevant to the aesthetic appreciation of human environments, which is at the very heart of not only the ecological approach but also the whole of the aesthetics of environments. This is the significance of the notion of things *looking as they should*. When environments look as they should, they appear necessary to us, and this is a means by which the ecological approach together with the idea of functional fit help to give a kind of parallel necessity to culture and nature. Indeed, the ecological approach is fruitful in part because it brings out the significance of this notion in the appreciation of human environments, by drawing the parallel with natural environments that evolutionary and ecological forces have shaped such that they look as they should. Of course, having such a look is largely a function of our own expectations; things look as they should, if they do, in part because they look as we expect them to look. But in the case of typical works of art or other objects that we experience as the products of deliberate design, our expectations are dictated by assumptions about the design and the designer's intentions, and our normal expectations about how things should look are marginalized.[18] By contrast, when we do not experience things primarily as products of deliberate design, our normal, day-to-day expectations about how they should look come to the foreground in our aesthetic experience. Aesthetic appreciation is facilitated when such expectations are satisfied, when things do in fact simply look as they should.[19] For this reason, the notion of things looking as they should is a central feature of environmental aesthetics in general, and of the aesthetics of human environments in particular, since with the latter especially we should be suspicious of looking for or in light of deliberate design. This opens the door for looking at human environments and, indeed, the whole of human life in terms of functional fit, which brings to the fore and reinforces certain of our normal expectations and thereby facilitates our sense of things looking as they should.

In light of these remarks, it is now possible to understand the fundamental problem with the designer landscape approach to the appreciation of human environments. The difficulties presented by this approach when it is embodied in the traditional aesthetics of architecture and is applied to its most plausible target, buildings, are only symptoms of the deeper problem. This problem is that the designer landscape approach, in construing human environments either as being in general deliberately designed or as being worthy of aesthetic consideration only insofar as they are so designed, shapes our expectations about how human environments should look. Moreover, it shapes our expectations in a particular way: our expectations are dictated by assumptions about a putative designer and his or her intentions, and thereby our normal expectations about how human environments should look are marginalized. Since most human environments are not in fact deliberately designed, however, expectations that are shaped by the designer landscape approach are typically not satisfied. That is to say, when seen through the eyes of the designer landscape approach to human environments, such environments typically do not look as they should.

The upshot is that, with the designer landscape approach, we frequently find human environments aesthetically unsatisfactory, missing much that is of potential aesthetic interest and merit. In short, there is a danger that, since we bring a misleading model to the aesthetic appreciation of human environments, we will find little to appreciate and thus little to value. This defect of the designer landscape approach mirrors those of the Object Model and the Landscape Model for the aesthetic appreciation of natural environments. Just as those models do for natural environments, the designer landscape model encourages us to approach human environments in the wrong way, such that we, to again quote Ronald Hepburn, "will look—and of course look in vain—for what can be found and enjoyed only in art."[20]

AN OBJECTION TO THE ECOLOGICAL APPROACH

The fundamental problem with the designer landscape approach points toward a possible objection to the alternative ecological approach. The designer landscape approach sets up expectations about human environments that are frequently frustrated, resulting in such environments seeming not to look as they should and thus appearing to offer little of aesthetic interest and merit. What is in a way the converse of this problem may be regarded as an objection to the ecological approach.

This approach, by means of the notion of functional fit, facilitates seeing human environments as the products of "natural" processes akin to those that shape natural environments. The result, as noted, is an ambience of human environments being and looking right or appropriate, an ambience of their looking as they should. Therefore, when seen through the eyes of the ecological approach, human environments offer much to aesthetically appreciate and value. The possible objection is that, to put it succinctly, with the ecological approach human environments may offer *too much* to aesthetically appreciate and value. In other words, perhaps the ecological approach makes possible, by means of facilitating human environments' looking as they should, the aesthetic appreciation and valuing of environments that for other reasons should not be appreciated and valued.

An example will help to clarify both this problem and its possible solutions. Consider a human environment such as an exclusive, upper-middle-class suburban neighborhood that has developed "naturally" over time in response to certain human needs, interests, and concerns. It is a human environment that has grown "organically" in line with social, economic, and political forces that have shaped it such that a functional fit of the different components has come into being. Such an environment will most likely look as it should and in this way offer much that is of aesthetic interest and merit. Nonetheless, the forces that have shaped such an environment to look as it should may *not* be ones of which we should approve and thus value. There may be, for example, moral grounds for not condoning the forces that have shaped it: the social forces may be racist; the economic forces, exploitive; and the political forces, corrupt. However, the ecological approach, in bringing to the forefront the way in which, in light of these forces, this human environment has a functional fit and thus looks as it should, thereby facilitates our finding it of aesthetic interest and merit and so fosters our valuing it. But does not such valuing implicitly condone those racist, exploitive, and corrupt forces that have helped shape it? Is not an aesthetic theory that facilitates such valuing at least morally irresponsible, if not completely morally bankrupt?

There are two lines of response to this concern about an ecological approach to the aesthetics of natural environments. The first is traditional, but not in the last analysis satisfactory; the second is more promising. The traditional response depends on the position known as "aestheticism," the view that aesthetics and ethics are two separate realms and thus that aesthetic appreciation is not subject to moral constraints. This view is often associated with such nineteenth-century thinkers as Théophile Gautier, Walter Pater, and, especially, Oscar Wilde, who claimed: "I must admit that . . . I am quite incapable of understanding how any work of art can be criticized from a moral standpoint. The sphere of art and the sphere of ethics are absolutely distinct and separate."[21] Aestheticism, of course, constitutes a powerful response to the problem faced by the ecological approach. Concerning the upper-middle-class suburban neighborhood, for example, aestheticism simply replies that it is irrelevant to the aesthetic interest and merit of this neighborhood that it is the result of racist, exploitive, and corrupt forces; only the former is the concern of the realm of aesthetics, while the latter is the business of the realm of ethics, and the two realms are "absolutely distinct and separate."

However, in the last analysis, aestheticism does not offer an adequate response to problems such as those confronted by the ecological approach to the aesthetics of human environments. Note that Wilde's remarks are focused primarily on art, and although aestheticism may have some plausibility when applied to "pure" works of art, which have been, at least within some traditions, regarded as isolated, people- and culture-free entities, it has much less plausibility when applied to the world beyond the artworld. To aesthetically appreciate human environments without any reference to moral concerns seems morally irresponsible, if not morally bankrupt, and if aestheticism condones such appreciation, then it too appears to be a morally bankrupt position. Moreover, aestheticism is incompatible with the basic assumptions of the ecological approach to the aesthetics of human environments. Recall that the ecological approach, following the lead suggested by the field of landscape ecology, is designed to emphasize ecological factors as a basis for appreciating human environments not as analogous to works of art, but as integral human ecosystems comparable to natural ecosystems. The idea of appreciating human environments in such a holistic manner, initially introduced to counter the culture-centric focus of the designer landscape approach, counts equally against aestheticism. If human environments cannot be appreciated fully without reference to ecological considerations, they likewise cannot be appreciated fully without reference to the complete gamut of cultural considerations, and at the heart of culture is morality. In short, aestheticism is ruled out from the start by an ecological approach to the aesthetics of human environments and, I might add, seemingly has in general no place in environmental aesthetics.

Before leaving aestheticism, it should be noted that the position is deeply problematic in regard to not only the aesthetics of human environments—indeed, the whole of environmental aesthetics—but also the aesthetics of art. This is most evident with the kinds of works of art—such as placement pieces, earthworks, and other environmental works of art—that have intimate ties with the natural and human environments in which they exist.[22] For example, consider a hypothetical work of art suggested by Peter Humphrey. It is called *Asian Floodwork,* and certainly it constitutes a complete reductio ad absurdum of aestheticism:

> Imagine that Christo [famous for environmental works such as *Running Fence* (1972–1976) and *Surrounded Islands* (1983)] announces at a press conference that he's going to dam the entire river system of an Asian alluvial valley. The object of the art project is to show Third-World agriculture under water. Jacques Cousteau will make photographs which will be shown in the Tate Gallery. At the end of the press conference Christo points out, "I know some of you object to this because of the billion people living there who are dependent on that agriculture. Such concerns, I must remind you, are irrelevant. This is a work of art."[23]

I now turn to the second line of response to the concern that an ecological approach to the aesthetics of natural environments makes possible, by means of facilitating such environments looking as they should, the aesthetic appreciation and valuing of human environments that for moral reasons perhaps should not be appreciated and valued. Unlike aestheticism, which attempts to drive a wedge between the aesthetic and the moral, the second line of response takes the two to be closely intertwined. Elaborating it requires introducing a distinction and some accompanying concepts. The distinction is between two senses of being aesthetically appreciable, or two senses of aesthetic value. One version that is adequate for our purposes was advanced by the early-twentieth-century aesthetician D. W. Prall and, following him, John Hospers.[24] Hospers describes it as that between the "thin sense" and the "thick sense" of "the aesthetic." According to Hospers, the thin sense is relevant when we aesthetically appreciate and value objects primarily because of their physical appearances, while the thick sense involves not merely the appearances of objects, but also certain qualities that they express or convey to the viewer. Prall calls this the "expressive beauty" of objects, while Hospers speaks of objects expressing "life values."

The distinction between the thin and the thick sense of the aesthetic may be elaborated by examples. It has relevance to works of art such as musical compositions that are frequently aesthetically appreciated and valued not only because of their pleasing patterns of sound, but also because of their expression of melancholy or joy. The distinction, as well as the significance of the thick sense, is also clearly evident in regard to both the human environment and the things that occupy it. Consider an older house. We may aesthetically appreciate it because of, for example, the design of the windows or the color of the woodwork, but this is typically only part of the matter. We also may aesthetically appreciate it because it gives the general impression of or has the ambience of a less hectic, more genteel way of life, or because it shows more signs of careful construction and craftsmanship than do many newer houses. Similarly, Hospers offers another example:

> We enjoy not merely the shining black and silver of the streamlined automobile . . . but rather these surfaces and forms as expressing certain life-values, and adapted to certain life-purposes. The design of the streamlined automobile seems to express speed, efficiency, ease, power (all of them values from life, dependent upon our knowledge from everyday experience of what an automobile is and does).[25]

Before applying the distinction between the thin and the thick sense of the aesthetic to the objection to the ecological approach, some additional remarks about the thick sense are useful, for it is this sense that is more relevant to the aesthetic appreciation of human environments. Following Hospers, I speak of objects as expressing "life values." This term refers to a wide range of human emotions, attitudes, dispositions, and the like that are associated with objects in such a way that it is appropriate to say that they express these emotions, attitudes, and dispositions. The relevant concept of "expression" is of the kind initially clarified by George Santayana, who was introduced to elucidate the central problem of the aesthetics of nature (chap. 2).[26] Thus for an object to express a life value, the value must be not simply suggested by the object, but associated with it in such a way that the life value is felt or perceived to be a quality of the object itself. Understood in this way, expression is not due to unique associations that result from an individual's own personal history. Rather, it involves more general and deep-seated associations characteristically held in common by the members of a human environment, associations by and large derived from what is in general perceived by them as the "true" nature and function of an expressive object.[27] Thus the life values that an object expresses often reflect the factors and forces that are responsible for the object's nature and function.[28]

How, then, is the distinction between the thin and the thick sense of the aesthetic and the expression of life values relevant to the concern that an ecological approach to the aesthetics of natural environments makes possible the aesthetic appreciation and valuing of human environments that for moral reasons should not be appreciated and valued? It should be clear that, given its commitment to aesthetically appreciating human environments in a holistic manner that involves both ecological and cultural considerations, an ecological approach presupposes a thick sense of the aesthetic. Consequently, with the ecological approach, part of what is involved in the aesthetic appreciation of human environments is the acceptance of the life values that such environments express. In short, a human environment's looking as it should involves not simply how it looks, but also why it looks as it does. For example, if the upper-middle-class neighborhood is indeed the result of racist, exploitive, and corrupt forces, then it may well express them. Given our moral views, a human environment that expresses such life values will be difficult, if not impossible, to aesthetically appreciate and value. The upshot is that, rather than facilitating the aesthetic appreciation of such an environment, the ecological approach actually makes such appreciation extremely difficult. In essence, the ecological approach, by the recognition of the role of expressed life values in aesthetic appreciation, dictates that insofar as the moral and the aesthetic initially appear to come into conflict, the former ultimately trumps the latter.

APPRECIATING HUMAN ENVIRONMENTS

Having developed and defended the ecological approach to the aesthetics of human environments, I now turn to some of its ramifications. As noted, the ecological approach proposes and promotes the appreciation of human environments under the concept of functional fit and thereby focuses our attention on human environments looking as they should. This approach has a number of what might be called appreciative consequences. They suggest the ways and means of actual aesthetic appreciation of human environments, and thus they are well worth reviewing.

The first and foremost of these consequences is obvious, especially given the rejection of the assumptions of the designer landscape approach as they are embodied in the traditional aesthetics of architecture. In the aesthetic appreciation of buildings, there must be an emphasis on all buildings, rather than simply on the magnificent or the specially designed. This emphasis follows from the fact that the functional fit of the ecosystem gives importance to each of its components. Thus according to an ecological approach to the aesthetics of human environments, all buildings—houses, stores, gas stations, banks, apartment buildings, shopping centers, factories, and refineries—are integral parts of the "natural" human environment and are viable candidates for aesthetic appreciation equal to the traditional paradigmatic works of architecture. Related to this consequence is a second point that also follows from the fact that functional fit gives importance to all the constituents of an ecosystem: an equal emphasis on nonbuildings—for example, roads, bridges, rail yards, harbors, and power and communication lines. These components of the infrastructure of environments help to complete the functional fit of the everyday human environment, and thus their appreciation is a vital dimension of its aesthetic appreciation. None of them in isolation may look as it should, but when the whole is seen as functionally fitting together, the result is frequently a total human environment that does (see, for example, the cover photograph).

These remarks not only emphasize the significance that an ecological approach gives to each of the various components of human environments, but also point in the direction of an equally important consequence: the ecological approach also stresses the interrelationships among these components. Given the importance of functional fit, whole complexes in human environments, like the ecosystems of natural environments, become focuses of aesthetic appreciation. Rather than emphasizing this or that particular object, appreciation shifts to larger units of appreciation, to cityscapes and landscapes—for example, the downtown, banking district, neighborhood, city park, suburb, urban sprawl, industrial park, and countryside. The fit within and between such places and spaces—together with their ambience, their feel, and their expressed life values—takes on greater aesthetic significance. This point has been fruitfully pursued by research in landscape ecology, cultural geography, and landscape architecture, among other fields, and thus it is not necessary to discuss here.[29]

The appreciative ramifications of the ecological approach noted thus far can be seen more clearly by considering a particular example. Given functional fit, buildings and other components of our human environments typically look as they should when they are in what might be called their "natural" human environment—that is, the one in which they were originally built in order to carry out a particular function. As noted, they are not easily portable, as are typical works of art, and thus if severed from the human environments in which they originally existed and functioned, buildings and other structures frequently appear at best highly artificial and at worst quite absurd; in short, they seldom look as they should. An example that nicely brings out this kind of aesthetic absurdity is London Bridge, formally in London, England (figure 4.1). In 1967/1968, the 1,005-foot, 137-year-old bridge was dismantled at its site on the Thames, and its 10,000-ton granite facing was shipped, block by block, to Lake Havasu City, Arizona. There it was reassembled over a mile-long artificial waterway called, no surprises, the Little Thames (figure 4.2). It has since become the second most popular tourist attraction in Arizona, surpassed by only the Grand Canyon.[30] This

Figure 4.1 London Bridge in London, England. (Postcard courtesy of the author)

is clearly a case of aesthetic absurdity, which does not necessarily lead to a decline in tourist popularity. After all, in spite of whether or not the new London Bridge environment looks as it should, it may yet express fairly interesting, and not necessarily immoral, life values, such as playfulness or just sheer silliness. Moreover, tourists, like those who frequent freak shows, often like to look at things just because they do not look as they should.

Another consequence of the ecological approach is perhaps ultimately more significant than those that have been noted thus far: the relationships between any human environment and the actual people whose environment it is. The tradition of appreciating pure works of art as isolated, people- and culture-free entities is probably wrongheaded, and the related tradition of appreciating works of architecture in a similar way is, as noted, deeply problematic. However, a parallel tradition concerning human environments in general is clearly both wrongheaded and deeply problematic. As noted, in a holistic ecological approach, the life values that an environment expresses are given a central place. Thus questions of how human environments reflect and express not only people, but also their emotions, attitudes, and dispositions, and even their whole cultures, acquire new importance. Such questions become a part of the essence of aesthetic appreciation rather than a curious sideline of such appreciation. Again, other writers have

Figure 4.2 London Bridge in Lake Havasu City, Arizona. (Photograph courtesy of Alex Neill)

stressed this point with great eloquence, and thus it probably needs no further development here.[31] However, it does bring out another dimension of the aesthetic absurdity of having moved London Bridge from London to Lake Havasu City. This lies in having taken it not simply through space, from one human environment to another, but also across time, from one culture to another. It is little wonder that in spite of both its popularity and whatever life values it expresses, the bridge, as well as the whole new human environment in which it now resides, does not look quite as it should.

A further consequence of an ecological approach to the aesthetics of human environments that is worth making more explicit has to do with a certain kind of "functionalism." Given the importance of functional fit, human environments must be appreciated in terms of the functions they perform. This point can be understood by noting the ways in which—in the appreciation of human environments, as in the appreciation of nature—functional descriptions are especially significant. Unfortunately, many English words for different human environments and their components do not always emphasize functional roles. Some of the labels for the internal parts of one small ecosystem, the house, certainly do; we refer to the living room, the dining room, the bathroom, and so on. However, such words as "building," "house," and "church" are not as suggestive. Perhaps phrases like "dwelling place" and "place of worship" would better facilitate appreciation in light of functional fit. Consider the aesthetic appreciation of churches under a description such as "place of worship." Unlike "church," "place of worship" forces function to the forefront of our minds, and certain kinds of questions become a part of our appreciation of the structure: Is this place conducive to worship? Does it make one humble? Does it inspire awe or even fear? Likewise, to the extent that entire human environments serve particular functions, they are also more easily appreciated under functional descriptions. Consider the degree of functional content of such words and phrases as "field," "farm," "harbor," "neighborhood," "banking district," "junkyard," "suburb," "urban sprawl," "industrial park," "market," and "nuisance grounds" and note that, given an ecological approach, some nurture and reinforce our aesthetic appreciation better than others.

It should be noted, however, that the "functionalism" of the ecological approach cannot simply be equated with the functionalism of twentieth-century modern architecture. Different versions of the latter were stressed by such architects as Louis Sullivan, Frank Lloyd Wright, Walter Gropius, Le Corbusier, and Ludwig Mies van der Rohe. The basic idea concerned the importance of attention to function in architectural design. It was often articulated with the slogan "form follows function," which is typically attributed to Sullivan. One of Sullivan's stronger statements of the idea is in "The Tall Office Building Artistically Considered," in which he states that "the shape, form, outward expression, design or whatever we may choose, of the tall office building should in the very nature of things follow the functions of the building."[32] He generalizes the idea:

When native instinct and sensibility shall govern the exercise of our beloved art; when the known law, the respected law, shall be that form ever follows function; then it may be proclaimed that we are on the high-road to a natural and satisfying art, an architecture that will soon become a fine art in the true, best sense of the word, an art that will live because it will be of the people, for the people, and by the people.[33]

As suggested by Sullivan's remarks, the emphasis on function in modern architecture has gone hand in hand with the traditional view of the aesthetics of architecture, according to which architecture is considered to be an art form. Thus the emphasis on function in modern architecture has more in common with the designer landscape approach than with the ecological approach. For example, in spite of the generalized construal that Sullivan gives the "law . . . that form ever follows function," his emphasis is on particular, quite grand buildings, such as the tall office building. And the emphases of those who followed him, such as Wright, remained in part on specific, magnificent, art-like buildings—although with Wright, perhaps more famously on dwelling places, such as Fallingwater (1935–1937) and Taliesin West (1934–1938), than on commercial structures. Moreover, the general theoretical aim seemingly remains to bring architecture into the fold of the fine arts. In spite of his sentiments about "the people," it appears that, in Sullivan's mind, functionalism was significant at least in part because it would put architecture "on the high-road to a natural and satisfying art, an architecture that will soon become a fine art." In short, the focus is on the function of individual structures, and the aim is to artistically design such structures to suit their functions. Thus the contrast with an ecological approach is significant, for the latter emphasizes not only, and not mainly, the functions of particular buildings, but the functional fit of all the components within the whole of the human environment.

THE SURVIVAL OF THE AESTHETICALLY FITTEST

I have attempted to move the aesthetics of human environments away from a cluster of ideas and assumptions embodied in the designer landscape approach: that human environments are correctly construed as being in general deliberately designed and worthy of aesthetic consideration only insofar as they are so designed; that human environments are in this way importantly akin to works of art; and that the aesthetics of human environments is thus closely aligned with the philosophy of art. Instead, I have suggested that the aesthetics of human environments be seen as a major area of environmental aesthetics. To facilitate this shift, I developed the idea of an ecological approach to the aesthetics of human environments and the attendant notion of functional fit. An ecological approach employs an analogy with natural ecosystems and, by stressing the role of functional fit in each, facilitates the appreciation of both natural and human environments as looking as they should. The upshot is a set of appreciative consequences that, hopefully, results in a more satisfying aesthetic experience of our human environments.

The hub of this set of appreciative consequences is the idea that, as in natural environments, nothing in human environments can be appreciated adequately in isolation. Each building, cityscape, or landscape must instead be appreciated by virtue of the fit that exists within it and with its larger human environment. To fail to do so is often to miss much that is of aesthetic interest and merit. Keeping with an ecological approach, we may reemphasize this point by reminding ourselves that natural environments work on the principle of the survival of the fittest and that, ecologically interpreted, this principle can be taken to mean the survival of that which best fits within its environment. For the aesthetic appreciation of human environments, a comparable principle suggests that we may find the greatest aesthetic interest and merit in that which best fits within its environment and therefore looks as it should.

5 / APPRECIATION OF THE HUMAN ENVIRONMENT
UNDER DIFFERENT CONCEPTIONS

Having argued that the human environment is better appreciated in terms of an ecological approach than in those of the designer landscape approach, I now expand the discussion. For purposes of clarity, I previously rather artificially presupposed that there is one standard and uniform manner in which we conceptualize "the human environment." This assumption is not fully warranted. Philosopher and aesthetician Francis Sparshott, in one of the truly groundbreaking essays in environment aesthetics, distinguishes several ways of thinking about our relationships to our environments. Such different conceptualizations, he argues, deeply influence the ways in which we aesthetically experience both environments and the things that occupy them.[1]

In this chapter, I follow up some of Sparshott's insights by considering the ways in which a number of rather common conceptualizations of environments relate to a feature of the contemporary human environment that is commonly referred to as environmental buildings or environmental architecture. The appreciation of such structures is an increasingly important issue for environmental aesthetics, especially given its relationship with environmentalism.

TWO CAVEATS

Initially, two caveats are in order. First, in view of this emphasis on environmental buildings and architecture, it is important to continue to resist the idea that architecture must be thought of principally as a fine art. Traditionally, architecture—along with painting, sculpture, poetry, and music—was regarded as one of the five founding art forms of the so-called modern system of the arts.[2] Given its functional features, however, architecture often has been the poor sibling of the famous five. Nonetheless, some critics still regard it as essentially a fine art.[3] Be that as it may, given my concern with environmental buildings and architecture and in light of the ecological approach to human environments, I focus on buildings in general and on what is sometimes referred to as vernacular architecture.

Second, phrases such as "environmental architecture," "building with the environment," and "environmentally friendly buildings" bring to mind ideas about ecological design, sustainable development, and environmental health. They are associated with design and building practices that rely on renewable energy and materials, stress recycling and efficient use of resources, and attempt to maintain the long-term integrity of both natural and human environments. Consequently, whether exemplified in the "fine art" of architecture or in vernacular buildings, such design and building practices point initially to ecological and, more broadly, ethical issues associated with architecture, which are best approached within environmental ethics or traditional ethical theory.[4] Although such ethical matters are of the greatest importance, and are touched on at the end of this chapter, I address primarily aesthetic issues involved in environmental buildings and architecture.

AESTHETICS AND ENVIRONMENTAL BUILDINGS AND ARCHITECTURE

The aesthetics of environmental architecture, like the ethics of environmental architecture, concerns most generally the relationships between structures and their environments, especially the environmental effects of the former on the latter. Of course, unlike ethics, which considers the actual environmental benefits or harms brought about by design and building practices and by the resultant structures, aesthetics focuses first and foremost on appearances. Although some aestheticians, such as the formalists (chap. 3), dwell almost exclusively on appearances, recognizing that aesthetics is concerned with appearances need not relegate it to the realm of the superficial.

Thus the aesthetics of environmental buildings and architecture, which initially focuses on the appearances of the relationships between structures and their environments, is not restricted to questions about whether the relationships are simply "pleasing to the eye" or "pretty." To do so would be to ignore the previously reached conclusions about the life values expressed by objects and to disregard considerations analogous to those captured by Hepburn's Serious Beauty Intuition.

Rather, the basic question for the aesthetics of environmental buildings and architecture is the same as that for the human environment in general: whether structures reside in their environments such that they *look as they should*. In essence, the idea is that structures and their environments are related in such a way that the structures appear appropriate or proper within their environments. Such an emphasis immediately moves the matter beyond simple appearances because the appearance of the appropriateness of a thing—of a thing looking as it should—depends not simply on how it looks to us, but also on what we know about it. And this, in turn, depends not only on its appearance, but also on its true nature. Thus a structure looking appropriate within its environment is a function of both the nature of the structure and the nature of the environment in which it resides. Consequently, appropriately aesthetically appreciating environmental architecture and buildings involves, rather than simply looking, looking with an eye and a mind educated about the nature, history, and function of both structures and environments. This requires knowing why and how structures are made as they are and why and how environments have come to be as they are.

How, then, are we to aesthetically appreciate and assess environmental buildings and architecture as exemplified in various environments? The answers lie in knowledge not only of the why and the how of structures themselves, but also of the why and the how of environments as they are understood under different concepts. Thus clarifying the most basic conceptualizations under which we understand our environments is of the utmost importance. It is here that Sparshott's remarks are illuminating. He distinguishes six ways in which we might conceptualize our relationships to other things: I/ Thou, thinker/problem, user/used, traveler/scene, subject/object, and self/setting. Clearly, not all these conceptualizations apply to environments, although Sparshott recognizes that many individuals might initially think that at least the last four clearly do. However, he suggests that "those who talk about the environment have in mind primarily the relation of self to setting, and secondarily that of traveler to scene."[5] Concerning user/used, he argues that "someone who looks on the world strictly as an object of exploitation is not thinking of it as an environment at all . . . he is blind to all the aspects that make it an environment."[6] Such a "consumer's view," he charges, "reduces the whole world to fodder and feces."[7] Likewise, although he notes that when aestheticians talk about the object of aesthetic appreciation, they are "usually thinking of it as entering into a subject/object relation," he argues, in line with some of the observations I made in chapter 2, that this conceptualization does not easily apply to the environment either.[8] He concludes: "If an exploiter fails to recognize his environment, perhaps aestheticians also necessarily fail to think environmentally."[9]

Sparshott's analysis is central to the field of environmental aesthetics. It demonstrates that if we are to do *environmental* aesthetics, to consider the aesthetic experience of *environments*, we have to conceptualize the environment in terms of one or the other of two relationships: self to setting or traveler to scene. As noted, Sparshott takes the former to be primary and the latter secondary. Moreover, there are other important differences between them. Sparshott connects the relationship of self to setting to the aesthetic appreciation of "the resident" and that of traveler to scene to the appreciation of "the transient." He notes that "a transient takes in the gross forms and qualities, or explores the detail, of what is there to be seen; but a resident reacts rather to what has taken shape in his mind."[10] Furthermore, "to the transient what he sees is mere façade with no inside and no past; to the resident it is the outcome of how it got there and the outside of what goes on inside."[11] The resident appreciates in terms of "what he knows happened or still goes on there."[12] Sparshott's remarks about the aesthetic appreciation of the resident underscore my argument that appropriate aesthetic appreciation is not simply a matter of looking; rather, it is looking with an eye and a mind informed about the nature, history, and function of the object of appreciation.

SELF TO SETTING

What, then, is the aesthetic significance of the primary conceptualization noted by Sparshott: self to setting? When we relate to structures within an environment understood as a setting, rather than as a scene, there are a few common ways in which we can further conceptualize that environmental setting. Perhaps the conceptualization that has received the most attention in the literature is *place*. There are also the conceptualizations of environmental settings as *territory*, a notion interestingly related to place, and as *terrain*, a more basic and less discussed concept that is nonetheless perhaps the most obviously and directly relevant to the consideration of environmental buildings and architecture. I investigate each of these three conceptualizations in turn.

A brief look at the word "terrain" is useful in coming to an understanding of how it structures the appreciation of environmental settings. The word derives from the Latin *terra*, which means "earth." It came to English by way of French, in which the emphasis is placed more centrally on the notion of land or ground. The idea is that of the actual ground, the physical surface and the resultant features of a tract of land. The notion of terrain is akin to that of topography. Thus to appreciate an environment conceptualized as terrain, to understand the why and the how of it, requires recourse to knowledge provided by the natural sciences, primarily geology and secondarily ecology, botany, and zoology. Such sciences tell us how an environment came to be as it is and why it looks as it does. It is here that the aesthetics of human environments overlaps with the aesthetics of natural environments, particularly with the Natural Environmental Model (chap. 2). Moreover, given that the natural sciences tell us about the natural environment conceptualized as terrain, they also reveal the kinds of structures that look as they should in an environment so conceptualized. Consequently, in terms of terrain, environmental buildings and architecture should be aesthetically appreciated and assessed in terms of whether they look as they should given their environments understood geologically and biologically. To be considered are such questions as whether the design—the actual shape, size, and proportions—of structures appears appropriate in light of the geological lay of the land and whether the building materials and methods appear appropriate in light of the geological and biological features of the land.

Within traditional architectural design, this is perhaps the most obvious and common way in which buildings and other architectural works might be considered environmentally friendly in the aesthetic sense of appearing appropriate in their environments. Moreover, many such works were environmentally friendly in this sense well before the current popularity of the idea of environmental architecture. For example, the classic styles and structures of certain architects, such as Frank Lloyd Wright's "prairie style" or some of his works, such as Fallingwater (1935–1937), seem to be aesthetically environmentally friendly within their environments considered only or mainly as terrain. Concerning the "prairie style," Wright observed, "A building should appear to grow easily from its site and be shaped to harmonize with its surroundings if nature is manifest there. The prairie has a beauty of its own and we should recognize and accentuate this natural beauty, its quiet level. Hence, gently sloping roofs, low proportions, quiet sky lines."[13] Likewise, the buildings of an early environmental development called Sea Ranch, with their low profiles and sod roofs, might be said to look as they should when their California environment is conceptualized primarily as terrain. The hallmark of Sea Ranch is "the attempt to blend man-made structures with their natural setting."[14] Moreover, in the realm of vernacular architecture, structures, especially less modern ones, are frequently aesthetically environmentally friendly in a somewhat similar way. Take, for example, the thatched-roofed, palm-fronded, or hide-covered dwellings of so-called primitive peoples the world over. Or consider the low, sod-roofed and -walled huts of the first European settlers on the western prairies of Canada and the United States. In regard to terrain, aesthetically appropriate vernacular environmental architecture is frequently more a matter of necessity than of design.

In thinking about an environment as a setting, the second relevant conceptualization is territory. Although the word "territory" has the same Latin source as "terrain," *terra*, and the same French connection, the Middle English meaning was not just any tract of land, but "terratory," the land around a town. Thus unlike terrain, with its topographical emphasis, territory takes on a geographic sense. It indicates an area of land surrounding, belonging to, and/or under the jurisdiction of a town or another source of authority. Consequently, there is the recognition of a distinct and central element of human (or another "territorial" animal) involvement and influence in an environment conceptualized as territory. Thus to appreciate an environment conceptualized as territory, to understand the why and the how of it, requires knowledge of more than the natural sciences. Equally important are history, geography, and such other social sciences as anthropology and sociology. When an environment is conceptualized as territory, knowledge about human history and culture tells us how it came to be as it is and why it looks as it does and thereby reveals what kinds of structures look as they should within an environment so conceptualized.

What, then, can be said of the aesthetic appreciation of environmental buildings and architecture in environments that are conceptualized as territory? What kinds of structures appear appropriate and look as they should within environments understood in light of relevant historical and cultural considerations? The answer is suggested by Sparshott's observation that "an environment is always *someone's* environment."[15] When we conceptualize an environment as a territory, we are typically thinking about it as *someone's* territory and thereby acknowledging that it belongs to a people. Consequently, the kinds of structures that typically look as they should within an environment so conceptualized are those that are characteristic of the people for whom it is the home environment: *their* territory. Moreover, this is true not simply for dwellings, but even more so for the other kinds of structures within a territory, for a people's territory is the environment in which they both live and make a living. Thus to understand and appreciate the *function* to which people put both their environments and the structures they build within them is especially relevant to the way in which and the extent to which the latter appear appropriate within the former.

As an example, consider again the western prairies of Canada and the United States. The land is flat and open and is ideal for the agricultural function to which it has been put: growing grain and other seed crops. Given this, the towering grain elevators and crop-storage depots that stand in sharp contrast to the environment considered as terrain nonetheless look precisely as they should within that environment conceptualized as territory—a territory of grain fields, belonging to farmers (figure 5.1).[16] Moreover, a people's territory is a place not simply

Figure 5.1 Horst Baender, *Prairie Sentinels*: grain storage elevators on the Canadian prairie. (Reprinted by permission of Horst Baender)

for work but also for worship, and thus the onion-domed Russian Orthodox churches that dot the grain fields of the western prairies of Canada also appear appropriate in this environment, for the land is the territory of immigrant farmers from Ukraine. In short, on the prairies of Canada, as we change our conceptualization of the environment from terrain to territory, grain elevators and onion-domed churches replace sod huts as the aesthetically appropriate vernacular environmental architecture—as the structures that look as they should. Moreover, the radical difference in the *raw* appearances, as it were, of grain elevators and onion-domed churches, on the one hand, and sod huts, on the other, underscores the importance to aesthetic appreciation of the way we conceptualize an environment and the knowledge that therefore plays the central role in how it appears to us.

Concerning an environment as a setting, the third relevant conceptualization is place. This concept is interesting as related to territory. Whereas territory is, as it were, a macro-concept, place is a closely analogous micro-concept. In the sense in which a geographic area of land can be a people's territory, there is a parallel sense in which a typically much smaller area can be a person's place. Thus some of the points about the concept of territory are equally relevant to that of place. In the ways in which a people's structures typically look appropriate in their territory, a person's house (and things) typically look (more or less) appropriate as his or her place. However, other than this kind of observation, the concept of place, although in general very aesthetically significant, may have limited application to the issues concerning the aesthetic appreciation of environmental buildings and architecture.[17] When it is not more or less synonymous with the concept of territory, the notion of place perhaps indicates an area that is typically somewhat too small and too private for such issues to arise. Its connotation of smallness is suggested by the connection of the word "place" to the Latin *planta*, which means "the sole of the foot." Thus one's place is where one puts down one's feet. Smallness is also evidenced by such senses of the word as "niche," "seat," and "position." The relevance of the private nature of place is emphasized by Sparshott, who argues that since, as noted, "an environment is always *someone's* environment," it is necessary to distinguish between *public* and *private* environments. In regard to the aesthetic appreciation of the environment, he adds that we "seem mostly to be thinking in terms of the public," which is "fair enough," since "what people do for and by themselves is their own business, and there is no call for us to criticize."[18]

TRAVELER TO SCENE

I now return to Sparshott's other general way of understanding our relationship to the environment: traveler to scene. When we relate to the environment understood as a scene, rather than as a setting, our aesthetic experience is that of the transient. It seems that this way of thinking involves only one common and traditional conceptualization of the environment. As suggested by Sparshott's use of the word "scene," it is the conceptualization of the environment as *landscape*. As discussed in chapter 2, the concept of landscape has been and continues to be absolutely central to the aesthetic appreciation of the natural environment. However, in ways similar to those in which the appreciation of the transient differs from that of the resident, the concept of landscape is very different in kind from those of terrain, territory, and place. The origin of the concept of landscape is disputed. It is often claimed to derive from the Dutch *landschap*, which means "land and ship," but there is also a tradition that traces it to a combination of Old Irish and the Old English *landscipe*, or "tract," which suggests an open space that is divided or split apart. From this idea, it is a short step to the contemporary meaning: a prospect that is separated out by the eye, such as to constitute a view or a scene, especially an imposing one seen from a specific standpoint and distance. That a landscape, in contrast to a particular terrain or territory or place, is constituted by the eye, and the mind, of the appreciator is central to the concept. As previously noted, it was recognized more than a century ago by George Santayana, who characterized the landscape as "indeterminate," adding that "it almost always contains enough diversity to allow the eye a great liberty in selecting, emphasizing, and grouping its elements."[19] The upshot, Santayana concluded, is that a "landscape to be seen has to be composed. . . . [T]hen we feel that the landscape is beautiful" (chap. 2).[20]

As the origins of the concept, as well as Sparshott's use of the term "scene" and Santayana's general observations, suggest, a landscape is, in one sense, essentially a view or a scene composed by the appreciator. It is perhaps best thought of not as a particular stretch of actual land, but as more like an image, not unlike the more conventional images of landscape painting and photography. Thus the concept of landscape is not only quite unlike that of terrain, territory, or place, but is different in two very significant ways. First, the conceptualization of an environment as landscape—as opposed to terrain, territory, or place—does *not* dictate the relevance to aesthetic appreciation of any specific kinds of features either of environments so conceptualized or of the structures that occupy them. The concept of landscape is much more open, prescribing attention not to any particular actual features but at most only to more general compositional and formal qualities, as in the picturesque tradition of landscape appreciation (chap. 2).

This point has three closely related ramifications. First, environments that are conceptualized only or mainly as landscapes, whether they are natural or human environments, are in danger of giving rise to all the problems of appreciation discussed in connection with the picturesque-influenced Landscape Model of appreciation. Likewise, they are especially vulnerable to appreciation that runs afoul of Hepburn's Serious Beauty Intuition. Second, because the concept of landscape is open in regard to that to which it prescribes attention, it gives us less guidance in determining whether environmental buildings and architecture are in fact aesthetically environmentally friendly than do the conceptualization of an environment as terrain, territory, or place. Third, the upshot of the first two ramifications, somewhat paradoxically, is that when an environment is conceptualized as landscape, the role of knowledge becomes especially significant. This is because we must know not only how to appreciate an environment that is *not* more or less prefigured by a particular conceptualization—as are terrain, territory, and place—but also how to compose that environment into a landscape in the first place. Ironically, just because the transient traveler attends to an environment primarily as a landscape and therefore, as Sparshott puts it, takes in its "gross forms and qualities" and sees a "mere façade with no inside and no past," such an appreciator needs *more* rather than less knowledge in order to well compose it as a landscape and thus to *appropriately* aesthetically appreciate it and its structures.

The second significant way in which the concept of landscape differs from terrain, territory, or place is closely related to the first, although somewhat the converse of it in its ramifications. Since a landscape is best thought of as more like an image than like a particular stretch of actual land, the conceptualization of an environment as a landscape offers great potential to *enhance* its aesthetic dimensions as well as those of the buildings and architecture that reside within it. To *create* a landscape, we, the appreciators, take the raw aesthetic resources, as it were, that are available in an environment that could be conceptualized as terrain or as territory or as place—or, for that matter, simply as environment—and *compose* them into a landscape. And in composing a landscape, we may select a point of view, a scale, and a perspective and utilize standard artistic techniques such as framing, blocking, and cropping in order to put in the most favorable aesthetic light the way in which and the extent to which structures look as they should within their environment.

As an example of the potential for aesthetic enhancement in environments conceptualized as landscapes, consider again figure 5.1 and note the skill with which the photographer composed the landscape. Or consider how landscape appreciation in the tradition of the picturesque can emphasize certain compositional and formal qualities to enhance the aesthetic dimensions of a wide range of environments and the structures within them. The classic instances are such landscapes as a shady glen with a ruined abbey, a rugged highland cliff with a humble cottage, or an expanse of parkland with a stately country house. Or think about the sketches and models that architects use to present proposed buildings and developments to their clients. Just as such sketches and models typically present the future structures as looking completely appropriate in their future environments, so too can the landscapes that we compose make the best of the appearance of environmental buildings and architecture.

Implicit in these examples, however, is a concern about the aesthetic appreciation of environmental structures when environments are conceptualized as landscapes. Consider again architectural sketches and models. It a well-known and notorious fact that when well designed, such sketches and models can make not only environmental buildings and architecture appear appropriate in their environments, but almost any structure, environmentally friendly or not, look as it should in its environment. In a similar fashion, well-composed landscapes can make almost any relationships between structures and their environments appear, if not completely appropriate, at least more appropriate than they are. Likewise, Sparshott notes what he calls a "subtle danger" in understanding the aesthetic appreciation of the environment mainly in terms of the relationship of the traveler to the scene: "that in emphasizing aesthetic values of 'the environment' we shall be endorsing transient values, favoring bright façades drained of all meaning."[21] Another way to bring out this "subtle danger" is to note that such an understanding of environments may result in an aesthetic approach that may fail to satisfy theoretical requirements analogous to Hepburn's Serious Beauty Intuition and perhaps even Budd's As Nature Constraint.

There is also a more practical, and thus perhaps more important, side to this concern about the aesthetic appreciation of environmental structures when environments are conceptualized as landscapes. When so appreciated, buildings and architecture that are aesthetically environmental—that look as they should, aesthetically speaking—can sometimes part company with buildings and architecture that may or

may not be environmental in other senses. This point is a particular instance of the more general point of contention between certain traditions of aesthetic appreciation, such as the picturesque, and environmentalism (chap. 1). It is most evident from the perspective of the
transient, when environments are conceptualized as landscapes, but it
also holds, although to a lesser extent, for environments understood as
place, territory, or terrain. Environmental buildings and architecture
that appear appropriate in their place, territory, or, especially, terrain
typically are environmentally friendly in a number of other ways, but
this is not necessarily so. Grain elevators, however appropriate they
may appear within an agricultural landscape of farms and fields, could
yet be resource wasteful and energy inefficient. A little house on the
prairie could perfectly exemplify Wright's "prairie style" and yet be an
ecological disaster. And while Sea Ranch attempts to "blend man-made
structures with their natural setting," it recognizes that "to live lightly
on the land," although completely desirable, is yet a separate matter.

THE AESTHETIC AND THE ETHICAL

In light of such concerns about the aesthetic appreciation of environmental buildings and architecture, especially when environments are
conceptualized as landscapes, I conclude by briefly returning to the
point noted at the beginning of this chapter: environmental buildings
and architecture are meant to utilize design and building practices that
rely on renewable resources, stress recycling and efficiency, and promote the integrity of environments. Although these ecological and
ethical matters were separated from aesthetic considerations in order to
achieve a degree of clarity, what should now be evident is that the two
must not be completely divorced.[22] We should keep in mind the broader
conception of environmental buildings and architecture that includes
the ecological and the ethical as well as the aesthetic and requires that
all these considerations be taken into account in the appreciation and
assessment of structures within their environments. When this is done,
some of the ecological and ethical dimensions can become aspects of
the aesthetic dimensions as life values expressed by the structures. In
such instances, when the aesthetic and the moral come into conflict,

the latter must ultimately trump the former (chap. 4) As Sparshott puts it, perhaps somewhat too cynically, what is important is "people's sense of what is a good place to be in and move through" and to protect it "not only from being flouted by greed and indifference, but also from being demeaned by aestheticians . . . in the interests of prettification."[23]

6 / AESTHETIC APPRECIATION AND
THE AGRICULTURAL LANDSCAPE

In this chapter, I investigate the aesthetic interest and merit of a particular human environment, one that, when we are neither in the city nor in pristine nature, typically surrounds us. Thus the consideration of its aesthetic appreciation is a matter that deserves much greater attention than it is typically given. This human environment is what is known as the agricultural landscape.[1] I argue, in line with the general position developed in chapter 4, that the landscapes of agriculture have great aesthetic value, much of which depends on their function and on how well or how poorly they fulfill it. Thus this dimension of their aesthetic interest and merit is determined by their productivity and sustainability.

The aesthetic appreciation of agricultural landscapes, like that of natural environments, has been problemitized by the overemphasis on the appreciation of scenic landscapes that stems from the tradition of the picturesque. This tradition has helped to characterize agricultural landscapes as lacking in aesthetic value, an assumption that can be countered by paying close attention to the ways in which the landscapes of contemporary agriculture, although not scenic in the classic picturesque sense, are landscapes of great formal and expressive beauty.

I relate these two lines of thought by showing that although formal beauty is an important dimension of the aesthetic value of contemporary agricultural landscapes, the more significant dimension is expressive beauty, which takes into account the aesthetic qualities of agricultural landscapes that depend on their productively and sustainability. But in the last analysis, the nature and full extent of the expressive aesthetic value of agricultural landscapes remains, for various reasons, ambiguous.

THE TRADITION OF THE PICTURESQUE

The tradition of the picturesque has its roots in the momentous developments in aesthetics that took place throughout the eighteenth century. Given the earlier discussion of the picturesque (chaps. 1 and 2), it is necessary to only briefly emphasize some aspects of those developments. The main point is that during the eighteenth century, due in large part to the work of such thinkers as Shaftesbury (Anthony Ashley Cooper), Francis Hutcheson, Archibald Alison, and finally Immanuel Kant, aesthetic theory came into its own and aesthetic experience became a recognized feature of the good life. This blossoming of the aesthetic culminated at the end of the century in what may be called the eighteenth-century aesthetic synthesis. This synthesis had a number of components, three of which are significant in regard to the aesthetic appreciation of agricultural landscapes. First, the synthesis solidified disinterestedness as the central concept of aesthetic theory and the characteristic feature of aesthetic experience. This concept provided the means both for defining the aesthetic and for separating aesthetic experience from other forms of experience, such as the moral, the economic, and the personal. Second, the synthesis firmly entrenched landscapes rather than works of art as the central focus of aesthetic theory and as the paradigmatic objects of aesthetic experience. Third, and most important for the aesthetic value of agricultural landscapes, the synthesis replaced the older ideal of simple appreciation of beauty with a new mode of aesthetic experience that not only was disinterested but also involved three distinct ideas: the beautiful, the sublime, and the picturesque.

The upshot of the synthesis is the idea of a paradigmatic aesthetic appreciator who disinterestedly experiences primarily landscapes and experiences them as beautiful, sublime, or picturesque. Landscape scholar John Conron claims that "in eighteenth-century theory, the boundaries between aesthetic categories are relatively clear and stable. For the most part, the beautiful, the sublime, and the picturesque are all distinguishable from one another."[2] He characterizes them as follows: "beautiful forms tend to be small . . . ; smooth . . . , but also subtly varied . . . ; delicate . . . ; and 'clean and fair' . . . of color."[3] By contrast, "sublime forms . . . are the source of the most powerful feelings, from horror and terror . . . to the most muted intensities of awe and admiration."[4] Thus the sublime is the idea relevant to the aesthetic experience of landscapes that are powerful, intense, or terrifying. Finally, "the picturesque [is] typically . . . in the middle ground between the sublime and the beautiful . . . complex and eccentric . . . , varied and irregular."[5]

Rather than the distinctions among the beautiful, the sublime, and the picturesque, however, what is more important in regard to agricultural landscapes is the way in which these distinct ideas gave rise to what Conron calls "nineteenth-century fusions," especially "picturesque beauty" and "picturesque sublimity."[6] As the names for these "fusions" suggest, the picturesque gradually became, throughout the nineteenth century, the dominant idea concerning the appreciation of landscapes. This central position of the picturesque was solidified by the work of the three significant theoreticians of the picturesque: William Gilpin, Uvedale Price, and Richard Payne Knight. They not only furthered the development of the theoretical underpinnings of the picturesque as the basic conception of the aesthetic experience of landscape, but also actively promoted and popularized picturesque-influenced appreciation as the favored means by which to appreciate landscapes. For example, Knight glamorized the picturesque in his long poem *The Landscape*, and Gilpin, in popular essays such as "On Picturesque Travel" and "On Sketching Landscapes," gave the picturesque pride of place in the aesthetic appreciation of such landscapes as those of the English Lake District and the Scottish Highlands.[7]

One of the significant ramifications of the popularization of the idea of the picturesque was to unequivocally tie picturesque-influenced appreciation, and thus aesthetic appreciation of landscapes in general, to the scenic. The idea of the picturesque gave rise to a mode of appreciation by which the natural world is experienced as divided into something like artistic scenes—scenes that aim in subject matter or in composition at ideals dictated by the arts.[8] Moreover, the tie between the picturesque and the scenic was also solidly underwritten by the other key concept of the eighteenth-century aesthetic synthesis: disinterestedness. Just as paintings and works of poetry invite disinterested appreciation, so do scenic landscape views from which an appreciator is appropriately separated by both emotional and physical distance.

Consequently, the focus of the aesthetic experience of landscapes gradually shifted toward and narrowed to those landscapes that facilitated disinterested appreciation and were considered scenic, such as the rolling mountains and valleys of the Lake District and the rugged cliffs and barren outcroppings of the Scottish Highlands. As noted in chapter 2, geographer Ronald Rees makes the point in his essay "The Taste for Mountain Scenery":

> The picturesque . . . simply confirmed . . . the taste . . . for a view, for scenery, not for landscape in the original Dutch—and the present geographical—meaning of the term, which denotes our ordinary, everyday surroundings. The average modern sightseer . . . is interested not in natural forms and processes, but in a prospect. . . . It is an unfortunate lapse which allows us to abuse our local environments and venerate the Alps and the Rockies.[9]

AGRICULTURAL LANDSCAPES AS LACKING IN AESTHETIC VALUE

As Rees suggests, the ascendancy of the disinterested picturesque-influenced appreciation of landscapes has both favorable and unfavorable consequences. On the one hand, it invites us to "venerate" landscapes such as those of the Lake District, Highlands, Alps, and Rockies. On the other, it diverts us from "our ordinary, everyday surroundings" and even "allows us to abuse our local environments." The kind of abuse that is relevant here is what might be termed "aesthetic abuse"— that is, the failure to aesthetically appreciate our local environments, "our ordinary, everyday surroundings." Such landscapes are considered to be, as philosopher Yuriko Saito succinctly puts it, echoing Rees's reservations about the picturesque, "lacking in aesthetic values":

> The picturesque . . . approach to nature has . . . encouraged us to look for and appreciate primarily the *scenically* interesting and beautiful parts of our environment. As a result those environments devoid of effective pictorial composition, excitement, or amusement (that is, those not worthy of being represented in a picture) are considered lacking in aesthetic values.[10]

What are the particular landscapes that are objects of "aesthetic abuse" and "considered lacking in aesthetic values"? Until recently, unfortunately, the answer has been almost any landscapes that are not stereotypically scenic—not only, as Rees stresses, "our ordinary, everyday surroundings," but also landscapes that are not dominated by mountains, cliffs, lakes, and waterfalls. For example, wetlands in all their forms—bogs, swamps, mires, marshes, fens, sloughs, peat lands, salt marshes, and lagoons (in short, any wetlands other than pristine mountain lakes)—have long been "considered lacking in aesthetic values."[11] Likewise, dense stands of unbroken forest, which allow too little opportunity for panoramic views, as well as vast expanses of open prairie, which apparently allow too much of such opportunity, are frequently objects of "aesthetic abuse." However, the most significant landscapes that generally have been considered lacking in aesthetic values are precisely those that inherit the land once the wetlands have been drained, the forests felled, and the prairies broken: the landscapes of agriculture.

Aldo Leopold, a visionary thinker about both our abuse and our appreciation of the land, saw clearly the myopic and aesthetically incompetent nature of what he called our "taste for country":

> The taste for country displays the same diversity in aesthetic competence among individuals as the taste for opera, or oils. There are those who are willing to be herded in droves through "scenic" places; who find mountains grand if they be proper mountains with waterfalls, cliffs, and lakes. To such the Kansas plains are tedious. They see the endless corn, but not the heave and the grunt of ox teams breaking the prairie. . . . They look at the low horizon, but they cannot see it, as de Vaca did, under the bellies of the buffalo.[12]

THE FORMAL BEAUTY OF AGRICULTURAL LANDSCAPES

What is the cure for finding the Kansas plains, the endless fields of corn, and agricultural landscapes in general to be, as Saito says, "lacking in aesthetic values" or simply, as Leopold concisely puts it, "tedious"? It is important that such a cure be forthcoming and not only for the aesthetic sake, as it were, of agricultural landscapes or simply for the enrichment of our aesthetic experience. It is also important from the point of view of aesthetic theory, for without such a remedy agricultural landscapes and other environments that are taken to be "lacking in aesthetic values" would seemingly constitute counter-examples to Ziff's Anything Viewed Doctrine (chap. 3). Given the centrality of this doctrine to Western aesthetic theory, this would be an unfortunate outcome.

Such an outcome can be avoided, however. The first step to addressing the issue is to retreat somewhat from the disinterested, picturesque paradigm of landscape appreciation and to return, to some extent, to the earlier ideal of simple appreciation of beauty. Conron characterizes the beautiful as small, smooth, subtly varied, delicate, and "'clean and fair' . . . of color." This does not, of course, perfectly fit the landscapes of contemporary agriculture, but it certainly comes closer to doing so than either the powerful and terrifying intensity of the sublime or the complex and irregular eccentricity of the classic picturesque. Although not always small, agricultural landscapes, especially when well tended, are quite often smooth and delicate, subtly varied, and "'clean and fair' . . . of color."

The primary way in which agricultural landscapes can be simply beautiful—the way in which they best exemplify some of the characteristics that Conron attributes to beauty rather than to the sublime or the picturesque—is in terms of their formal aesthetic qualities. Clive Bell was perhaps the greatest advocate of formal beauty as the proper focus of aesthetic experience (chap. 3). He found such beauty mainly in what he termed the "significant form" of works of art. However, even Bell, whose aesthetic interest was almost exclusively devoted to art, could find aesthetic value in the landscape when it was experienced as, in his words, "a pure formal combination of lines and colours." And significantly, his example is an agricultural landscape, a landscape of "fields and cottages":

All of us, I imagine, do, from time to time, get a vision of material objects as pure forms. . . . We see things . . . with the eye of an artist. Who has not, once at least in his life, had a sudden vision of landscape as pure form? For once, instead of seeing it as fields and cottages, he has felt it as lines and colours. . . . [H]e has contrived to see it as a pure formal combination of lines and colours."[13]

Bell recommended that we see things "with the eye of an artist" in order to discover their aesthetic value. This may not be the best way to aesthetically appreciate natural environments and many human environments, but it is a way to begin to administer the cure for finding agricultural landscapes "lacking in aesthetic values" or simply "tedious." For such landscapes, it is a means by which to retreat from the disinterested, picturesque paradigm of landscape appreciation and to return to the ideal of simple appreciation of beauty. This is because many artistic treatments of agricultural landscapes, in contrast to such treatments of classic scenic landscapes, do not cling to the disinterested, picturesque paradigm, but are more straightforward exercises in presenting the formal beauty of such landscapes, perhaps because agricultural landscapes simply have greater formal beauty than do scenic natural environments. Be that as it may, this tendency for artistic treatments of agricultural landscapes to emphasize the formal beauty of line, shape, and color is particularly evident in the work of artists who pursue more abstract kinds of painting. When they turn their attention to the landscapes of contemporary agriculture, they frequently bring out many of the characteristics that Conron attributes to beauty: smoothness, delicacy, subtle variation, and "clean and fair" color. For example, the work of Canadian artist Takao Tanabe, such as *The Land, #26* (1972) and *The Land, 4/75—East of Calgary* (1975), illustrate this general point (figure 6.1).

Once we begin to see agricultural landscapes "with the eye of an artist," their formal beauty becomes strikingly obvious. This is especially clear in the case of fieldscapes, as is indicated by Tanabe's paintings. In the grain fields of the North American Midwest, for example, subtly of color and boldness of line combine with scale and scope to produce landscapes of breathtaking formal beauty: great checkerboard squares of green and gold, vast rectangles of infinitesimally different shades of gray, or "immense stripes of sepia and ocher stretching mile upon mile to the margins of the sky."[14] Such features are well exemplified in any overview of the great grain-farming landscapes of western Canada (figure 6.2). Moreover, they are also evident in agricultural landscapes of less vast dimension, such as those of northern Europe (figure 6.3). In

Figure 6.1 Takao Tanabe, *The Land, 4/75—East of Calgary* (1975). (Reprinted by permission of Takao Tanabe)

Figure 6.2 An agricultural landscape, Saskatchewan, Canada. (Postcard courtesy of the author)

Figure 6.3 An agricultural landscape, Häme, Finland. (Photograph by the author)

such landscapes, there is smaller scale and perhaps greater delicacy and subtler variation, and thus they even more clearly exemplify the characteristics that Conron attributes to beauty.[15]

THE EXPRESSIVE BEAUTY OF AGRICULTURAL LANDSCAPES

Formal beauty is an impressive and important dimension of the aesthetic value of agricultural landscapes and constitutes part of the solution to the problems posed by such landscapes being taken to be "lacking in aesthetic value," but it does not exhaust their aesthetic value. Unlike Bell and other formalists, we should not limit the aesthetic value of either works of art or landscapes simply to their formal aesthetic qualities. Recall that after he disparages the aesthetic competence of those "who are willing to be herded in droves through 'scenic' places" and who find agricultural landscapes only "tedious," Leopold does *not* go on to praise the formal beauty of such landscapes. Rather, he recommends that we see, in our mind's eye, the "ox teams breaking the prairie" and "the low horizon, . . . as de Vaca did, under the bellies of the buffalo." Leopold is emphasizing that there is much more to the aesthetic value of landscapes than simply the formal beauty that most immediately strikes the eye. Philosopher John Hospers makes a similar point concerning the aesthetic value of natural landscapes: "When we contemplate a starry night or a mountain lake we see it not merely as an arrangement of pleasing colors, shapes, and volumes, but as expressive of many things in life, drenched with the fused association of many scenes and emotions from memory and experience."[16]

Elaborating the point suggested by Leopold and made explicit by Hospers requires returning to the distinction and accompanying concepts introduced in chapter 4. Recall that the distinction is between two senses of aesthetic value, as clarified by D. W. Prall and Hospers.[17] Hospers describes it as the distinction between the "thin sense" and the "thick sense" of "the aesthetic." The thin sense is relevant when we, following Bell and other formalists, aesthetically appreciate and value objects primarily in terms of their physical appearances and their resultant formal aesthetic qualities, while the thick sense involves not merely appearances but also certain qualities that objects express to the appreciator. Prall calls this the "expressive beauty" of objects, while Hospers speaks of objects expressing "life values."[18] Although I use the phrase "expressive beauty," I mainly employ the notion of life values, since, as will become clear, not all life values are appropriately characterized as "beautiful." Life values involve a wide range of characteristics that are associated with objects such that they are felt or perceived to be qualities of the objects themselves. They are connected with objects by deep-seated and commonly held beliefs and thus depend on what is in general taken to be the "true" nature of the objects said to express them.[19]

Before applying the distinction between the thin and the thick sense of aesthetic value to agricultural landscapes, it is useful to note that in focusing on the expressive beauty of these landscapes and the life values that they express, we take another step away from the eighteenth-century aesthetic synthesis, which ultimately led to the "aesthetic abuse" of finding agricultural landscapes "lacking in aesthetic value." As noted, this "aesthetic abuse" is rooted in the disinterested, picturesque paradigm of landscape appreciation. Although the appreciation of the formal beauty of agricultural landscapes is an antidote to the exclusive emphasis on scenic picturesque landscapes, it does not fully address the problemization of the appreciation of agricultural landscapes, for formal beauty and disinterestedness are fully compatible. However, focusing on expressive beauty and life values calls into question the overly dominant and restrictive role that disinterestedness plays in aesthetic experience. This is because the life values that an object seems to express are ultimately tied to what is generally taken to be the object's "true" nature, which not only has little to do with whether it is "scenic," but also is unlikely to be revealed if our experience of that object is *totally* disinterested. Aesthetic experience requires a degree of disinterestedness, but not so much as to make it impossible to appreciate the expressive beauty of objects of appreciation.

FUNCTION, PRODUCTIVITY, SUSTAINABILITY, AND EXPRESSIVE BEAUTY

Given that the expressive beauty of an object—the life values that it seems to expresses—is connected with and by and large derived from what is taken to be its "true" nature, it follows that the life values expressed by agricultural landscapes depend on their particular functions and on how well or how poorly they fulfill them. In short, the expressed life values of agricultural landscapes depend on their productivity and sustainability. This is because part of the "true" nature of any agricultural landscape is that it is *functional*. In general, functional landscapes are created by humans in order to achieve certain goals. Consequently, functional landscapes are to various degrees designed, and the degree to which they are designed, together with how well they are designed, in large part determines the life values that they express.[20] In other words, the life values expressed by functional landscapes depend largely on how well their designs facilitate the accomplishment of their functions—that is, how productive and sustainable they are.

These considerations are especially pertinent to contemporary agricultural landscapes, for they are typically both highly designed and well designed—and they are typically very productive. I have developed this line of thought elsewhere and consequently will only summarize my conclusions.[21] The kind of functions that contemporary

Figure 6.4 Grain-storage units, Alberta, Canada. (Photograph by the author)

agricultural landscapes perform and the way that they perform them—
using the land itself to produce food and fiber—lead to the creation of
highly designed landscapes. Moreover, such landscapes are in general
very well designed. Years of trial and error, together with the pressures
for production, have resulted in landscapes that are paradigms of good
design—crisp, clean, uncluttered, and expressive of such life values as
ingenuity, efficiency, and economy. Not only the fields, but also both
the machines that work them and the buildings that occupy them
should be appreciated in terms of how and how well they perform their
functions. Consider the self-propelled pickers and combines or the si-
los and storage structures that populate contemporary agricultural
landscapes. They are examples of machines designed to collect, sort,
and clean in one continuous flow of activity and of storage units designed to follow the natural "angle of repose" of that which they contain
(figure 6.4). Such machines and buildings not only express life values
associated with good design, but also possess a style, grace, and ele-
gance seldom exceeded anywhere else. In short, agricultural landscapes
have great expressive beauty. Although the formal beauty of the land-

scapes of agriculture is an impressive and important dimension of their aesthetic value, it is ultimately overshadowed by their expressive beauty.

According to this line of thought, the expressive beauty of agricultural landscapes depends on their productivity, their being paradigms of good design that are expressive of such life values as ingenuity, efficiency, and economy. But since the life values expressed by functional landscapes depend on how well their designs facilitate the accomplishment of their functions—that is, how productive *and sustainable* they are—to fully determine the expressive beauty of agricultural landscapes, we must consider not only their productivity but also their sustainability. The issues that touch on sustainability are less clear and perhaps the life values expressed less positive than are those that relate to productivity. The point is put forcefully by environmental philosopher Ned Hettinger:

> If aesthetically appreciating modern agricultural landscapes involves focusing on their functions, and if such landscapes are unsustainable—as the environmentalist critics of agriculture charge—then instead of a positive aesthetic response to well-functioning landscapes, the appropriate response will be dismay at a massively dysfunctional system. Modern agriculture is fossil-fuel and fossil-water reliant, it is soil eroding, it is a prime water polluter, and it destroys rural communities. . . . In light of this focus on the purposes, goals, and functions of modern industrial agriculture, such landscapes are expressive of waste, short-sightedness, and profligacy.[22]

Hettinger's view is that rather than being paradigms of good design expressive of such life values as ingenuity, efficiency, and economy, contemporary agricultural landscapes are "massively dysfunctional system[s] . . . expressive of waste, short-sightedness, and profligacy." Certainly, if this opinion is correct, then the so-called expressive beauty of the landscapes of contemporary agriculture is badly tarnished and perhaps should be termed "expressive ugliness" rather than "expressive beauty." In essence, Hettinger's concerns are about the social and environmental costs of the continual development of modern agriculture, and these costs are, of course, evidenced in the landscapes of

Figure 6.5 Abandoned farm buildings, Alberta, Canada. (Photograph by the author)

agriculture. Many such landscapes were once home to small family farms, which, although perhaps not fully paradigms of good design, were at least not "massively dysfunctional system[s]." However, such landscapes are now all too frequently the sites of deserted farmsteads and abandoned and dilapidated farm buildings (figure 6.5). Indeed, they bespeak the social costs of modern agriculture and can easily be regarded as expressing such life values as "waste, short-sightedness, and profligacy." Moreover, if these landscapes are occupied by anything other than the decaying remains of once-thriving farms, it is too frequently only the fertilizer and pesticide operations that signify the environmental costs of contemporary agriculture and thus reinforce the expression of negative life values, such as "short-sightedness" and "profligacy."

The upshot is that once we fully recognize the significance of the expressive beauty of the landscapes of agriculture and appreciate the fact that they are functional landscapes with expressive aesthetic qualities dependent on their productivity and sustainability, we are left with the following question: Are the landscapes of contemporary agriculture paradigms of good design expressive of ingenuity, efficiency, and economy, or "massively dysfunctional system[s] . . . expressive of waste, short-sightedness, and profligacy"? Concerning this question, three related points are relevant. First, since the life values that a landscape *seems* to express are ultimately tied to what is generally taken to be its "true" nature, it follows that the life values that it actually expresses depend not simply on what is perceived to be its "true" nature, but on what is *in fact* its true nature. Second, as a consequence of this, it becomes clear that the question of whether contemporary agricultural landscapes express ingenuity, efficiency, and economy or "waste, short-sightedness, and profligacy" cannot be answered simply by aesthetic analysis and philosophical debate. Rather, it is an *empirical* question that ultimately must be settled by a determination of the facts about the landscapes of contemporary agriculture and the agricultural practices that produce them. And third, it thus becomes evident that once all the facts are determined, there probably will be no black-and-white, across-the-board answer to this question. Not only will some of the landscapes of agriculture express mainly positive life values while others express mainly negative ones, but, and perhaps more important, many, if not most, will express some positive and some negative life values. In short, appreciating the expressive aesthetic value of the landscapes of contemporary agriculture is truly a matter of, as cultural geographer Peirce Lewis nicely puts it, "facing up to ambiguity."[23]

AESTHETIC AMBIGUITY AND THE HUMAN ENVIRONMENT

These three points, as well as the ambiguity of the aesthetic value of agricultural landscapes to which they lead us, have both theoretical and appreciative consequences.

On the theoretical level, they reinforce the main theme that I have emphasized when developing such ideas as the Natural Environmental Model, concerning natural environments, and the ecological approach, concerning human environments. The theme is that to fully and appropriately aesthetically appreciate such environments requires knowledge: first, that provided by the natural sciences of geology, ecology, botany, and zoology; and, second, that offered by the social sciences of history, geography, anthropology, and sociology. When confronted with landscapes, such as those of agriculture, that are complex mixtures of natural and human elements and that are especially ambiguous in regard to their aesthetic value, it becomes evident not only why all such knowledge is relevant, but also how very relevant it is if we wish to get at what might be called the aesthetic truth of the matter. Closely related to this is a second theoretical consequence, which is that landscapes such as those of agriculture fully bring out the usefulness of the methodological framework developed in chapter 3. Although such landscapes initially seem to challenge Ziff's Anything Viewed Doctrine, they ultimately reinforce it once their aesthetic value is brought to light. More important, when the full extent of their aesthetic ambiguity is revealed, such landscapes strongly underwrite the importance of, in line with Budd's As Nature Constraint, appreciating environments for what they truly are and, in line with Hepburn's Serious Beauty Intuition, attempting to achieve as deep and as serious an aesthetic appreciation as possible. And, somewhat paradoxically, aesthetically ambiguous landscapes highlight the significance of trying to meet Thompson's Objectivity Desideratum, for their ambiguity, unless and until it is resolved, poses a serious challenge to the possibility of reaching objective aesthetic judgments about them.

The appreciative consequences of the aesthetic ambiguity of agricultural landscapes can be summarized in the five main points. First, when brought out from under the shadow of the disinterested, picturesque paradigm of landscape appreciation, the landscapes of contemporary agriculture, rather than lacking aesthetic value, are of exceptional formal and expressive beauty. Second, while the impressive formal beauty of many agricultural landscapes is simply given in their appearances, their expressive beauty depends on other factors, such as their function, productivity, and sustainability. Therefore, third, pinpointing this more significant dimension of the aesthetic value of agricultural landscapes depends on determining their true nature, finding out whether they are in fact paradigms of good design or "massively dysfunctional system[s]." Fourth, this, however, is an empirical issue that must be settled by recourse to knowledge provided by both the natural and the social sciences. This, in turn, suggests, fifth, that the exact nature and extent of the more significant dimension of the aesthetic value of the landscapes of contemporary agriculture are far from clear and may vary considerably from case to case.

Although this conclusion may be unsettling to some, it is important to keep in mind in our attempts to fully and appropriately aesthetically appreciate human environments, for the ambiguity of aesthetic value that is apparent in the landscapes of agriculture is also evident in other human environments. For example, it is a feature of such previously discussed cases as both exclusive, upper-middle-class suburban neighborhoods (chap. 4) and some environmental buildings and architecture (chap. 5). In short, the aesthetic ambiguity that we confront in contemporary agricultural landscapes can be found, to a greater or lesser degree, in all the landscapes that humans have created.

7 / WHAT IS THE CORRECT WAY TO
AESTHETICALLY APPRECIATE LANDSCAPES?

In his book *Aesthetics and the Philosophy of Art Criticism*, aesthetician Jerome Stolnitz presents a particular formulation of the issue that I have been addressing, both implicitly and explicitly, throughout this book. He calls it the question of aesthetic relevance. He asks: "Is it ever 'relevant' to aesthetic experience to have thoughts or images or bits of knowledge which are not present within the object itself? If these are even relevant, under what conditions are they so?"[1] In this final chapter, I use Stolnitz's question as a means to focus and bring together several ideas and themes discussed in earlier chapters. In doing so, I hope to not only summarize my own point of view, but also begin to answer a reformulation of Stolnitz's question: What is the correct way to aesthetically appreciate landscapes?

THE QUESTION OF AESTHETIC RELEVANCE

Stolnitz asks his version of the question of aesthetic relevance mainly about works of art, and his treatment of it reflects the particular nature of art.[2] Although the question is complex and confusing in regard to the aesthetic experience of art, it is even more so for landscapes. Concerning the aesthetic appreciation of landscapes, the question of aesthetic relevance is doubly ramified. First, recall that landscapes are famously characterized by George Santayana as "indeterminate" and "promiscuous," containing "enough diversity to allow the eye a great liberty in selecting, emphasizing, and grouping its elements." Thus to be appreciated, landscapes must be "composed," even though such appreciation depends on all that is vague and whimsical, on reverie, fancy, and emotion (chaps. 2 and 5).[3] Second, in addition to indeterminacy, contemporary human landscapes in particular are especially prone to aesthetic ambiguity resulting from a mix of negative and positive expressed life values. As discussed in chapter 6, appreciating the aesthetic value of human landscapes, such as those of contemporary agriculture, frequently involves, as Peirce Lewis puts it, "facing up to ambiguity."[4] Consequently, the question of aesthetic relevance in regard to landscapes is not simply the question of what is relevant to appreciation. It is the question of how, *in light of indeterminacy and ambiguity*, a landscape is to be composed in order to facilitate its appropriate aesthetic appreciation. Among all the vague and whimsical stuff and all the positive and negative life values on which appreciation might depend, what "thoughts or images or bits of knowledge" are really relevant?

Throughout this chapter, I approach the question of aesthetic relevance as an issue in aesthetic education about landscapes. If aesthetic education is the business of teaching appropriate aesthetic appreciation, then, concerning the landscape, the question is what to teach those in whom we wish to instill the appreciation of landscapes. What skills, what talents, what thoughts, what images, what information, what bits of knowledge must we give our children—and, indeed, our peers and even ourselves—in order to engender a rich, appropriate appreciation of landscapes? To put the question explicitly in terms of aesthetic education: What is the correct *curriculum* for teaching the appropriate aesthetic appreciation of landscapes? I approach this question by considering several topics, each of which might be a candidate for inclusion in such a curriculum: form, common knowledge, science, history, contemporary use, myth, symbol, and art.

A POSTMODERN VIEW OF LANDSCAPE APPRECIATION?

Before considering the eight topics, it is useful to note one point of view that, if correct, would seemingly render pointless the whole question of a correct curriculum for the appropriate appreciation of landscapes. It might be argued that if, as Santayana and Lewis suggest, the landscape is indeterminate and ambiguous—if its appreciation depends

on that which is vague and whimsical, on reverie, fancy, and emotion—
it follows that anything and everything, and nothing in particular,
should be included in the curriculum. When it comes to the aesthetic
appreciation of landscapes, this position suggests, it is not a matter of
relevant or irrelevant information and appropriate or inappropriate
appreciation, but simply a matter of "whatever" and perhaps "the more,
the merrier." The view seemingly involves a sort of radical landscape
relativism. According to it, as the saying goes, "It's all relative."

I call this perspective, without, I hope, doing *too much* injustice to all
concerned parties, the postmodern view of landscape appreciation. I
use this label for two reasons: first, because of the obvious and frequently made comparison between the landscape and a text and, second, because of one postmodern position on the reading of a text. In
reading a text, according to this view, we rightly find not just the
meaning that its author intended, but any of various meanings that the
text may in one way or another have acquired or that we may for one
reason or another find in it. Moreover, and this is the important point,
none of these possible meanings has priority; no reading of a text is
privileged. On the postmodern view of landscape appreciation, whatever of Santayana's vague and whimsical reverie, fancy, and emotional
response we may bring to the landscape is seemingly as good as any
other; no reading of a landscape is privileged. According to this view, it
is perfectly fine, to return to Ronald Hepburn's example, that if "the
outline of a cumulo-nimbus cloud resembles that of a basket of washing, . . . we [simply] amuse ourselves in dwelling upon this resemblance"
(chap. 3).[5] In short, there is no appropriate appreciation of landscapes,
no correct way to aesthetically appreciate them, and thus no correct
curriculum for landscape appreciation.

Those who subscribe to the postmodern view of landscape appreciation might find support for their position not only in Santayana's
remarks about the landscape as indeterminate and promiscuous, but
also in some of his comments on aesthetic education. He says, for example, "Aesthetic education consists in training ourselves to see the
maximum of beauty."[6] And, indeed, looking for the *maximum* of
beauty certainly sounds a lot like "the more, the merrier." One might
think that to obtain the *maximum* of beauty—that is, the fullest and
richest appreciation—everything is relevant and nothing should be

excluded. However, Santayana's comments on aesthetic education also contain the seeds of a refutation of the postmodern view. We must *train* ourselves to see, he says, the maximum of beauty. The implication is that seeing the maximum of beauty, attaining the fullest and richest appreciation, is a matter of training, of learning. Vague and whimsical reverie and fancy may give us an occasional thrill, a delight in this or that possible reading, or a chuckle at a puffy, floating-by basket of washing. But ultimately, it will give us only titillating chaos, not the fullest and richest possible appreciation of landscapes. For such appreciation, we need training; and for training, we need a correct curriculum, not just anything, everything, and nothing in particular.

Thus I leave the postmodern view, at least for now, and suggest that insofar as we maintain the parallel between the landscape and a text, we should do so, at least initially, with the somewhat out-of-fashion, modernist notion of the reading of a text. On this view, at least some readings of a text are mistaken: misinterpretations that are simply read into it, rather than, as it were, read out of it. Likewise, some readings of the landscape are mistaken: misinterpretations that are not a basis for appropriate appreciation. Thus there is the possibility of mistaken, inappropriate aesthetic appreciation of landscapes. I accept this view of landscape appreciation for now and use it as the background assumption as we work through the eight topics, asking which should be included in a curriculum for appropriate aesthetic appreciation of landscapes and which are only dimensions of postmodern landscape appreciation.

FORM, CONTENT, AND COMMON KNOWLEDGE

The first of the eight topics is form. By this term, I mean something like that which traditional formalist theoreticians, such as Clive Bell, refer to as significant form—that is, aesthetically moving combinations of lines, shapes, and colors (chaps. 3 and 6). It is difficult to deny that the appreciation of form in this sense is a dimension of the aesthetic appreciation of landscapes. Even Bell, who focused almost exclusively on art, entertained the possibility of seeing the landscape as, in his words, "a pure formal combination of lines and colours." Recall that he asked: "Who has not, once at least in his life, had a sudden vision of landscape as pure form? For once, instead of seeing it as fields and cottages, he has felt it as lines and colours."[7] Bell had in mind something like seeing a landscape as it might look in a painting by Cézanne, for example.

Bell was correct in thinking that we can and do appreciate landscapes in this formal manner. Moreover, the appreciation of formal beauty can be a first step toward the aesthetic appreciation of landscapes thought to be "lacking in aesthetic value," especially when it is guided by certain kinds of landscape painting (chap. 6). However, this mode of appreciation is not simply encouraged by landscape painting, but also in a less subtle way imposed on the landscape by many popular presentations of landscapes, such as postcard and calendar images, in which dominant shapes, strong lines, and striking colors are emphasized to the near exclusion of other aesthetic qualities. Such images can promote a misleading and superficial form of appreciation of the natural environment that, nonetheless, continues to be a common dimension of popular aesthetic appreciation (chap. 2). Consequently, the curriculum for teaching the appropriate aesthetic appreciation of landscapes must include those skills and that information necessary for formal appreciation. If we persist in seeing landscapes in formal terms, it is important that we do it well—or at least as well as possible, given all the pitfalls and perils inherent in such appreciation.

Having granted this much, however, it is important, to resist the additional step that many formalists have taken. This is to insist that the formal dimension is the fundamental, perhaps even the only, dimension of aesthetic appreciation. Bell and other pure formalists are notorious for holding that formal appreciation exhausts aesthetic appreciation. The view is that consideration of form is all that is involved in aesthetic appreciation and that, by contrast, consideration of content is irrelevant. As is well known, Bell claimed that for aesthetic appreciation, "we need bring with us nothing from life, no knowledge of its ideas and affairs, no familiarity with its emotions."[8] As is also well known, however, there are many problems with this kind of pure formalism.[9] For example, some versions of formalism seem to violate Budd's As Nature Constraint.

Moreover, one problem concerning the pure formalist appreciation of landscapes is especially relevant here. On the one hand, landscapes, as noted, are indeterminate and ambiguous and therefore must be composed to be appreciated; on the other, formal elements in themselves typically do not provide adequate resources to compose a landscape. This is in part because by reference to only themselves, the formal elements of a landscape can hardly even be identified. The way in which they are identified is by reference to something other than themselves, typically content. For example, consider any formally impressive landscape—say, a forested mountain landscape with one major peak and two minor ones. Then ask yourself: How many shapes does it have? one? three? or about three hundred? How many lines does it have? The point is that in order to identify the shapes and the lines in a landscape, we make reference to content. If we decide that there is one basic shape, it is in part because one major thing, the major mountain peak, is present. If we decide that there are three, it is because three things, the major peak and two minor ones, are taken as constituting its content. If we decide that there are about three hundred, it is because we are counting each identifiable tree as a particular shape. These examples demonstrate that the formal appreciation of a landscape in terms of lines, shapes, and colors necessitates the consideration of the content of that landscape. In short, in landscape appreciation, we cannot appreciate form without including content.

If formal appreciation requires us to consider content as well as form, this takes us beyond pure formalism and beyond the first item in the suggested curriculum. It shows that the curriculum must include content as well as form. However, it should be clear that all the remaining seven candidates for inclusion in the curriculum are in one sense or other content items. Thus, the question is: Which and how many of these are relevant?

Consider the second topic: common knowledge. By this term, I mean the normal classifications that we employ in our commonsense conceptualization of the world. This is the kind of knowledge that pure formalists such as Bell seek to exclude from aesthetic appreciation. He wanted us to see the landscape in terms of lines, shapes, and colors and *not* in terms of fields and cottages. Ironically, however, this is the knowledge required for the formal appreciation of landscapes, for it is by reference to these commonsense conceptualizations that we typically organize or, to use Santayana's term, "compose" a landscape. We compose the mountain landscape by reference to that which we have categorized as, for example, mountain peak or tree. Thus this basic kind of content is seemingly required for any aesthetic appreciation of landscapes. It must be an essential part of the correct curriculum. However, it hardly needs extensive treatment in teaching the curriculum, for it is the kind of knowledge we acquire in our language learning and socialization. Indeed, we need it not just for aesthetic appreciation, but for life itself.

SCIENCE AND LANDSCAPE APPRECIATION

The third topic is science. By this term, I mean the natural history of a landscape as it is elaborated by the natural sciences, especially geology, biology, and ecology. Since the role of scientific knowledge in the aesthetic appreciation of landscapes, especially natural landscapes, has been discussed (chaps. 2 and 3), I do not dwell on it here.[10] But I do briefly note two arguments that demonstrate that scientific knowledge of landscapes is as vital to their aesthetic appreciation as is common knowledge and thus must have an equally central place in the curriculum.

The first argument depends on the fact that, in one important sense, scientific knowledge is simply an extension of common knowledge. The scientific classifications of a landscape may be finer-grained and theoretically richer than commonsense ones, but they are not essentially different in kind. Compare two descriptions of a typical mountain landscape: first, a commonsense description of it as a series of rocky peaks jutting from a rolling valley and, second, a scientific description of it as a series of faulted igneous uplifts exposed by the erosion of surrounding sedimentary deposits. There is, of course, some of what might be called conceptual movement from the commonsense to the scientific description. What is important, however, is that insofar as this movement makes any difference in the appreciation of the landscape, it does not involve a change from aesthetic appreciation to something else. Rather, if there is a difference in appreciation, it is a movement from superficial to deeper aesthetic appreciation—that is, what Hepburn describes as "a passage . . . from easy beauty to difficult and more serious beauty," or, in other words, a movement away from the appreciation of clouds as a "basket of washing."[11] According to this line of argument, scientific knowledge deepens and enhances the appropriate aesthetic appreciation of landscapes that is initiated by common knowledge. Thus its addition to the curriculum for teaching appropriate aesthetic appreciation is essential, in part because it helps to ensure that the curriculum will accord with Hepburn's Serious Beauty Intuition.

The second argument involves a comparison with the aesthetic appreciation of art. I employed this kind of argument in developing the Natural Environmental Model for the appreciation of natural environments (chap. 2), so give only a brief sketch of it here. The argument takes for granted that the knowledge provided by such disciplines as art history and art criticism is essential to the appropriate aesthetic appreciation of works of art. These subjects are, without doubt, included in any curriculum for art appreciation, and they impart knowledge about the nature of and creation of works of art—in short, knowledge about the categorization of artworks and about what might be called their histories of production. And this is the kind of knowledge that science provides about landscapes. For example, geology classifies the elements of landscapes and tells the story of how they came to be—their histories of production, as it were. Thus for the same reasons that art historical and art critical knowledge is given a prominent place in any curriculum for the aesthetic appreciation of art, scientific knowledge must be given an analogous place in a curriculum for the aesthetic appreciation of landscapes.

In light of these two arguments, as well as what I have argued in previous chapters, I conclude that scientific knowledge is necessary for the appropriate aesthetic appreciation of landscapes. Therefore, the essential reading list for the correct curriculum must include works of natural science, especially the writings of those natural historians and scientifically informed nature writers who specifically treat the understanding and appreciation of the natural world—for example, Henry David Thoreau, John Muir, John Burroughs, Aldo Leopold, Joseph Kurtch, Marston Bates, Sally Carrighar, Sigurd Olson, Loren Eiseley, Barry Lopez, and David Quammen.[12]

HISTORICAL AND CONTEMPORARY USES OF LANDSCAPES

We now have what might be thought of as the heart of the correct curriculum for the appropriate aesthetic appreciation of landscapes. It includes the first three proposed topics: form, common knowledge, and scientific knowledge. Does it follow that the remaining five items—history, contemporary use, myth, symbol, and art—are not essential to the curriculum? Does it follow that they should be involved only in postmodern appreciation?

The comparison with art appreciation would seem to indicate that these five topics should not be included in the curriculum. Consider history. By this term, I mean the historical use, not the natural history, of a landscape. The comparison with art appreciation seemingly suggests that the history of a particular landscape in this sense is indeed irrelevant. The history of a particular work of art is usually thought to be irrelevant to its aesthetic appreciation. For example, for most standard works of art, historical facts such as that the work first was displayed in a certain museum, then was shipped here and there, and now hangs in a particular gallery would not normally be considered relevant to its appropriate aesthetic appreciation. Is knowing that after its completion Picasso's *Guernica* (1937) was displayed in a number of European capitals and resided at the Museum of Modern Art in New York City for many years before it was finally moved to Madrid in 1981 significant for its aesthetic appreciation? It seems that such information is at least not obviously relevant. Or that it is relevant only if we embrace the postmodern view, according to which no appreciation is privileged and any information that happens to interest us can be accepted as relevant.

On the issue of the relevance of landscape history to landscape appreciation, however, the comparison with art appreciation is somewhat misleading. There is an important disanalogy between landscapes and works of art that must be considered. A work of art usually is *completed* at a specific time. What happens to it before this point is what I call its history of production and, alternatively, what happens to it after the time of completion is its history. And typically with a work of art, while its history of production, like the natural history of a landscape, is clearly relevant to its aesthetic appreciation, its later history, as suggested by the example of *Guernica*, is not. By contrast, there is no specific time at which most landscapes are completed. For this reason, their natural histories and their actual histories—their historical uses—are in a sense continuous, since both constitute a single ongoing history of production. This is another sense in which landscapes can be thought to be, using Santayana's term, "promiscuous": most landscapes are continuously in the process of being made and remade. All that happens to them, their ongoing histories, continues to shape them.

The upshot is that knowledge of the ongoing histories of most landscapes is vital to their aesthetic appreciation—indeed, often the most important key to such appreciation. Consequently, the knowledge about landscapes provided by the social sciences—history itself, as well as geography, anthropology, and sociology—is an essential component of the curriculum for the appreciation of landscapes. Especially relevant are particular kinds of studies that employ the knowledge gained from such sciences specifically to tell the stories of the long-term development of landscapes. Thus, for example, consider works such as W. G. Hoskins's seminal volume, *The Making of the English Landscape*; John Brinckerhoff Jackson's classic reflections on the American landscape; and May Theilgaard Watts's near-perfect blend of natural and cultural history in her landscape guidebook, *Reading the Landscape of America*.[13] A familiarity with such writings, as well as those of the naturalists listed earlier, is absolutely necessary for the appropriate aesthetic appreciation of landscapes. The social sciences, especially in the hands of such thinkers as Hoskins, Jackson, and Watts, generally tell the story of landscapes over long spans of time. However, less gradual and more dramatic changes in the history of a landscape, again because of how they shape it, are equally a part of the history of production and therefore equally aesthetically relevant. For example, consider two monuments in the western United States: Devils Tower in Wyoming and Mount Rushmore in South Dakota. The former was set aside as the first United States National Monument in 1906 (figure 7.1). By this act, it was removed from further development, and thus the act is in a negative sense extremely relevant to appreciating the present, somewhat pristine state of Devils Tower. Indeed, without this moment in its history, Devils Tower today might be crowned with golden arches or sculpted into a great stone Mickey Mouse. Mount Rushmore, as is well

Figure 7.1 Devils Tower National Monument, Wyoming. (Photograph by the author)

known, was indeed sculpted, not into a stone mouse, but into likenesses of four United States presidents. Such a momentous event in a landscape's history is obviously relevant to its appropriate aesthetic appreciation. Similarly, another mountain in South Dakota's Black Hills is in the process of being turned into a sculpture of the great Sioux leader Crazy Horse. Without knowledge of this, it is impossible to appropriately appreciate the mountain's somewhat chaotic current state.

This brings us to the fifth candidate for inclusion in the curriculum: the contemporary use of landscapes. By this phrase, I mean all the various functions and roles in human life that environments have in the modern world. The relevance of knowledge of the contemporary use of landscapes to their aesthetic appreciation should be clear from discussions in previous chapters, but it also follows from the relevance of the history of landscapes. The contemporary use of a landscape is continuous with its actual history, just as that history is continuous with its natural history. All three are a part of the ongoing history of production of a landscape. Thus those aspects of the social sciences, especially geography and sociology, that focus on the recent and current factors that are shaping landscapes are particularly significant parts of the curriculum for the appreciation of landscapes.

However, there is an important difference between the history of a landscape and its contemporary use that is worth noting, if only because the difference tends to obscure the similarity of the two. It is that, seemingly in part because of our closeness to it, we as appreciators of landscapes are much more apt to regard as negative the contemporary use of a landscape and the making and remaking that it brings to the landscape. We frequently consider the contemporary remaking of landscapes to be *abuse* rather than simply *use* and look on it with aesthetic dismay. This is certainly true of some current uses of many natural landscapes. Consider, for example, the remaking of landscapes brought about by strip-mining or clear-cutting. Few individuals, except perhaps the odd developer, would view the resultant new landscapes in an aesthetically positive way.[14] This is also true of many recent changes that are visited on some traditional human landscapes, such as those that result from the application of modern agricultural techniques in traditional farming landscapes (chap. 6). In fact, the aesthetic ambiguity, in addition to indeterminacy, to which human environments are particularly predisposed is typically most evident in light of their contemporary use.

Be that as it may, what must be stressed is that even if we regard the contemporary making and remaking of a landscape primarily in a negative manner, our reaction does *not* make knowledge of this part of its history of production *irrelevant* to its aesthetic appreciation. Another analogy with a work of art is helpful. Consider Michelangelo's *Pietà* (1498–1499). On May 21, 1972, a mentally disturbed geologist attacked it with a hammer. After the attack, the sculpture was reconstructed, and missing fragments were replaced with a mixture of ground marble and polyester resin. Most likely, we regard these dramatic events in the contemporary history of this work negatively. However, given the way in which the destruction and subsequent reconstruction of the *Pietà* necessarily brought about changes in the statue and its appearance, knowledge of this episode in its contemporary history is absolutely essential to its appropriate aesthetic appreciation. Without this knowledge, when we view the contemporary *Pietà*, we will surely misunderstand and misappreciate it.

Along the same lines, consider the recent alterations of Michelangelo's frescoes on the ceiling of the Sistine Chapel, brought about by cleaning, not vandalism. However one regards the results, it must be admitted that knowledge of their cleaning is vital to the appropriate aesthetic appreciation of the paintings in their present state. Indeed, the knowledge not only may be essential to appropriate appreciation, but actually may help to make possible more positive appreciation. For example, the bright, shiny, nearly pastel frescoes on the ceiling of the Sistine Chapel are much easier to positively appreciate in light of the knowledge that their new look is the result of restoration, rather than of, say, retouching or, worse, updating. Thus knowledge of the contemporary use of landscapes has an essential, perhaps even somewhat special, place in the curriculum for the appropriate aesthetic appreciation of landscapes, especially since it is particularly useful in dealing with the ambiguity of aesthetic value that infects much of the contemporary human environment.[15]

MYTH, SYMBOL, AND ART

The last three items are myth, symbol, and art. By these terms, I indicate what are also *uses* of landscapes, particularly their uses in the mythical, symbolic, and artistic creations of different peoples and cultures. These uses, unlike the physical ones, do not seem to be directly involved in the making and remaking of landscapes. Thus the issue is whether we have finally left the essential curriculum and come, with these three uses, to topics that play a role only in the postmodern view of landscape appreciation: Is knowledge of these three uses of the landscape unessential and therefore best omitted from the curriculum?

The use of landscapes in mythical and folk traditions is common to most cultures. For example, consider again the landscape of Devils Tower. In the traditions of some Native American cultures, principally the Cheyenne and Kiowa, it is the landscape of Mateo Tepee, or Bear Lodge (figure 7.2). One version of the mythological account of the formation of the rock tower goes as follows:

Eight children were there at play, seven sisters and their brother. Suddenly the boy was struck dumb; he trembled and began to run upon his hands and feet. His fingers became claws, and his body was covered

Figure 7.2 Devils Tower as Mateo Tepee, or Bear Lodge. (Postcard courtesy of the author)

with fur. Directly there was a bear where the boy had been. The sisters were terrified; they ran, and the bear after them. They came to the stump of a great tree, and the tree spoke to them. It bade them climb upon it, and as they did so it began to rise into the air. The bear came to kill them, but they were just beyond its reach. It reared against the tree and scored the bark all around with its claws. The seven sisters were borne into the sky, and they became the stars of the Big Dipper.[16]

Such mythical accounts are frequently closely related to the symbolic uses of landscapes. For example, in part because of its place in this myth, Devils Tower is considered a sacred place by some Native American cultures, symbolic of the creation of the earth and the sky. It is said that when Mateo Tepee rose from the earth, it was the "birth of time" and "the motion of the world was begun."[17]

Other landscapes have comparable symbolic roles in different cultures. Mountains and similar formations seem to be particularly good bearers of such symbolic import. For instance, Mount Fuji, as is well known, has a special symbolic role in the culture of Japan. Likewise, what were called the Shining Mountains by the early explorers of North America, actually the eastern faces of the Rockies as they caught the morning sun, are still for many the symbol of the American West as the ever-beckoning land of opportunity. And, of course, a landscape formation such as Mount Rushmore has, for obvious reasons, powerful symbolic importance for many Americans. Such examples could be multiplied almost endlessly. Consider not just Mount Rushmore, Mount Fuji, and Devils Tower, but the Matterhorn, Pikes Peak, Mount Kilimanjaro, the Black Hills, Mount Edith Cavell, Mont-Saint-Victoire, Ayers Rock, Half Dome, Mount Ararat, Ship Rock, and Mount Olympus. Each has symbolic significance for certain individuals, groups, or cultures.

This brings us to the eighth topic: art. The use of landscapes in art is often connected to that in myth or as symbol. For example, the very common use of images of Mount Fuji in Japanese art is closely linked to its symbolic role in Japanese culture; each continually reinforces the other. Other examples have somewhat less intimate cultural ties. Many works of art, like those that depict Mount Fuji, involve mainly images of landscapes, while others employ actual landscapes. On the one hand, Mont-Saint-Victoire is only a basis for numerous paintings by Cézanne. On the other, the landscape itself was part of the work in environmental pieces such as Christo's Running Fence (1972–1976) and Valley Curtain (1971–1972).[18] Perhaps somewhat intermediate examples are the use of actual landscapes in realistic photographic and cinematic works of art. The images by photographers such as Edward Weston and Ansel

Figure 7.3 Devils Tower as the landing site for visitors from outer space. (Photograph by the author)

Adams are for many the classic presentations of the natural landscapes of western North America. Equally classic, although perhaps in a somewhat different sense, is the appearance of landscapes in film. Consider the use of Mount Rushmore by Alfred Hitchcock in his thriller *North by Northwest* (1959) or that of Devils Tower by Steven Spielberg in his immensely popular science-fiction film *Close Encounters of the Third Kind* (1977), in which Devils Tower is the landing site for visitors from outer space (figure 7.3).

Is knowledge of the mythical, symbolic, and artistic uses of landscapes an essential part of the correct curriculum for landscape appreciation? Indeed, does such knowledge have any place in such a curriculum? Initially, a negative answer to this question seems intuitive. After all, who would want to hold that in order to appropriately aesthetically appreciate, for example, the landscape of Devils Tower, we have to know about the Cheyenne and Kiowa myth of the creation of Mateo Tepee, let alone about Spielberg's story of humankind's first "third kind" close encounter with aliens from outer space. Likewise, to suggest that to appropriately appreciate Mount Rushmore, we must recall *North by Northwest* seems ludicrous, and perhaps even unpatriotic. Intuitively, it seems plausible to abandon such information to the vague and whimsical reverie and fancy favored by the postmodern view of landscape appreciation. Indeed, these seem to be just the right kinds of associations for this perspective.

This intuition is particularly well illustrated by Devils Tower and *Close Encounters of the Third Kind*. The guidebook to Devils Tower in the National Park Service's series The Story Behind the Scenery remarks, in a somewhat disapproving tone, that since its "cameo role" in *Close Encounters,* the tower "has been host to millions of curious moviegoers."[19] The guidebook confirms that the Park Service considers such interest on the part of "moviegoers" to be no more than vague and whimsical reverie and fancy. It quickly adds, with obvious approval, that the movie fans "soon leave memories of the film behind to capture the geological, historical, and natural stories of the Devils Tower National Monument."[20] The guidebook further tacks down the intuition by emphatically concluding that "soon the *commotion* over the motion picture died down," and "today the 450,000 yearly visitors are in awe of the Tower for its own dramatic presence and *not* as the setting for an imaginary spaceship landing."[21]

In addition to this intuition, there is a more substantial reason for skepticism about the place of knowledge about mythical, symbolic, and artistic uses of landscape in the curriculum. Myth, symbol, and art appear to be essentially different in kind from the five other topics. As noted, form and common knowledge are at the very foundation of the aesthetic appreciation of landscapes, and science, history, and contemporary use involve matters that directly influence the nature of actual landscapes. They constitute the histories of production of landscapes. Consequently, these items are relevant to the appropriate aesthetic appreciation of landscapes at least in part because they explain the way landscapes are and thus the way they look to us. By contrast, the mythical, symbolic, and artistic uses of landscapes seemingly have nothing to do with the histories of production of landscapes. Landscapes are not made and remade by them; they seem to leave landscapes just as they find them. The landscape of Devils Tower was not altered by being called Mateo Tepee or by fictionally hosting humankind's first big close encounter of the third kind. Mont-Saint-Victoire was not changed by Cézanne, nor was Half Dome remade by Ansel Adams. And even

Christo, after his environmental works of art are completed, religiously restores the landscapes he has used to their original condition.

In light of this seemingly significant difference between the last three topics and the first five, it seems reasonable to conclude that myth, symbol, and art have no essential place in the curriculum. Moreover, this determination is reinforced by recalling the ways in which art-based approaches to environmental appreciation, such as the Object Model and the Landscape Model (chap. 2) and the designer landscape approach (chap. 4), frequently mislead aesthetic appreciation. It should be obvious that mythological, symbolic, and artistic uses of landscapes can be similarly misleading to appropriate aesthetic appreciation. Consequently, concerning these uses of landscapes, it is tempting to simply follow the postmodern view of landscape appreciation. Recall that this approach contends that we may read in the landscape any of various meanings that it may in one way or another have acquired or that we may for one reason or another find in it. Moreover, none of these possible meanings has priority; no reading of the landscape is privileged. Thus the mythical, symbolic, and artistic uses are relegated to the realm of vague and whimsical reverie and fancy. Just as we may, if we wish to do so, see Hepburn's cumulo-nimbus cloud as a puffy "basket of washing," we may read the landscape text of Devils Tower in light of the myth of Mateo Tepee and its great clawing bear or the whimsical tale of close encounters with childlike aliens. But there is absolutely nothing to choose between these readings; neither is privileged. Therefore, knowledge of neither belongs in the correct curriculum for the appropriate aesthetic appreciation of landscapes.

THE "CLOSE ENCOUNTERS PHENOMENON" AND LANDSCAPE PLURALISM

There is, however, something wrong with the postmodern view even for the mythical, symbolic, and artistic uses of landscapes. It does not appear to do justice to the seeming importance and vitality of such uses. The difficulty is illuminated by what I call, after Spielberg's film, the "Close Encounters Phenomenon." Even if we believe that knowledge of, for example, the use of Devils Tower in *Close Encounters of the Third Kind* is absolutely irrelevant to the appropriate aesthetic appreciation of the monument, we may find, if we have seen the film, that it is almost impossible to free ourselves from its images. The situation is similar to that experienced by the main character in *Close Encounters*, played by Richard Dreyfuss, who, because of an encounter with a flying saucer that "imprints" the image of the tower in him, cannot shake it from his mind. He finds himself possessed by the image: he sculpts it in mashed potatoes on his dinner plate; he models it in mud in his living room. Likewise, once we have had an "imprinting" encounter with the film, it is difficult to shake its images from our minds. For instance, having seen the film, I find it almost impossible to look at a photograph of a nice family standing at the base of Devils Tower without imagining a large, ominous-looking space ship with flashing lights rising over the rock (figure 7.4)!

Obviously, the "Close Encounters Phenomenon" is quite common. The guidebook *Devils Tower: The Story Behind the Scenery* reports that after the release of *Close Encounters* "the monument's attendance rates skyrocketed. For quite some time, the most frequent question became, 'Now, where did the spaceship land?' "[22] Similarly, having seen *North by Northwest*, only once and many years ago, I yet have difficulty looking at Mount Rushmore without imagining Cary Grant and Eva Marie Saint scrambling in the moonlight over the faces of Roosevelt, Lincoln, Washington, and Jefferson. And I expect that there are Native Americans who imagine Mateo Tepee and its great clawing bear when they look at Devils Tower. Moreover, this phenomenon has not escaped the notice of artists. For example, even though Christo faithfully restores the landscape sites of his works to their original states, when he was asked "whether he thought that the canyon at Rifle Gap remained unaffected by having hosted *Valley Curtain*, he replied: 'Perhaps not. Was Mont-Saint-Victoire ever the same after Cézanne?' "[23]

The "Close Encounters Phenomenon" reminds us of the extent to which, to paraphrase a remark made by philosopher Ludwig Wittgenstein in a different context, our pictures hold us captive.[24] Its significance to the aesthetic appreciation of landscapes is that, because many mythical, symbolic, and artistic images of landscapes do hold us captive, these uses of landscapes are after all somewhat more like the other uses than they at first appear to be. It is true that these uses are not a part of the histories of production of landscapes. They do not make

Figure 7.4 A family at Devils Tower: the "Close Encounters Phenomenon"? (Photograph by the author)

and remake landscapes and by this means explain how such landscapes look to us. Nonetheless, they have explanatory power concerning the way landscapes look, at least with respect to the way they look to those who are held captive by the relevant images.

Consequently, we might say that the mythical, symbolic, and artistic uses of landscapes make and remake not the actual landscapes, but the landscape images of individuals, groups, or whole cultures. We might characterize them as making and remaking imaginary landscapes in the individual or the collective mind. And thus knowledge of these uses does indeed explain the way landscapes look to certain individuals or to members of certain groups or cultures. Of course, the explanatory power of the knowledge of the mythical, symbolic, and artistic uses of landscapes is somewhat limited because it is relative to specific contexts. Nonetheless, it seems relevant to the aesthetic appreciation of landscapes. Thus the "Close Encounters Phenomenon" suggests yet another way in which landscapes can be said to be promiscuous, indeterminate, and ambiguous: they lend themselves to and allow themselves to be appreciated in terms of the different images that various individuals and cultures bring to them.

Moreover, the "Close Encounters Phenomenon" also suggests that in regard to this dimension of landscape appreciation, the postmodern view is not quite suitable after all. Rather than the landscape relativism of the postmodern approach, what might be called landscape pluralism seems more appropriate. Like the postmodern view, the pluralist view accepts something like the comparison between the landscape and a text and recognizes that we can read in a landscape many of various meanings that it may have acquired or that we may find in it. Unlike landscape relativism, however, landscape pluralism holds that for particular individuals, groups, or cultures, some of these possible meanings have priority and thus constitute privileged readings of a landscape. Which readings are privileged depends on which landscapes of the mind hold sway for individuals, groups, or cultures—that is, which images of landscapes hold them captive. Consequently, the pluralist view gives a contextually constrained role in appropriate aesthetic appreciation to mythical, symbolic, and artistic uses of landscapes, which, by means of contributing to landscapes of the mind, form the basis for a contextually privileged aesthetic appreciation of landscapes.[25]

It is important to note, however, that the information required for such contextually privileged aesthetic appreciation will not contribute to appropriate aesthetic appreciation in the same way that knowledge of the histories of production of actual landscapes contributes to such appreciation. The latter is essential to the appropriate aesthetic appreciation of landscapes by any appreciator, while the former is relevant to only certain individuals, groups, or cultures. Moreover, and perhaps of more theoretical importance, the knowledge of the histories of production of actual landscapes is a central component of any account that meets requirements for an adequate aesthetics of environments, whether natural or human, comparable to, especially, Budd's As Nature Constraint, Hepburn's Serious Beauty Intuition, and perhaps even Thompson's Objectivity Desideratum (chap. 3). By contrast, information required only for contextually privileged aesthetic appreciation, although significant for certain individuals, groups, or cultures, always poses the danger of misleading aesthetic appreciation in ways similar to those of various art-based approaches to the aesthetic appreciation of environments (chaps. 2, 4, and 6). This is an important defect of landscape pluralism that must not be underestimated. To do so is to miss the point of much of what I have argued throughout this book.

THE CORRECT CURRICULUM FOR LANDSCAPE APPRECIATION

In conclusion, in light of the "Close Encounters Phenomenon" and the pluralist view of landscape appreciation, I return to the issue of the correct curriculum for the appropriate aesthetic appreciation of landscapes and to Stolnitz's question of aesthetic relevance. I have argued that matters of form and common knowledge, together with information about the histories of production of actual landscapes, are essential to the appropriate aesthetic appreciation of landscapes by any appreciators, while knowledge of various mythical, symbolic, and artistic uses is significant only in certain contexts. This difference suggests a model for a correct curriculum that includes one core curriculum together with a number of alternative curricula. The core curriculum would include only material about the first five topics (form, common knowledge, science, history, and contemporary use), while the supplementary curricula would cover the last three (myth, symbol, and art). In aesthetic education, the core curriculum would be taught in every situation, while different supplementary curricula would be relevant or not, depending on the context.

What are the ramifications of an approach to aesthetic education that requires such a combination of curricula? On the one hand, in light of this approach, we may not be able to give one universal and unequivocal answer to Stolnitz's question about the conditions under which "images or bits of knowledge which are not present within the object itself" are relevant to aesthetic appreciation. We may have to conclude that although some of such "images or bits of knowledge" are always relevant, others are relevant only in certain contexts and may be irrelevant and even misleading in others. In short, we may have to accept both the fact that landscapes are promiscuous, indeterminate, and ambiguous and the dangers to aesthetic appreciation that this fact entails. On the other hand, provided that we are wary of such dangers, we may, by utilizing such a combination of curricula in our aesthetic education, avoid resigning ourselves to the landscape relativism of the postmodern approach and instead instill the richest and most appropriate aesthetic appreciation of landscapes. Moreover, in doing so we may realize, in others and even in ourselves, what Santayana calls the "maximum of beauty." If so, we move toward achieving what he characterizes as the "marriage of the imagination with reality" and identifies as the ultimate aim of contemplation:

> Aesthetic education consists in training ourselves to see the maximum of beauty. To see it in the physical world, which must continually be about us, is a great progress toward that marriage of the imagination with reality which is the goal of contemplation.[26]

NOTES

1. THE DEVELOPMENT AND NATURE OF ENVIRONMENTAL AESTHETICS

I thank Arlene Kwasniak and Alex Neill for suggesting a number of improvements to this chapter.

1. Other overviews of the field of environmental aesthetics include Allen Carlson, "Environmental Aesthetics," in David Cooper, ed., *A Companion to Aesthetics* (Oxford: Blackwell, 1992), 142–144; "Environmental Aesthetics," in Edward Craig, ed., *Routledge Encyclopedia of Philosophy Online* (London: Routledge, 2002) (available at www.rep.routledge.com/views/home/html); "Environmental Aesthetics," in Berys Gaut and Dominic McIver Lopes, eds., *The Routledge Companion to Aesthetics*, 2nd ed. (London: Routledge, 2005), 541–555; and "Environmental Aesthetics," in Edward N. Zalta, ed., *The Stanford Encyclopedia of Philosophy* (Stanford, Calif.: Metaphysics Research Lab, Center for the Study of Language and Information, 2007) (available at http://plato.stanford.edu/entries/environmental-aesthetics/); Yrjö Sepänmaa, "Environmental Aesthetics," in Robert Paehlke, ed., *Conservation and Environmentalism: An Encyclopedia* (New York: Garland, 1995), 221–223; Arnold Berleant, "Environmental Aesthetics," in Michael Kelly, ed., *Encyclopedia of Aesthetics* (New York: Oxford University Press, 1998), 2:114–120; John A. Fisher, "Environmental Aesthetics," in Jerrold Levinson, ed., *The Oxford Handbook of Aesthetics* (Oxford: Oxford University Press, 2002), 667–678; Donald Crawford, "The Aesthetics of Nature and the Environment," in Peter Kivy, ed., *Blackwell Guide to Aesthetics* (Oxford: Blackwell, 2003), 306–324; and Stephanie Ross, "Environmental Aesthetics," in Donald M. Borchert, ed., *The Encyclopedia of Philosophy*, 2nd ed. (New York: Macmillan, 2006), 254–258.

2. Jerome Stolnitz, "On the Origins of 'Aesthetic Disinterestedness,'" *Journal of Aesthetics and Art Criticism* 20 (1961): 131–143. The historical sources are Anthony Ashley Cooper, third Earl of Shaftesbury, *Characteristics of Men, Manners, Opinions, Times*, ed. Lawrence E. Klein (1711; Cambridge: Cambridge

University Press, 1999); Francis Hutcheson, *An Inquiry Concerning Beauty, Order, Harmony, Design* (1725; Glasgow: Robert and Andrew Foulis, 1772); and Archibald Alison, *Essays on the Nature and Principles of Taste* (Dublin: Byrne, 1790).

3. Immanuel Kant, *Critique of the Power of Judgment*, ed. Paul Guyer, trans. Paul Guyer and Eric Matthews (1790; Cambridge: Cambridge University Press, 2000). For a concise discussion of Kant on the aesthetics of natural environments, see Malcolm Budd, "Delight in the Natural World: Kant on the Aesthetic Appreciation of Nature: Part I: Natural Beauty," *British Journal of Aesthetics* 38 (1998): 1–18; "Delight in the Natural World: Kant on the Aesthetic Appreciation of Nature: Part II: Natural Beauty and Morality," *British Journal of Aesthetics* 38 (1998): 117–126; and "Delight in the Natural World: Kant on the Aesthetic Appreciation of Nature: Part III: The Sublime in Nature," *British Journal of Aesthetics* 38 (1998): 233–250, all reprinted in *The Aesthetic Appreciation of Nature: Essays on the Aesthetics of Nature* (Oxford: Oxford University Press, 2002), 24–47, 48–65, 66–89.

4. Edmund Burke, *A Philosophical Enquiry into the Origin of Our Ideas of the Sublime and the Beautiful*, ed. James T. Boulton (1757; London: Routledge & Kegan Paul, 1958); Immanuel Kant, *Observations on the Feeling of the Beautiful and Sublime*, trans. John T. Goldthwait (1764; Berkeley: University of California Press, 1960).

5. John Conron, *American Picturesque* (University Park: Pennsylvania State University Press, 2000), 17–18.

6. Two standard treatments of the subject are Christopher Hussey, *The Picturesque: Studies in a Point of View* (London: Putnam, 1927), and Walter John Hipple, Jr., *The Beautiful, the Sublime, and the Picturesque in Eighteenth-Century British Aesthetic Theory* (Carbondale: Southern Illinois University Press, 1957). For more recent accounts, see Malcolm Andrews, *The Search for the Picturesque: Landscape Aesthetics and Tourism in Britain, 1760–1800* (Stanford, Calif.: Stanford University Press, 1989), and Dabney Townsend, "The Picturesque," *Journal of Aesthetics and Art Criticism* 55 (1997): 365–376.

7. Their major works are William Gilpin, *Three Essays: On Picturesque Beauty, On Picturesque Travel, and On Sketching Landscape* (London: Blamire, 1792); Uvedale Price, *An Essay on the Picturesque* (London: Robson, 1794); and Richard Payne Knight, *The Landscape* (London: Bulmer, 1794), and *Analytical Inquiry into the Principles of Taste* (1805; Westmead, Eng.: Gregg International, 1972).

8. Georg Wilhelm Friedrich Hegel, *Hegel's Aesthetics: Lectures on Fine Arts*, trans. T. M. Knox (1835; Oxford: Oxford University Press, 1975).

9. A standard edition is Henry David Thoreau, *The Works of Thoreau*, ed. Henry Seiden Canby (Boston: Houghton Mifflin, 1937).

10. George Perkins Marsh, *Man and Nature* (1864; Cambridge, Mass.: Harvard University Press, 1965), 8–9.

11. Lewis Mumford, *The Brown Decades: A Study of the Arts in America, 1865–1895* (New York: Harcourt, Brace, 1931), 78.

12. John Muir, "A Near View of the High Sierra," in *The Mountains of California* (New York: Century, 1894), 26–39.

13. John Muir, *A Thousand-Mile Walk to the Gulf* (Boston: Houghton Mifflin, 1916), 98.

14. John Muir, *The Wilderness World of John Muir*, ed. Edwin Way Teale (Boston: Houghton Mifflin, 1954), 166–167.

15. George Santayana, *The Sense of Beauty: Being the Outline of Aesthetic Theory* (1896; New York: Collier, 1961).

16. John Dewey, *Art as Experience* (1934; New York: Putnam, 1958); Curt Ducasse, *Art, the Critics, and You* (1944; Indianapolis: Bobbs-Merrill, 1955).

17. R. G. Collingwood, *Principles of Art* (1938; New York: Oxford University Press, 1958), and *The Idea of Nature* (1945; New York: Oxford University Press, 1960).

18. Arthur Lovejoy, " 'Nature' as Aesthetic Norm," *Modern Language Notes* 42 (1927): 444–450; Harold Osborne, "The Use of Nature in Art," *British Journal of Aesthetics* 2 (1962): 318–327.

19. The major exception among expressionist approaches was Dewey, *Art as Experience*.

20. Edward Bullough, " 'Psychical Distance' as a Factor in Art and as an Aesthetic Principle," *British Journal of Psychology* 5 (1912): 87–98; Jerome Stolnitz, *Aesthetics and the Philosophy of Art Criticism: A Critical Introduction* (Boston: Houghton Mifflin, 1960).

21. The most famous example of the attack on disinterestedness is George Dickie, "The Myth of the Aesthetic Attitude," *American Philosophical Quarterly* 1 (1964): 56–65.

22. The classic statement of the initial version of the institutional theory is George Dickie, *Art and the Aesthetic: An Institutional Analysis* (Ithaca, N.Y.: Cornell University Press, 1974).

23. The term "artworld" is coined in Arthur Danto, "The Artworld," *Journal of Philosophy* (1964): 571–584.

24. Monroe C. Beardsley, *Aesthetics: Problems in the Philosophy of Criticism* (New York: Harcourt, Brace & World, 1958); Joseph Margolis, ed., *Philosophy Looks at the Arts: Contemporary Readings in Aesthetics* (New York: Scribner, 1962); W. E. Kennick, ed., *Art and Philosophy: Readings in Aesthetics* (New York: St. Martin's Press, 1964).

25. Beardsley, *Aesthetics*, 1.

26. See, for example, Kendall Walton, "Categories of Art," *Philosophical Review* 79 (1970): 334–367, and Dickie, *Art and the Aesthetic*, 169–199

27. Don Mannison, "A Prolegomenon to a Human Chauvinistic Aesthetic," in Don S. Mannison, Michael A. McRobbie, and Richard Routley, eds., *Environmental*

Philosophy (Canberra: Australian National University, 1980), 212–216; Robert Elliot, "Faking Nature," *Inquiry* 25 (1982): 81–93. Elliot later rejects this position in favor of one closer to positive aesthetics in *Faking Nature: The Ethics of Environmental Restoration* (London: Routledge, 1997).

28. See such classic studies as Alfred Biese, *The Development of the Feeling for Nature in the Middle Ages and Modern Times* (1905; New York: Burt Franklin, 1964), and Marjory Hope Nicolson, *Mountain Gloom and Mountain Glory: The Development of the Aesthetics of the Infinite* (Ithaca, N.Y.: Cornell University Press, 1959).

29. See, for example, Robert Stecker, "The Correct and the Appropriate in the Appreciation of Nature," *British Journal of Aesthetics* 37 (1997): 393–402; Donald Crawford, "Scenery and the Aesthetics of Nature," in Allen Carlson and Arnold Berleant, eds., *The Aesthetics of Natural Environments* (Peterborough, Ont.: Broadview Press, 2004), 253–268; and Thomas Leddy, "A Defense of Arts-Based Appreciation of Nature," *Environmental Ethics* 27 (2005): 299–315.

30. Nick Zangwill, "Formal Natural Beauty," *Proceedings of the Aristotelian Society* 101 (2001): 209–224, reprinted in *The Metaphysics of Beauty* (Ithaca, N.Y.: Cornell University Press, 2001), 112–126. For follow-up discussion, see Glenn Parsons, "Natural Functions and the Aesthetic Appreciation of Inorganic Nature," *British Journal of Aesthetics* 44 (2004): 44–56, and Nick Zangwill, "In Defence of Extreme Formalism About Inorganic Nature: Reply to Parsons," *British Journal of Aesthetics* 45 (2005): 185–191.

31. Paul Ziff, "Anything Viewed," in Esa Saarinen, Risto Hilpinen, Ilkka Niiniluoto, and Merrill B. Provence Hintikka, eds., *Essays in Honour of Jaakko Hintikka on the Occasion of His Fiftieth Birthday on January 12, 1979* (Dordrecht: Reidel, 1979), 285–293.

32. Malcolm Budd, "The Aesthetics of Nature," *Proceedings of the Aristotelian Society* 100 (2000): 137–157, reprinted in *Aesthetic Appreciation of Nature*, 90–109.

33. Concerning North America, this development is both fostered by and documented in works such as Christopher Tunnard and Boris Pushkarev, *Man-Made America: Chaos or Control? An Inquiry into Selected Problems of Design in the Urbanized Landscape* (New Haven, Conn.: Yale University Press, 1963); Peter Blake, *God's Own Junkyard: The Planned Deterioration of America's Landscape* (New York: Holt, Rinehart and Winston, 1964); and Peirce F. Lewis, David Lowenthal, and Yi-Fu Tuan, eds., *Visual Blight in America* (Washington, D.C.: Association of American Geographers, 1973).

34. Two examples of empirical approaches from the time are R. Burton Litton, Jr., *Forest Landscape Description and Inventories: A Basis for Land Planning and Design* (Berkeley, Calif.: Pacific Southwest Forest and Range Experimental Station, 1968), and Elwood L. Shafer, Jr., and James Mietz, *It Seems Possible to Quan-*

tify Scenic Beauty in Photographs (Upper Darby, Pa.: Northeastern Forest Experiment Station, 1970). For insight into how this type of research has changed over the past thirty years, see, for example, Jim Bedwell, Larry Blocker, Paul Gobster, Terry Slider, and Tom Atzet, "Beyond the Picturesque: Integrating Aesthetics and Ecology in Forest Service Scenery Management," in Cheryl Wagner, ed., *ASLA 1997: Annual Meeting Proceedings* (Washington, D.C.: American Society of Landscape Architects, 1997), 86–90; Simon Bell, *Landscape: Pattern, Perception and Process* (London: Routledge, 1999); and Stephen R. J. Sheppard and Howard W. Harshaw, eds., *Forests and Landscapes: Linking Ecology, Sustainability, and Aesthetics* (New York: CAB International, 2001).

35. Mark Sagoff, "On Preserving the Natural Environment," *Yale Law Journal* 84 (1974): 205–267; Allen Carlson, "Environmental Aesthetics and the Dilemma of Aesthetic Education," *Journal of Aesthetic Education* 10 (1976): 69–82.

36. Allen Carlson, "On the Possibility of Quantifying Scenic Beauty," *Landscape Planning* 4 (1977): 131–172, and "Formal Qualities and the Natural Environment," *Journal of Aesthetic Education* 13 (1979): 99–114.

37. Jay Appleton, "Landscape Evaluation: The Theoretical Vacuum," *Transactions of the Institute of British Geographers* 66 (1975): 120–123.

38. On "prospect-refuge theory," see Jay Appleton, *The Experience of Landscape* (London: Wiley, 1975). For a shorter account of the theory, see Jay Appleton, "Pleasure and the Perception of Habitat: A Conceptual Framework," in Barry Sadler and Allen Carlson, eds., *Environmental Aesthetics: Essays in Interpretation* (Victoria, B.C.: Department of Geography, University of Victoria, 1982), 27–45. Appleton attempts to extend his theory to human influenced and human created environments as well as to the arts in *The Symbolism of Habitat: An Interpretation of Landscape in the Arts* (Seattle: University of Washington Press, 1990). Another attempt at an evolution-related theory can be found in Gordon H. Orians and Judith H. Heerwagen, "An Ecological and Evolutionary Approach to Landscape Aesthetics," in Edmund C. Penning-Rowsell and David Lowenthal, eds., *Landscape Meanings and Values* (London: Allen and Unwin, 1986), 3–25. See also Gordon H. Orians and Judith H. Heerwagen, "Evolved Responses to Landscapes," in Jerome H. Barkow, Leda Cosmides, and John Tooby, eds., *The Adapted Mind: Evolutionary Psychology and the Generation of Culture* (New York: Oxford University Press, 1992), 555–579, and "Humans, Habitats, and Aesthetics," in Stephen R. Kellert and Edward O. Wilson, eds., *The Biophilia Hypothesis* (Washington, D.C.: Island Press, 1993), 138–172.

39. See, for example, James L. Sell, Jonathan G. Taylor, and Ervin H. Zube, "Toward a Theoretical Framework for Landscape Perception," in Thomas E. Saarinen, David Seamon, and James L. Sell, eds., *Environmental Perception and Behavior: An Inventory and Prospect* (Chicago: Department of Geography, University of Chicago, 1984), 61–83; Rachel Kaplan and Stephen Kaplan, *The Experience*

of Nature: A Psychological Perspective (Cambridge: Cambridge University Press, 1989); and Steven C. Bourassa, *The Aesthetics of Landscape* (London: Belhaven, 1991).

40. For overviews, see, for example, Ervin H. Zube, James L. Sell, and Jonathan G. Taylor, "Landscape Perception: Research, Application and Theory," *Landscape Planning* 9 (1982): 1–33; Ervin H. Zube, "Themes in Landscape Assessment Theory," *Landscape Journal* 3 (1984): 104–110; William L. Cats-Barrel and Linda Gibson, "Evaluating Aesthetics: The Major Issues and a Bibliography," *Landscape Journal* 5 (1986): 93–102; Allen Carlson, "Recent Landscape Assessment Research," in Kelly, ed., *Encyclopedia of Aesthetics*, 3:102–105; and Terry C. Daniel, "Whither Scenic Beauty? Visual Landscape Quality Assessment in the 21st Century," *Landscape and Urban Planning* 54 (2001): 276–281. In addition, Bourassa has a number of overview chapters as well as an extensive bibliography in *Aesthetics of Landscape*. Some noteworthy collections include Gary H. Elsner and Richard C. Smardon, eds., *The Proceedings of Our National Landscape: A Conference on Applied Techniques for Analysis and Management of the Visual Resource* (Berkeley, Calif.: Pacific Southwest Forest and Range Experimental Station, 1979); Saarinen, Seamon, and Sell, eds., *Environmental Perception and Behavior*; and Jack L. Nasar, ed., *Environmental Aesthetics: Theory, Research, and Applications* (Cambridge: Cambridge University Press, 1988). Although now somewhat dated, the last is a very useful collection of thirty-two articles of differing lengths and technical detail, mainly by individuals representing various empirical and applied approaches, together with an excellent bibliography of empirical work.

41. See, for example, Arnold Berleant, "Aesthetic Perception in Environmental Design," in Nasar, ed., *Environmental Aesthetics*, 84–97; Marcia Eaton, *Aesthetics and the Good Life* (Cranbury, N.J.: Associated University Presses, 1989), chaps. 4 and 5, and "The Role of Aesthetics in Designing Sustainable Landscapes," in Yrjö Sepänmaa, ed., *Real World Design: The Foundations and Practice of Environmental Aesthetics* (Helsinki: University of Helsinki, 1997), 51–63; Allen Carlson, "Whose Vision? Whose Meanings? Whose Values? Pluralism and Objectivity in Landscape Analysis," in Paul Groth, ed., *Vision, Culture, and Landscape: The Berkeley Symposium on Cultural Landscape Interpretation* (Berkeley: Department of Landscape Architecture, University of California, 1990), 157–168; "On the Theoretical Vacuum in Landscape Assessment," *Landscape Journal* 12 (1993): 51–56; and "Aesthetic Preferences for Sustainable Landscapes: Seeing and Knowing," in Sheppard and Harshaw, eds., *Forests and Landscapes*, 31–41; and Douglas J. Porteous, *Environmental Aesthetics: Ideas, Politics and Planning* (London: Routledge, 1996).

42. Ronald W. Hepburn, "Contemporary Aesthetics and the Neglect of Natural Beauty," in Bernard Williams and Alan Montefiore, eds., *British Analytical*

Philosophy (London: Routledge & Kegan Paul, 1966), 285–310, reprinted in Ronald W. Hepburn, *"Wonder" and Other Essays: Eight Studies in Aesthetics and Neighboring Fields* (Edinburgh: Edinburgh University Press, 1984), 9–35, and Carlson and Berleant, eds., *Aesthetics of Natural Environments*, 43–62. For a shorter version of this essay, see Ronald W. Hepburn, "Aesthetic Appreciation of Nature," in Harold Osborne, ed., *Aesthetics and the Modern World* (London: Thames and Hudson, 1968), 49–66.

43. This point is also pursued in Ronald W. Hepburn, "Trivial and Serious in Aesthetic Appreciation of Nature," in Salim Kemal and Ivan Gaskell, eds., *Landscape, Natural Beauty and the Arts* (Cambridge: Cambridge University Press, 1993), 65–80.

44. The labels "cognitive" and "noncognitive" are used by, among others, Carlson and Berleant, eds., *Aesthetics of Natural Environments*. The terms "conceptual" and "nonconceptual" are introduced in Ronald Moore, "Appreciating Natural Beauty as Natural," *Journal of Aesthetic Education* 33 (1999): 42–59. The words "narrative" and "ambient" are employed in Cheryl Foster, "The Narrative and the Ambient in Environmental Aesthetics," *Journal of Aesthetics and Art Criticism* 56 (1998): 127–137, reprinted in Carlson and Berleant, eds., *Aesthetics of Natural Environments*, 197–213. For an excellent overview of the whole of the aesthetics of nature, see Glenn Parsons, *Aesthetics and Nature* (London: Continuum, 2008).

45. Yuriko Saito, "Appreciating Nature on Its Own Terms," *Environmental Ethics* 20 (1998): 135–149.

46. This kind of approach to art appreciation is defended by a number of contemporary philosophers. An early, concise version is presented in Walton, "Categories of Art."

47. I introduced the label "Natural Environmental Model" in "Appreciation and the Natural Environment," *Journal of Aesthetics and Art Criticism* 37 (1979): 267–276, which is updated in Allen Carlson, "Aesthetic Appreciation of the Natural Environment," in Richard G. Botzler and Susan J. Armstrong, eds., *Environmental Ethics: Divergence and Convergence*, 2nd ed. (Boston: McGraw-Hill, 1998), 108–114. The term "scientific cognitivism" is used by, among others, Glenn Parsons, "Nature Appreciation, Science, and Positive Aesthetics," *British Journal of Aesthetics* 42 (2002): 279–295.

48. Carlson, "Appreciation and the Natural Environment"; Allen Carlson, "Nature, Aesthetic Judgment, and Objectivity," *Journal of Aesthetics and Art Criticism* 40 (1981): 15–27; "Saito on the Correct Aesthetic Appreciation of Nature," *Journal of Aesthetic Education* 20 (1986): 85–93; "Aesthetic Appreciation of the Natural Environment," in Susan L. Feagin and Patrick Maynard, eds., *Aesthetics* (Oxford: Oxford University Press, 1997), 30–40; "Nature Appreciation and the Question of Aesthetic Relevance," in Arnold Berleant, ed., *Environment and the*

Arts: Perspectives on Environmental Aesthetics (Aldershot, Eng.: Ashgate, 2002), 62–75; and *Aesthetics and the Environment: The Appreciation of Nature, Art and Architecture* (London: Routledge, 2000). A science-based approach to the aesthetic appreciation of nature is also defended in Holmes Rolston, III, "Does Aesthetic Appreciation of Landscapes Need to Be Science-Based?" *British Journal of Aesthetics* 35 (1995): 374–386; Marcia Eaton, "Fact and Fiction in the Aesthetic Appreciation of Nature," *Journal of Aesthetics and Art Criticism* 56 (1998): 149–156, reprinted in Carlson and Berleant, eds., *Aesthetics of Natural Environments*, 170–181; Patricia Matthews, "Scientific Knowledge and the Aesthetic Appreciation of Nature," *Journal of Aesthetics and Art Criticism* 60 (2002): 37–48; and Glenn Parsons, "Theory, Observation, and the Role of Scientific Understanding in the Aesthetic Appreciation of Nature," *Canadian Journal of Philosophy* 36 (2006): 165–186, and "Nature Appreciation, Science, and Positive Aesthetics."

49. A moderate position of this kind is endorsed in Saito, "Appreciating Nature on Its Own Terms." A more extreme view is defended in Thomas Heyd, "Aesthetic Appreciation and the Many Stories About Nature," *British Journal of Aesthetics* 41 (2001): 125–137, reprinted in Carlson and Berleant, eds., *Aesthetics of Natural Environments*, 269–282.

50. Malcolm Budd, "The Aesthetic Appreciation of Nature," *British Journal of Aesthetics* 36 (1996): 207–222, reprinted in *Aesthetic Appreciation of Nature*, 1–23, and "The Aesthetics of Nature." A somewhat similar position concerning the sounds of nature is developed in John A. Fisher, "What the Hills Are Alive With: In Defense of the Sounds of Nature," *Journal of Aesthetics and Art Criticism* 56 (1998): 167–179, reprinted in Carlson and Berleant, eds., *Aesthetics of Natural Environments*, 232–252.

51. Arnold Berleant, *The Aesthetics of Environment* (Philadelphia: Temple University Press, 1992). See also Arnold Berleant, *Art and Engagement* (Philadelphia: Temple University Press, 1991); *Living in the Landscape: Toward an Aesthetics of Environment* (Lawrence: University Press of Kansas, 1997); and *Aesthetics and Environment: Variations on a Theme* (Aldershot, Eng.: Ashgate, 2005).

52. Noël Carroll, "On Being Moved by Nature: Between Religion and Natural History," in Kemal and Gaskell, eds., *Landscape, Natural Beauty and the Arts*, 244–266, reprinted in Carlson and Berleant, eds., *Aesthetics of Natural Environments*, 89–107.

53. Stan Godlovitch, "Icebreakers: Environmentalism and Natural Aesthetics," *Journal of Applied Philosophy* 11 (1994): 15–30, reprinted in Carlson and Berleant, eds., *Aesthetics of Natural Environments*, 108–126. See also Stan Godlovitch, "Offending Against Nature," *Environmental Values* 7 (1998): 131–150, and "Theoretical Options for Environmental Aesthetics," *Journal of Aesthetic Education* 31 (1998): 17–27.

54. Emily Brady, "Imagination and the Aesthetic Appreciation of Nature," *Journal of Aesthetics and Art Criticism* 56 (1998): 139–147. See also Emily Brady, *Aesthetics of the Natural Environment* (Edinburgh: Edinburgh University Press, 2003).

55. Ronald W. Hepburn, "Landscape and the Metaphysical Imagination," *Environmental Values* 5 (1996): 191–204.

56. Allen Carlson, "Aesthetics and Engagement," *British Journal of Aesthetics* 33 (1993): 220–227; "Beyond the Aesthetic," *Journal of Aesthetics and Art Criticism* 52 (1994): 239–241; "Nature, Aesthetic Appreciation, and Knowledge," *Journal of Aesthetics and Art Criticism* 53 (1995): 393–400; "Appreciating Godlovitch," *Journal of Aesthetics and Art Criticism* 55 (1997): 55–57; and "Arnold Berleant's Environmental Aesthetics," *Ethics, Place and Environment* 10 (2007): 217–225.

57. See, for example, Allen Carlson, "On Appreciating Agricultural Landscapes," *Journal of Aesthetics and Art Criticism* 43 (1985): 301–312, and "Viljelysmaisemien Esteettinen Arvo Ja Touttavuus" [Productivity and the Aesthetic Value of Agricultural Landscapes], in Yrjö Sepänmaa and Liisa Heikkilä-Palo, eds., *Pellossa Perihopeat* [*Fields: The Family Silver*] (Helsinki: Maahenki, 2005), 52–61.

58. Allen Carlson, "On Aesthetically Appreciating Human Environments," *Philosophy and Geography* 4 (2001): 9–24, and "The Aesthetic Appreciation of Architecture Under Different Conceptions of the Environment," *Journal of Aesthetic Education* 40 (2006): 77–88.

59. This sense of place is investigated by cultural geographers such as Yi-Fu Tuan, who discusses it in such works as *Topophilia: A Study of Environmental Perception, Attitudes, and Values* (Englewood Cliffs, N.J.: Prentice-Hall, 1974); *Space and Place: The Perspective of Experience* (Minneapolis: University of Minnesota Press, 1977); and *Passing Strange and Wonderful: Aesthetics, Nature, and Culture* (Washington, D.C.: Island Press, 1993). Similarly, Finnish aesthetician Yrjö Sepänmaa notes the influence of Finnish nature mythology on the aesthetic appreciation of the landscapes of Finland in *The Beauty of Environment: A General Model for Environmental Aesthetics*, 2nd ed. (Denton, Tex.: Environmental Ethics Books, 1993). Sepänmaa's book is an extensive study of a wide range of important issues in environmental aesthetics and includes an excellent bibliography of relevant philosophical research. The aesthetic relevance of mythologically influenced descriptions of landscapes in popular fiction—for example, those of the American Southwest in the novels of Tony Hillerman—are discussed in Allen Carlson, "Landscape and Literature," in *Aesthetics and the Environment*, 216–240.

60. See, for example, Ronald W. Hepburn's work on Christianity and aesthetics, such as "Aesthetic and Religious: Boundaries, Overlaps, and Intrusions," in

Sepänmaa, ed., *Real World Design*, 42–48, and "Restoring the Sacred: Sacred as a Concept of Aesthetics," in Pauline von Bonsdorff and Arto Haapala, eds., *Aesthetics in the Human Environment* (Lahti, Finland: International Institute of Applied Aesthetics, 1999), 166–185; or Yuriko Saito's work on Buddhism and environmental aesthetics, such as "The Japanese Appreciation of Nature," *British Journal of Aesthetics* 25 (1985): 239–251, and "The Japanese Love of Nature: A Paradox," *Landscape* 31 (1991): 1–8.

61. Arnold Berleant, "Aesthetic Paradigms for an Urban Ecology," *Diogenes* 103 (1978): 1–28; "Aesthetic Participation and the Urban Environment," *Urban Resources* 1 (1984): 37–42; "Cultivating an Urban Aesthetic," *Diogenes* 136 (1986): 1–18; and "The Critical Aesthetics of Disney World," *Journal of Applied Philosophy* 11 (1994): 171–180. Similar ideas are presented in Berleant, *Living in the Landscape* and *Aesthetics and Environment*.

62. Berleant, *Aesthetics and Environment*, part 2, and *Re-thinking Aesthetics: Rogue Essays on Aesthetics and the Arts* (Aldershot, Eng.: Ashgate, 2004).

63. See, for example, Emily Brady, "Aesthetic Character and Aesthetic Integrity in Environmental Conservation," *Environmental Ethics* 24 (2002): 75–91, and "Sniffing and Savoring: The Aesthetics of Smells and Tastes," in Andrew Light and Jonathan M. Smith, eds., *The Aesthetics of Everyday Life* (New York: Columbia University Press, 2005), 177–193.

64. See, for example, Foster, "Narrative and the Ambient in Environmental Aesthetics," and Ronald Moore, *Natural Beauty: A Theory of Aesthetics Beyond the Arts* (Peterborough, Ont.: Broadview Press, 2007), and "Appreciating Natural Beauty as Natural." Also relevant to this point is Arnold Berleant and Allen Carlson, eds., *The Aesthetics of Human Environments* (Peterborough, Ont.: Broadview Press, 2007).

65. See, for example, Malcolm Andrews, "The View from the Road and the Picturesque," 272–298; Pauline von Bonsdorff, "Urban Richness and the Art of Building," 57–68; David Macauley, "Walking the City," 100–118; and Mikita Brottman, "The Last Stop of Desire: The Aesthetics of the Shopping Center," 119–138, all in Berleant and Carlson, eds., *Aesthetics of Human Environments*.

66. Two introductions to the area are Yuriko Saito, "Everyday Aesthetics," *Philosophy and Literature* 25 (2001): 87–95, and Tom Leddy, "The Nature of Everyday Aesthetics," in Light and Smith, eds., *Aesthetics of Everyday Life*, 3–22. The first major study of the area is Yuriko Saito, *Everyday Aesthetics* (Oxford: Oxford University Press, 2008).

67. The aesthetics of smaller living spaces is discussed in Kevin Melchionne, "Living in Glass Houses: Domesticity, Interior Decoration, and Environmental Aesthetics," *Journal of Aesthetics and Art Criticism* 56 (1998): 191–200, and "Front Yards," in Berleant, ed., *Environment and the Arts*, 102–111, as well as in Tom

Leddy "Everyday Surface Qualities: Neat, Messy, Clean, Dirty," *Journal of Aesthetics and Art Criticism* 53 (1995): 259–268.

68. See, for example, Carolyn Korsmeyer, "Food and the Taste of Meaning," in von Bonsdorff and Haapala, eds., *Aesthetics in the Human Environment*, 90–105; *Making Sense of Taste: Food and Philosophy* (Ithaca, N.Y.: Cornell University Press, 1999); and "Delightful, Delicious, Disgusting," *Journal of Aesthetics and Art Criticism* 60 (2002): 217–225. Also note Glenn Kuehn, "How Can Food Be Art?" 194–212, and Wolfgang Welsch, "Sport Viewed Aesthetically, and Even as Art?" 135–155, both in Light and Smith, eds., *Aesthetics of Everyday Life*.

69. See, for example, Arto Haapala, ed., *The City as Cultural Metaphor: Studies in Urban Aesthetics* (Lahti, Finland: International Institute of Applied Aesthetics, 1998); von Bonsdorff and Haapala, eds., *Aesthetics in the Human Environment*; Light and Smith, eds., *Aesthetics of Everyday Life*; and Berleant and Carlson, eds., *Aesthetics of Human Environments*.

70. Three important philosophical studies of gardens are Mara Miller, *The Garden as Art* (Albany: State University of New York Press, 1993); Stephanie Ross, *What Gardens Mean* (Chicago: University of Chicago Press, 1998); and David E. Cooper, *A Philosophy of Gardens* (Oxford: Oxford University Press, 2006). Also of interest are Michael Pollan, *Second Nature: A Gardener's Education* (New York: Dell, 1991), and John Dixon Hunt, *Greater Perfections: The Practice of Garden Theory* (Philadelphia: University of Pennsylvania Press, 2000), and *The Afterlife of Gardens* (Philadelphia: University of Pennsylvania Press, 2004).

71. The standard philosophical treatment of architecture is Roger Scruton, *The Aesthetics of Architecture* (Princeton, N.J.: Princeton University Press, 1979). Two useful overviews of the area are Edward Winters, "Architecture," in Gaut and Lopes, eds., *Routledge Companion to Aesthetics*, 655–668, and Gordon Graham, "Architecture," in Levinson, ed., *Oxford Handbook of Aesthetics*, 555–571. On the relationship between the aesthetic appreciation of environments and architecture, see Arnold Berleant, "Architecture and the Aesthetics of Continuity," 21–30, and Allen Carlson, "Existence, Location, and Function: The Appreciation of Architecture," 141–164, both in Michael Mitias, ed., *Philosophy and Architecture* (Amsterdam: Rodopi, 1994), and Robert Stecker, "Reflections on Architecture: Buildings as Artworks, Aesthetic Objects, and Artificial Environments," 81–93, and Allen Carlson, "The Aesthetic Appreciation of Everyday Architecture," 107–121, both in Michael Mitias, ed., *Architecture and Civilization* (Amsterdam: Rodopi, 1999). Both of these collections have a number of interesting studies of the aesthetics of architecture, although most do not explicitly address its relationship to environmental aesthetics.

72. The research by cultural geographers and landscape ecologists is especially kindred to that of environmental aestheticians. The following collections are useful: Donald W. Meinig, ed., *The Interpretation of Ordinary Landscapes:*

Geographical Essays (New York: Oxford University Press, 1979); Penning-Rowsell and Lowenthal, eds., *Landscape Meanings and Values*; Michael P. Conzen, ed., *The Making of the American Landscape* (Boston: Unwin Hyman, 1990); Groth, ed., *Vision, Culture, and Landscape*; Paul Groth and Todd W. Bressi, eds., *Understanding Ordinary Landscapes* (New Haven, Conn.: Yale University Press, 1997); and Joan Iverson Nassauer, ed., *Placing Nature: Culture and Landscape Ecology* (Washington, D.C.: Island Press, 1997).

73. Three landscape critics who excel as sensitive and perceptive apprecia-tors of the human environment are W. G. Hoskins, John Brinckerhoff Jackson, and May Theilgaard Watts. Hoskins's classic work is *The Making of the English Landscape* (London: Hodder & Stoughton, 1955). There are a number of collec-tions of Jackson's essays: *Landscapes: Selected Writings of J. B. Jackson*, ed. Ervin H. Zube (Amherst: University of Massachusetts Press, 1970); *The Necessity for Ruins, and Other Topics* (Amherst: University of Massachusetts Press, 1980); *Discovering the Vernacular Landscape* (New Haven, Conn.: Yale University Press, 1984); and *A Sense of Place, a Sense of Time* (New Haven, Conn.: Yale University Press, 1994). An excellent guide to the landscape is Watts's classic work, *Reading the Landscape of America* (1957; New York: Collier, 1975).

74. Traditional art forms are discussed in Berleant, *Art and Engagement*, and Ross, *What Gardens Mean*. Two recent studies of the influence of painting on environmental appreciation by nonphilosophers are Gina Crandell, *Nature Pictorialized: "The View" in Landscape History* (Baltimore: Johns Hopkins University Press, 1993), and Charlotte Klonk, *Science and the Perception of Nature: British Landscape Art in the Late Eighteenth and Early Nineteenth Centuries* (New Haven, Conn.: Yale University Press, 1996).

75. On film, see Kenneth I. Helphand, "Landscape Films," *Landscape Journal* 5 (1986): 1–8, and P. Adams Sitney, "Landscape in the Cinema: The Rhythms of the World and the Camera," in Kemal and Gaskell, eds., *Landscape, Natural Beauty and the Arts*, 103–126. On environmental art, see Donald Crawford, "Nature and Art: Some Dialectical Relationships," *Journal of Aesthetics and Art Criticism* 62 (1983): 49–58; Allen Carlson, "Is Environmental Art an Aesthetic Affront to Nature?" *Canadian Journal of Philosophy* 16 (1986): 635–650; and Stephanie Ross, "Gardens, Earthworks, and Environmental Art," in Kemal and Gaskell, eds., *Landscape, Natural Beauty and the Arts*, 158–182.

76. A number of significant essays on the relationship between environmen-tal aesthetics and environmentalism are in Allen Carlson and Sheila Lintott, eds., *Nature, Aesthetics, and Environmentalism: From Beauty to Duty* (New York: Columbia University Press, 2008).

77. Two excellent short accounts of these developments are Ronald Rees, "The Taste for Mountain Scenery," *History Today* 25 (1975): 305–312, and "The

Scenery Cult: Changing Landscape Tastes over Three Centuries," *Landscape* 19 (1975): 39–47.

78. For an overview of several of the factors that influenced North American environmental appreciation, see Eugene C. Hargrove, "The Historical Foundations of American Environmental Attitudes," *Environmental Ethics* 1 (1979): 209–240.

79. On the problems of aesthetically appreciating wetlands, see Allen Carlson, "Soiden Ihaileminen: Kosteikkojen Vaikea Kauneus" [Admiring Mirelands: The Difficult Beauty of Wetlands], in Liisa Heikkilä-Palo, ed., *Suo on Kaunis* [*Beauty in the Bog*] (Helsinki: Maahenki, 1999), 173–181; Holmes Rolston, III, "Aesthetics in the Swamps," *Perspectives in Biology and Medicine* 43 (2000): 584–597; and J. Baird Callicott, "Wetland Gloom and Wetland Glory," *Philosophy and Geography* 6 (2003): 33–45.

80. On anthropocentricity, see Godlovitch, "Icebreakers"; on obsession with scenery, Yuriko Saito, "The Aesthetics of Unscenic Nature," *Journal of Aesthetics and Art Criticism* 56 (1998): 101–111; on triviality, J. Baird Callicott, "The Land Aesthetic," in J. Baird Callicott, ed., *Companion to A Sand County Almanac: Interpretive and Critical Essays* (Madison: University of Wisconsin Press, 1987), 157–171; on subjectivity, Janna Thompson, "Aesthetics and the Value of Nature," *Environmental Ethics* 17 (1995): 291–305; and on moral vacuity, Andrews, *Search for the Picturesque.*

81. Carlson, "Aesthetics and Engagement"; Malcolm Budd, "Aesthetics of Nature," in Levinson, ed., *Oxford Handbook of Aesthetics*, 117–135, reprinted in *Aesthetic Appreciation of Nature*, 111–112; Allen Carlson, "Aesthetics and Environment," *British Journal of Aesthetics* 46 (2006): 416–427.

82. Brady, *Aesthetics of the Natural Environment.*

83. Godlovitch, "Icebreakers."

84. For example, although his overall position includes both cognitive and noncognitive elements, Holmes Rolston, III, suggests that engagement is an antidote to anthropocentricity and scenery-obsession in "Aesthetic Experience in Forests," *Journal of Aesthetics and Art Criticism* 56 (1998): 157–166, and "From Beauty to Duty: Aesthetics of Nature and Environmental Ethics," in Berleant, ed., *Environment and the Arts*, 127–141.

85. Ned Hettinger, "Carlson's Environmental Aesthetics and the Protection of the Environment," *Environmental Ethics* 27 (2005): 57–76, and "Objectivity in Environmental Aesthetics and Protection of the Environment," in Carlson and Lintott, eds., *Nature, Aesthetics, and Environmentalism*, 413–437; Glenn Parsons, "Freedom and Objectivity in the Aesthetic Appreciation of Nature," *British Journal of Aesthetics* 46 (2006): 17–37.

86. Aldo Leopold, *A Sand County Almanac, with Essays on Conservation from Round River* (New York: Oxford University Press, 1966). On Leopold's views about

the aesthetics of nature, see Callicott, "Land Aesthetic," and the updated "The Land Aesthetic," in Christopher Key Chapple, ed., *Ecological Prospects: Scientific, Religious, and Aesthetic Perspectives* (Albany: State University of New York Press, 1994), 169–183. See also Paul Gobster, "Aldo Leopold's Ecological Esthetic: Integrating Esthetic and Biodiversity Values," *Journal of Forestry* 93 (1995): 6–10.

87. See, for example, Rolston, "Does Aesthetic Appreciation of Landscapes Need to Be Science-Based?" and "From Beauty to Duty"; Marcia Eaton, "The Beauty that Requires Health," in Nassauer, ed., *Placing Nature*, 85–106, and "Fact and Fiction in the Aesthetic Appreciation of Nature"; and Sheila Lintott, "Toward Eco-Friendly Aesthetics," *Environmental Ethics* 28 (2006): 57–76.

88. The initial discussion of this issue is in Allen Carlson, "Nature and Positive Aesthetics," *Environmental Ethics* 6 (1984): 5–34. The view is endorsed in different ways and to various degrees in Holmes Rolston, III, *Environmental Ethics: Duties to and Values in the Natural World* (Philadelphia: Temple University Press, 1988), chap. 6; Eugene C. Hargrove, *Foundations of Environmental Ethics* (Englewood Cliffs, N.J.: Prentice-Hall, 1989), chap. 6, and "Carlson and the Aesthetic Appreciation of Nature," *Philosophy and Geography* 5 (2002): 213–223; and Parsons, "Nature Appreciation, Science, and Positive Aesthetics." On Hargrove's and Rolston's endorsement of positive aesthetics, see Allen Carlson, "Hargrove, Positive Aesthetics, and Indifferent Creativity," *Philosophy and Geography* 5 (2002): 224–234, and " 'We see beauty now where we could not see it before': Rolston's Aesthetics of Nature," in Christopher J. Preston and Wayne Ouderkirk, eds., *Nature, Value, Duty: Life on Earth with Holmes Rolston, III* (Dordrecht: Springer, 2006), 103–124.

89. Allen Carlson, "Appreciating Art and Appreciating Nature," in Kemal and Gaskell, eds., *Landscape, Natural Beauty and the Arts*, 199–227, and "Nature and Positive Aesthetics."

90. Parsons, "Nature Appreciation, Science, and Positive Aesthetics."

91. Thompson, "Aesthetics and the Value of Nature"; Stan Godlovitch, "Evaluating Nature Aesthetically," *Journal of Aesthetics and Art Criticism* 56 (1998): 113–125.

92. Stan Godlovitch, "Valuing Nature and the Autonomy of Natural Aesthetics," *British Journal of Aesthetics* 38 (1998): 180–197; Saito, "Aesthetics of Unscenic Nature"; Budd, "The Aesthetics of Nature."

93. See, for example, Joan Iverson Nassauer, "Cultural Sustainability: Aligning Aesthetics and Ecology," in Nassauer, ed., *Placing Nature*, 65–84; Eaton, "Beauty that Requires Health"; Lintott, "Toward Eco-Friendly Aesthetics"; and Allen Carlson, "What Is the Correct Curriculum for Landscape Appreciation?" *Journal of Aesthetic Education* 35 (2001): 97–112.

94. See, for example, Moore, "Appreciating Natural Beauty as Natural"; Robert Fudge, "Imagination and the Science-Based Aesthetic Appreciation of Un-

scenic Nature," *Journal of Aesthetics and Art Criticism* 59 (2001): 275–285; and Stephanie Ross, "Landscape Perception: Theory-Laden, Emotionally Resonant, Politically Correct," *Environmental Ethics* 27 (2005): 245–263.

95. See, for example, Rolston, "Aesthetic Experience in Forests," and Yuriko Saito, "The Role of Aesthetics in Civic Environmentalism," in Berleant and Carlson, eds., *Aesthetics of Human Environments*, 203–218.

96. In addition to the works cited in the previous notes, for further discussion of various issues involving links between environmental aesthetics and environmental ethics and environmentalism, see, for example, Robert Elliot, "Environmental Degradation, Vandalism and the Aesthetic Object Argument," *Australasian Journal of Philosophy* 67 (1989): 191–204; Stan Godlovitch, "Aesthetic Protectionism," *Journal of Applied Philosophy* 6 (1989): 171–180; Tony Lynch, "Deep Ecology as an Aesthetic Movement," *Environmental Values* 5 (1996): 147–160; Terry J. Diffey, "Arguing About the Environment," *British Journal of Aesthetics* 40 (2000): 133–148; Yuriko Saito, "Ecological Design: Promises and Challenges," *Environmental Ethics* 24 (2002): 243–261; and Emily Brady, "Aesthetics, Ethics and the Natural Environment," 113–126, and Yuriko Saito, "Environmental Directions for Aesthetics and the Arts," 171–185, both in Berleant, ed., *Environment and the Arts*.

2. AESTHETIC APPRECIATION AND THE NATURAL ENVIRONMENT

I thank Alex Neill for suggesting a number of improvements to this chapter, as well as several other individuals who commented on earlier versions of it.

1. George Santayana, *The Sense of Beauty: Being the Outline of Aesthetic Theory* (1896; New York: Collier, 1961), 99.

2. Paul Ziff, "Reasons in Art Criticism," in *Philosophical Turnings: Essays in Conceptual Appreciation* (Ithaca, N.Y.: Cornell University Press, 1966), 71. I examine Ziff's notion of appreciation more fully in "Critical Notice of Ziff, *Antiaesthetics: An Appreciation of the Cow with the Subtile Nose*," *Canadian Journal of Philosophy* 17 (1987): 919–933.

3. Ziff, "Reasons in Art Criticism," 71.

4. Santayana, *Sense of Beauty*, 100.

5. Arthur Danto, *The Transfiguration of the Commonplace: A Philosophy of Art* (Cambridge, Mass.: Harvard University Press, 1981), and "The Artworld," *Journal of Philosophy* (1964): 571–584. On turning nonart objects into art, see the classic account of the institutional theory of art: George Dickie, *Art and the Aesthetic: An Institutional Analysis* (Ithaca, N.Y.: Cornell University Press, 1974).

6. Yi-Fu Tuan, *Topophilia: A Study of Environmental Perception, Attitudes, and Values* (Englewood Cliffs, N.J.: Prentice Hall, 1974), 132–133.

7. For a good brief discussion, see Ronald Rees, "The Scenery Cult: Changing Landscape Tastes over Three Centuries," *Landscape* 19 (1975): 39–47.

8. Quoted in John T. Ogden, "From Spatial to Aesthetic Distance in the Eighteenth Century," *Journal of the History of Ideas* 35 (1974): 66–67.

9. Ronald Rees, "The Taste for Mountain Scenery," *History Today* 25 (1975): 312.

10. Paul Shepard, *The Tender Carnivore and the Sacred Game* (New York: Scribner, 1973), 147–148. See also Paul Shepard, *Man in the Landscape: A Historic View of the Esthetics of Nature* (New York: Knopf, 1967).

11. Rees, "Taste for Mountain Scenery," 312. Ethical concerns are also expressed in Tuan, *Topophilia*, chap. 8, and Ralph A. Smith and Christiana M. Smith, "Aesthetics and Environmental Education," *Journal of Aesthetic Education* (1970): 125–140, who find "a special form of arrogance in experiencing nature strictly in the categories of art" (131–132).

12. Ronald W. Hepburn, "Aesthetic Appreciation of Nature," in Harold Osborne, ed., *Aesthetics and the Modern World* (London: Thames and Hudson, 1968), 53. Hepburn suggests that aesthetic appreciation of nature is enhanced by "realizing" that an object is what it is and has the qualities it has (60–65). For a more substantial version of this essay, see Ronald W. Hepburn, "Contemporary Aesthetics and the Neglect of Natural Beauty," in Bernard Williams and Alan Montefiore, eds., *British Analytical Philosophy* (London: Routledge & Kegan Paul, 1966), 285–310, reprinted in Ronald W. Hepburn, *"Wonder" and Other Essays: Eight Studies in Aesthetics and Neighboring Fields* (Edinburgh: Edinburgh University Press, 1984), 9–35, and Allen Carlson and Arnold Berleant, eds., *The Aesthetics of Natural Environments* (Peterborough, Ont.: Broadview Press, 2004), 43–62.

13. This kind of position presupposes that a creationist account of the origins of the earth is either untenable or, if tenable, not an adequate foundation for understanding the aesthetic appreciation of nature. For a discussion of these issues, see Allen Carlson, "Nature and Positive Aesthetics," *Environmental Ethics* 6 (1984): 5–34.

14. Robert Elliot, "Faking Nature," *Inquiry* 25 (1982): 90. The label is from Don Mannison, "A Prolegomenon to a Human Chauvinistic Aesthetic," in Don S. Mannison, Michael A. McRobbie, and Richard Routley, eds., *Environmental Philosophy* (Canberra: Australian National University, 1980), 212–216. I examine the Human Chauvinistic Aesthetic more fully in "Nature and Positive Aesthetics."

15. Arnold Berleant, *The Aesthetics of Environment* (Philadelphia: Temple University Press, 1992), 169–170. See also Arnold Berleant, *Living in the Land-*

scape: Toward an Aesthetics of Environment (Lawrence: University Press of Kansas, 1997), and *Aesthetics and Environment: Variations on a Theme* (Aldershot, Eng.: Ashgate, 2005).

16. For a powerful statement of the orthodox view, see Paul Ziff, "Anything Viewed," in Esa Saarinen, Risto Hilpinen, Ilkka Niiniluoto, and Merrill B. Provence Hintikka, eds., *Essays in Honour of Jaakko Hintikka on the Occasion of His Fiftieth Birthday on January 12, 1979* (Dordrecht: Reidel, 1979), 285–293.

17. I discuss problems with the Aesthetics of Engagement in "Aesthetics and Engagement," *British Journal of Aesthetics* 33 (1993): 220–227; "Beyond the Aesthetic," *Journal of Aesthetics and Art Criticism* 52 (1994): 239–241; and "Aesthetics and Environment," *British Journal of Aesthetics* 46 (2006): 416–427.

18. Tuan, *Topophilia*, 96.

19. William James, *The Principles of Psychology* (1890; Cambridge, Mass.: Harvard University Press, 1981), 462.

20. This point suggests further problems for the Landscape Model as far as it encourages formalistic aesthetic appreciation. If boundaries and foci do not exist in nature itself, it is difficult to see how it has significant formal aesthetic properties. I pursue this idea in "Formal Qualities and the Natural Environment," *Journal of Aesthetic Education* 13 (1979): 99–114.

21. John Dewey, *Art as Experience* (1934; New York: Putnam, 1958), esp. 35–57.

22. For another account of the role of classification in art appreciation, see Kendall Walton, "Categories of Art," *Philosophical Review* 79 (1970): 334–367. I develop a Walton-like view for nature appreciation in "Nature, Aesthetic Judgment, and Objectivity," *Journal of Aesthetics and Art Criticism* 40 (1981): 15–27.

23. A paradigmatic exemplification of the aesthetic appreciation of nature enhanced by natural science is the writings of Aldo Leopold, such as his well-known *A Sand County Almanac, with Essays on Conservation from Round River* (New York: Oxford University Press, 1966).

24. The centrality of scientific knowledge in the aesthetic appreciation of nature is challenged in, for example, Stan Godlovitch, "Icebreakers: Environmentalism and Natural Aesthetics," *Journal of Applied Philosophy* 11 (1994): 15–30; Emily Brady, "Imagination and the Aesthetic Appreciation of Nature," *Journal of Aesthetics and Art Criticism* 56 (1998): 139–147; and Thomas Heyd, "Aesthetic Appreciation and the Many Stories About Nature," *British Journal of Aesthetics* 41 (2001): 125–137, all reprinted in Carlson and Berleant, eds., *Aesthetics of Natural Environments*, 108–126, 156–169, 269–282. It is defended in, for example, Holmes Rolston, III, "Does Aesthetic Appreciation of Nature Need to Be Science Based?" *British Journal of Aesthetics* 35 (1995): 374–386; Marcia Eaton, "Fact and Fiction in the Aesthetic Appreciation of Nature," *Journal of Aesthetics and Art Criticism* 56 (1998): 149–156, reprinted in Carlson and

Berleant, eds., *Aesthetics of Natural Environments*, 170–181; Patricia Matthews, "Scientific Knowledge and the Aesthetic Appreciation of Nature," *Journal of Aesthetics and Art Criticism* 60 (2002): 37–48; and Glenn Parsons, "Nature Appreciation, Science, and Positive Aesthetics," *British Journal of Aesthetics* 42 (2002): 279–295.

25. John Muir's view is well exemplified in his essays for *Atlantic Monthly* that are collected in *Our National Parks* (Boston: Houghton Mifflin, 1916). See also John Muir, *A Thousand-Mile Walk to the Gulf* (Boston: Houghton Mifflin, 1916), and *The Mountains of California* (New York: Century, 1894). For an introduction to his aesthetic views, see Philip G. Terrie, "John Muir on Mount Ritter: A New Wilderness Aesthetic," *Pacific Historian* 31 (1987): 135–144.

26. I consider positive aesthetics and its relationship to the development of Western science in "Nature and Positive Aesthetics."

27. I discuss objectivity in the appreciation of nature in "Nature, Aesthetic Judgment, and Objectivity," and "On the Possibility of Quantifying Scenic Beauty," *Landscape Planning* 4 (1977): 131–172.

28. I apply these ideas to other kinds of cases in, for example, "On Appreciating Agricultural Landscapes," *Journal of Aesthetics and Art Criticism* 43 (1985): 301–312; "Existence, Location, and Function: The Appreciation of Architecture," in Michael Mitias, ed., *Philosophy and Architecture* (Amsterdam: Rodopi, 1994), 141–164; and "On Aesthetically Appreciating Human Environments," *Philosophy and Geography* 4 (2001): 9–24.

29. I develop the idea of an object-centered aesthetics in "Appreciating Art and Appreciating Nature," in Salim Kemal and Ivan Gaskell, eds., *Landscape, Natural Beauty and the Arts* (Cambridge: Cambridge University Press, 1993), 199–227.

3. THE REQUIREMENTS FOR AN ADEQUATE AESTHETICS OF NATURE

The ideas in this chapter have been presented in various PowerPoint presentations at several universities and a few conferences. I thank the members of the audiences for comments that have proved most useful in writing the chapter, especially Renee Conroy, Ned Hettinger, Andrew Kania, Andrew Light, Ronald Moore, Christopher Preston, Ted Toadvine, and Alison Wylie.

1. Jerome Stolnitz, *Aesthetics and the Philosophy of Art Criticism: A Critical Introduction* (Boston: Houghton Mifflin, 1960), 35.

2. George Dickie, "A Response to Cohen: The Actuality of Art," in George Dickie and Richard J. Sclafani, eds., *Aesthetics: A Critical Anthology* (New York: St. Martin's Press, 1977), 200.

3. Paul Ziff, "Anything Viewed," in Esa Saarinen, Risto Hilpinen, Ilkka Niiniluoto, and Merrill B. Provence Hintikka, eds., *Essays in Honour of Jaakko Hintikka on the Occasion of His Fiftieth Birthday on January 12, 1979* (Dordrecht: Reidel, 1979), 286–287, 293.

4. Robert Elliot, "Faking Nature," *Inquiry* 25 (1982): 81–93.

5. Don Mannison, "A Prolegomenon to a Human Chauvinistic Aesthetic," in Don S. Mannison, Michael A. McRobbie, and Richard Routley, eds., *Environmental Philosophy* (Canberra: Australian National University, 1980), 212, 216.

6. Stan Godlovitch, "Icebreakers: Environmentalism and Natural Aesthetics," *Journal of Applied Philosophy* 11 (1994): 15–30, reprinted in Allen Carlson and Arnold Berleant, eds., *The Aesthetics of Natural Environments* (Peterborough, Ont.: Broadview Press, 2004), 108–126.

7. Allen Carlson, "Nature, Aesthetic Appreciation, and Knowledge," *Journal of Aesthetics and Art Criticism* 53 (1995): 393–400, and "Appreciating Godlovitch," *Journal of Aesthetics and Art Criticism* 55 (1997): 55–57.

8. Arnold Berleant, *Art and Engagement* (Philadelphia: Temple University Press, 1991), and *The Aesthetics of Environment* (Philadelphia: Temple University Press, 1992).

9. Allen Carlson, "Aesthetics and Engagement," *British Journal of Aesthetics* 33 (1993): 220–227; "Beyond the Aesthetic," *Journal of Aesthetics and Art Criticism* 52 (1994): 239–241; and "Aesthetics and Environment," *British Journal of Aesthetics* 46 (2006): 416–427.

10. Malcolm Budd, "The Aesthetics of Nature," *Proceedings of the Aristotelian Society* 100 (2000): 137–157, reprinted in *The Aesthetic Appreciation of Nature: Essays on the Aesthetics of Nature* (Oxford: Oxford University Press, 2002), 91.

11. For example, Budd notes that this "conception of the aesthetic appreciation of nature has long been recognized by Allen Carlson and Holmes Rolston III, among others" ("Aesthetics of Nature," 91).

12. See, for example, Robert Stecker, "The Correct and the Appropriate in the Appreciation of Nature," *British Journal of Aesthetics* 37 (1997): 393–402, and Donald Crawford, "Scenery and the Aesthetics of Nature," in Carlson and Berleant, eds., *Aesthetics of Natural Environments*, 253–268.

13. Anthony Savile, *The Test of Time: An Essay in Philosophical Aesthetics* (Oxford: Oxford University Press, 1982).

14. Nick Zangwill, "Formal Natural Beauty," *Proceedings of the Aristotelian Society* 101 (2001): 209–224, reprinted in *The Metaphysics of Beauty* (Ithaca, N.Y.: Cornell University Press, 2001), 112–126. Zangwill calls it the "weak Qua thesis," since he distinguishes it from the "strong Qua thesis," which he rightly attributes to me: "We can distinguish weak and strong versions of this 'Qua thesis.' According to the strong version, we must subsume things under either the correct scientific or the correct common-sense natural categories.

We must appreciate a natural thing as the *particular kind* of natural thing it is. But all the weak Qua thesis holds is that one need only appreciate a natural thing as a natural thing. . . . Carlson defends the strong thesis. Budd (I think) only endorses the weak thesis. But in my view, *both* theses should be resisted" (210).

15. Glenn Parsons, "Natural Functions and the Aesthetic Appreciation of In-organic Nature," *British Journal of Aesthetics* 44 (2004): 44–56. The new versions of formalism concerning the aesthetic appreciation of nature that are defended by Zangwell and others are discussed in Glenn Parsons and Allen Carlson, "New Formalism and the Aesthetic Appreciation of Nature," *Journal of Aesthetics and Art Criticism* 62 (2004): 363–376.

16. Thomas Heyd, "Aesthetic Appreciation and the Many Stories About Nature," *British Journal of Aesthetics* 41 (2001): 125, reprinted in Carlson and Berleant, eds., *Aesthetics of Natural Environments*, 269–282.

17. Berleant, *Aesthetics of Environment*, 161.

18. Clive Bell, *Art* (1913; New York: Putnam, 1958).

19. George Dickie, *Art and the Aesthetic: An Institutional Analysis* (Ithaca, N.Y.: Cornell University Press, 1974), 169, 199.

20. Kendall Walton, "Categories of Art," *Philosophical Review* 79 (1970): 334–367. I explicitly address Walton's treatment of aesthetic judgments about nature in "Nature, Aesthetic Judgement, and Objectivity," *Journal of Aesthetics and Art Criticism* 40 (1981): 15–27.

21. Budd, "Aesthetics of Nature," 108.

22. Ibid. Budd also has other reasons for holding that the aesthetic appreciation of nature is freer than that of art. For discussions of these reasons, see Glenn Parsons, "Nature Appreciation, Science, and Positive Aesthetics," *British Journal of Aesthetics* 42 (2002): 279–295, and "Freedom and Objectivity in the Aesthetic Appreciation of Nature," *British Journal of Aesthetics* 46 (2006): 17–37, and Allen Carlson, "Budd and Brady on the Aesthetics of Nature," *Philosophical Quarterly* 55 (2005): 107–114, and "Scientific Representations of Natural Landscapes and Appropriate Aesthetic Appreciation," *Rivista di estetica* 29 (2005): 41–51.

23. John Andrew Fisher, "What the Hills Are Alive With: In Defense of the Sounds of Nature," *Journal of Aesthetics and Art Criticism* 56 (1998): 177, reprinted in Carlson and Berleant, eds., *Aesthetics of Natural Environments*, 232–252.

24. Ronald W. Hepburn, "Contemporary Aesthetics and the Neglect of Natural Beauty," in Bernard Williams and Alan Montefiore, eds., *British Analytical Philosophy* (London: Routledge & Kegan Paul, 1966), 305, reprinted in Ronald W. Hepburn, *"Wonder" and Other Essays: Eight Studies in Aesthetics and Neighboring Fields* (Edinburgh: Edinburgh University Press, 1984), 9–35, and Carlson and Berleant, eds., *Aesthetics of Natural Environments*, 43–62. See also Ronald W.

Hepburn, "Trivial and Serious in Aesthetic Appreciation of Nature," in Salim Kemal and Ivan Gaskell, eds., *Landscape, Natural Beauty and the Arts* (Cambridge: Cambridge University Press, 1993), 65–80.

25. Noël Carroll, "On Being Moved by Nature: Between Religion and Natural History," in Kemal and Gaskell, eds., *Landscape, Natural Beauty and the Arts*, 245, reprinted in Carlson and Berleant, eds., *Aesthetics of Natural Environments*, 89–107.

26. Cheryl Foster, "The Narrative and the Ambient in Environmental Aesthetics," *Journal of Aesthetics and Art Criticism* 56 (1998): 132–133, reprinted in Carlson and Berleant, eds., *Aesthetics of Natural Environments*, 197–213. See also Cheryl Foster, "Aesthetic Disillusionment: Environment, Ethics, Art," *Environmental Values* 1 (1992): 205–215, and "I've Looked at Clouds from Both Sides Now: Can There Be Aesthetic Qualities in Nature?" in Emily Brady and Jerrold Levinson, eds., *Aesthetic Concepts: Essays After Sibley* (Oxford: Oxford University Press, 2001), 180–198.

27. Janna Thompson, "Aesthetics and the Value of Nature," *Environmental Ethics* 17 (1995): 292.

28. I argue for the objectivity of aesthetic judgments about nature on other grounds in "Nature, Aesthetic Judgment, and Objectivity."

29. Malcolm Budd, "Aesthetics of Nature," in Jerrold Levinson, ed., *The Oxford Handbook of Aesthetics* (Oxford: Oxford University Press, 2002), 117–135, reprinted in *Aesthetic Appreciation of Nature*, 147–148.

30. Fisher, "What the Hills Are Alive With," 171.

31. Foster, "Narrative and the Ambient in Environmental Aesthetics," 136.

32. Carroll, "On Being Moved by Nature," 245, 257.

33. Carroll does not advocate his arousal model as a complete account of the aesthetic appreciation of nature, but sees it as "coexisting" with more cognitively focused positions, such as the Natural Environmental Model (ibid., 257). Thus if the latter complements the former, a greater degree of objectivity is possible. I discuss the relationship between Carroll's view and scientific cognitivism in "Nature, Aesthetic Appreciation, and Knowledge."

34. Emily Brady, *Aesthetics of the Natural Environment* (Edinburgh: Edinburgh University Press, 2003). See also Emily Brady, "Aesthetic Character and Aesthetic Integrity in Environmental Conservation," *Environmental Ethics* 24 (2002): 75–91.

35. Marcia Eaton, "Fact and Fiction in the Aesthetic Appreciation of Nature," *Journal of Aesthetics and Art Criticism* 56 (1998): 149–156, reprinted in Carlson and Berleant, eds., *Aesthetics of Natural Environments*, 170–181; Robert Fudge, "Imagination and the Science-Based Aesthetic Appreciation of Unscenic Nature," *Journal of Aesthetics and Art Criticism* 59 (2001): 275–285.

36. Brady, *Aesthetics of the Natural Environment*, 185.

37. Ibid., 201–202. On the notion of "perceptual proof," see Frank Sibley, "Aesthetic Concepts," *Philosophical Review* 68 (1959): 421–450.

38. Carlson, "Budd and Brady on the Aesthetics of Nature."

39. Different versions of this kind of position are defended in Eaton, "Fact and Fiction in the Aesthetic Appreciation of Nature"; Patricia Matthews, "Scientific Knowledge and the Aesthetic Appreciation of Nature," *Journal of Aesthetics and Art Criticism* 60 (2002): 37–48; Parsons, "Nature Appreciation, Science, and Positive Aesthetics"; Holmes Rolston, III, "Does Aesthetic Appreciation of Landscapes Need to Be Science-Based?" *British Journal of Aesthetics* 35 (1995): 374–386; and Allen Carlson, *Aesthetics and the Environment: The Appreciation of Nature, Art and Architecture* (London: Routledge, 2000). For a number of essays discussing scientific cognitivism, including several that are cited in the notes for this chapter, see Carlson and Berleant, eds., *Aesthetics of Natural Environments*.

40. Allen Carlson, "Nature and Positive Aesthetics," *Environmental Ethics* 6 (1984): 27–28.

4. AESTHETIC APPRECIATION AND THE HUMAN ENVIRONMENT

I thank the editors, as well as the anonymous reviewers, of the journal *Philosophy and Geography* for suggesting improvements to an earlier version of this chapter. The example of "an exclusive, upper-middle-class suburban neighborhood" was suggested by one of the reviewers.

1. Geoffrey Jellicoe and Susan Jellicoe, *The Landscape of Man: Shaping the Environment from Prehistory to the Present Day* (London: Thames and Hudson, 1987), 8.

2. I apply the ideas of this chapter exclusively to architecture in "The Aesthetic Appreciation of Everyday Architecture," in Michael Mitias, ed., *Architecture and Civilization* (Amsterdam: Rodopi, 1999), 107–121.

3. Arthur Schopenhauer, *The World as Will and Representation*, trans. E. F. J. Payne (1844; New York: Dover, 1966), 1:214.

4. This point is nicely illustrated in the introduction, aptly titled "The Problem of Architecture," to Roger Scruton, *The Aesthetics of Architecture* (Princeton, N.J.: Princeton University Press, 1979), 1–19.

5. Stephen Bungay, *Beauty and Truth: A Study of Hegel's Aesthetics* (New York: Oxford University Press, 1984), 102.

6. Virgil C. Aldrich, *Philosophy of Art* (Englewood Cliffs, N.J.: Prentice-Hall, 1963), 56–60.

7. Larry L. Ligo, *The Concept of Function in Twentieth-Century Architectural Criticism* (Ann Arbor: University of Michigan Research Press, 1984), 3–4.

8. I develop this point in more detail in "Existence, Location, and Function: The Appreciation of Architecture," in Michael Mitias, ed., *Philosophy and Architecture* (Amsterdam: Rodopi, 1994), 141–164. For an extended treatment of the importance of function in the aesthetic appreciation of not simply buildings, but the whole human environment, as well as nature and art, see Glenn Parsons and Allen Carlson, *Functional Beauty* (Oxford: Oxford University Press, 2008).

9. Joan Iverson Nassauer, "Culture and Landscape Ecology: Insights for Action," in Joan Iverson Nassauer, ed., *Placing Nature: Culture and Landscape Ecology* (Washington D.C.: Island Press, 1997), 4.

10. Joan Iverson Nassauer, "Cultural Sustainability: Aligning Aesthetics and Ecology," in Nassauer, ed., *Placing Nature*, 68.

11. Ibid., 76–77.

12. Ibid., 69.

13. I introduce and develop this idea in "Reconsidering the Aesthetics of Architecture," *Journal of Aesthetic Education* 20 (1986): 21–27.

14. Plato, *Phaedrus* [360 B.C.E.], 264c.

15. Harold Osborne, *Aesthetics and Art Theory: An Historical Introduction* (New York: Dutton, 1980), 284–293.

16. John Hospers, *Understanding the Arts* (Englewood Cliffs, N.J.: Prentice-Hall, 1982), 104.

17. I consider the case of rural and agricultural environments in detail in "On Appreciating Agricultural Landscapes," *Journal of Aesthetics and Art Criticism* 43 (1985): 301–312, and "Viljelysmaisemien Esteettinen Arvo Ja Touttavuus" [Productivity and the Aesthetic Value of Agricultural Landscapes], in Yrjö Sepänmaa and Liisa Heikkilä-Palo, eds., *Pellossa Perihopeat* [Fields: The Family Silver] (Helsinki: Maahenki, 2005), 52–61.

18. I discuss the centrality of the role of designs and designers in the aesthetic appreciation of works of art as well as its lack of significance in the appreciation of nature in "Appreciating Art and Appreciating Nature," in Salim Kemal and Ivan Gaskell, eds., *Landscape, Natural Beauty and the Arts* (Cambridge: Cambridge University Press, 1993), 199–227.

19. I introduce the connection between aesthetic appreciation and things looking "natural" and "as they should" in "On the Aesthetic Appreciation of Japanese Gardens," *British Journal of Aesthetics* 37 (1997): 47–56.

20. Ronald W. Hepburn, "Aesthetic Appreciation of Nature," in Harold Osborne, ed., *Aesthetics and the Modern World* (London: Thames and Hudson, 1968), 53. The passage is quoted in full in chapter 2.

21. Oscar Wilde, "Letter to the Editor," *St. James Gazette*, June 25, 1890, in *The Artist as Critic: Critical Writings of Oscar Wilde*, ed. Richard Ellmann (New York: Vintage, 1969), 236.

22. I discuss related issues concerning environmental art in "Is Environmental Art an Aesthetic Affront to Nature?" *Canadian Journal of Philosophy* 16 (1986): 635–650.

23. Peter Humphrey, "The Ethics of Earthworks," *Environmental Ethics* 7 (1985): 7–8.

24. D.W. Prall, *Aesthetic Judgment* (New York: Crowell, 1929), 178–227; John Hospers, *Meaning and Truth in the Arts* (Chapel Hill: University of North Carolina Press, 1946), 11–15.

25. Hospers, *Meaning and Truth in the Arts*, 13.

26. George Santayana, *The Sense of Beauty: Being the Outline of Aesthetic Theory* (1896; New York: Collier, 1961).

27. I do not address here the important question of the possibility of objectivity concerning attributions of expressed life values. This is an issue within the general topic of the objective of aesthetic judgments. I address this topic with respect to natural environments in "Nature, Aesthetic Judgment, and Objectivity," *Journal of Aesthetics and Art Criticism* 40 (1981): 15–27.

28. I introduce and develop the distinction between the thin and the thick sense of the aesthetic and the role of life values in the aesthetic appreciation of environments in "Environmental Aesthetics and the Dilemma of Aesthetic Education," *Journal of Aesthetic Education* 10 (1976): 69–82.

29. See, for example, Nassauer, ed., *Placing Nature*; Richard T.T. Forman and Michael Godron, *Landscape Ecology* (New York: Wiley, 1986); Donald W. Meinig, ed., *The Interpretation of Ordinary Landscapes: Geographic Essays* (New York: Oxford University Press, 1979); Barry Sadler and Allen Carlson, eds., *Environmental Aesthetics: Essays in Interpretation* (Victoria, B.C.: Department of Geography, University of Victoria, 1982); Edmund C. Penning-Rowsell and David Lowenthal, eds., *Landscape Meanings and Values* (London: Allen and Unwin, 1986); Paul Groth, ed., *Vision, Culture, and Landscape: The Berkeley Symposium on Cultural Landscape Interpretation* (Berkeley: Department of Landscape Architecture, University of California, 1990); Michael P. Conzen, ed., *The Making of the American Landscape* (Boston: Unwin Hyman, 1990); J. Douglas Porteous, *Environmental Aesthetics: Ideas, Politics and Planning* (London: Routledge, 1996); and Paul Groth and Todd W. Bressi, eds., *Understanding Ordinary Landscapes* (New Haven, Conn.: Yale University Press, 1997).

30. Peter Jackson, *London Bridge* (London: Cassell, 1971); David Scott and Alden P. Armagnac, "London Bridge Comes to America," *Popular Science*, September 1968, 68–71.

31. See, for example, the writings of John Brinckerhoff Jackson, such as *Landscapes: Selected Writings of J.B. Jackson*, ed. Ervin H. Zube (Amherst: University of Massachusetts Press, 1970); *The Necessity of Ruins, and Other Topics* (Am-

herst: University of Massachusetts Press, 1980); *Discovering the Vernacular Landscape* (New Haven, Conn.: Yale University Press, 1984); and *A Sense of Place, a Sense of Time* (New Haven, Conn.: Yale University Press, 1994).

32. Louis Sullivan, "The Tall Office Building Artistically Considered" (1918), in *Kindergarten Chats and Other Writings* (New York: Dover, 1979), 208.

33. Ibid.

5. APPRECIATION OF THE HUMAN ENVIRONMENT UNDER DIFFERENT CONCEPTIONS

Some of my observations and examples concerning landscape, territory, and terrain are included in a discussion note in *Building Materials* 12 (2005): 60–63. I thank the editor of that journal for helpful comments.

1. Francis E. Sparshott, "Figuring the Ground: Notes on Some Theoretical Problems of the Aesthetic Environment," *Journal of Aesthetic Education* 6 (1972): 11–23.

2. See the seminal articles by Paul Oskar Kristeller, "The Modern System of the Arts: A Study in the History of Aesthetics I," *Journal of the History of Ideas* 12 (1951): 496–527, and "The Modern System of the Arts: A Study in the History of Aesthetics II," *Journal of the History of Ideas* 13 (1952): 17–46.

3. I discuss this more fully in "The Aesthetic Appreciation of Everyday Architecture," in Michael Mitias, ed., *Architecture and Civilization* (Amsterdam: Editions Rodopi, 1999), 107–121.

4. Two useful sets of essays in this area are Warwick Fox, ed., *Ethics and the Built Environment* (London: Routledge, 2000), and the issue on ethics and architecture of *Philosophical Forum* 35, no. 2 (2004).

5. Sparshott, "Figuring the Ground," 13.

6. Ibid.

7. Ibid.

8. Ibid.

9. Ibid., 14.

10. Ibid., 15

11. Ibid.

12. Ibid.

13. Frank Lloyd Wright, "In the Cause of Architecture" (1908), in *Frank Lloyd Wright on Architecture: Selected Writings, 1894–1940*, ed. Frederick Gutheim (New York: Duell, Sloan and Pearce, 1941), 34

14. For more on Sea Ranch, see http://www.tsra.org/.

15. Sparshott, "Figuring the Ground," 14.

16. For a magnificent photographic study of the grain elevators of the Canadian prairies, see Hans Dommasch, *Prairie Giants* (Saskatoon: Western Producer Prairie Books, 1986), or, for simply a lot of elevator images, see http://scaa.usask.ca/gallery/elevators/.

17. Although environments conceptualized as places may have limited application to the particular issues covered in this chapter, the concept of place is very aesthetically significant in our appreciation of our smaller living and working spaces and places. See the discussion of the aesthetics of everyday life in chapter 1, and Kevin Melchionne, "Living in Glass Houses: Domesticity, Interior Decoration, and Environmental Aesthetics," *Journal of Aesthetics and Art Criticism* 56 (1998): 191–200, and "Front Yards," in Arnold Berleant, ed., *Environment and the Arts: Perspectives on Environmental Aesthetics* (Aldershot, Eng.: Ashgate, 2002), 103–111.

18. Sparshott, "Figuring the Ground," 14–15.

19. George Santayana, *The Sense of Beauty: Being the Outline of Aesthetic Theory* (1896; New York: Collier, 1961), 99.

20. Ibid. The passage is quoted in full in chapter 2.

21. Sparshott, "Figuring the Ground," 15.

22. The way in which the conceptualization of the environment as landscape encourages the divorcing of the aesthetic from the moral is, as indicated in chapters 1 and 2, clearly illustrated by the picturesque tradition of landscape appreciation. In his study of the picturesque, Malcolm Andrews argues that there is a general moral fault with the picturesque: "[T]he trouble is that the Picturesque enterprise in its later stage, with its almost exclusive emphasis on visual appreciation, entailed a suppression of the spectator's moral response" (*The Search for the Picturesque: Landscape Aesthetics and Tourism in Britain, 1760–1800* [Stanford, Calif.: Stanford University Press, 1989], 59).

23. Sparshott, "Figuring the Ground," 23.

6. AESTHETIC APPRECIATION AND THE AGRICULTURAL LANDSCAPE

An overview of this chapter was presented as a PowerPoint presentation at the Fifth International Conference on Environmental Aesthetics, "The Aesthetics of Agriculture," at Häme Polytechnic, Lepaa Unit, Hattula, Finland, August 5–8, 2003. I thank the members of the audience for comments that proved most useful in writing the chapter, especially Emily Brady, Marcia Eaton, Joan Nassauer, and Glenn Parsons.

1. In this chapter, more so than previously in this book, I use the concept of landscape. However, I do not define it in the narrow sense introduced in

chapter 1 and elaborated in chapter 5. Rather, as in chapter 7, I intend it in the more general sense in which it is almost synonymous with "environment." I avoid using the phrase "agricultural environment," since it has connotations that I do not want to evoke.

2. John Conron, *American Picturesque* (University Park: Pennsylvania State University Press, 2000), 17.

3. Ibid.

4. Ibid., 18.

5. Ibid.

6. Ibid., 19.

7. Richard Payne Knight, *The Landscape* (London: Bummer, 1794); William Gilpin, *Three Essays: On Picturesque Beauty, On Picturesque Travel, and On Sketching Landscape* (London: Balmier, 1792). See also Uvedale Price, *An Essay on the Picturesque* (London: Robson, 1794), and Richard Payne Knight, *Analytical Inquiry into the Principles of Taste* (1805; Westmead, Eng.: Gregg International, 1972), as well as such secondary sources as Christopher Hussey, *The Picturesque: Studies in a Point of View* (London: Putnam, 1927); Walter John Hipple, Jr., *The Beautiful, the Sublime, and the Picturesque in Eighteenth-Century British Aesthetic Theory* (Carbondale: Southern Illinois University Press, 1957); and Malcolm Andrews, *The Search for the Picturesque: Landscape Aesthetics and Tourism in Britain, 1760–1800* (Stanford, Calif.: Stanford University Press, 1989).

8. Allen Carlson, "Aesthetic Appreciation of Nature," in Edward Craig, ed., *Routledge Encyclopedia of Philosophy* (London: Routledge, 1998), 6:731–735.

9. Ronald Rees, "The Taste for Mountain Scenery," *History Today* 25 (1975): 312.

10. Yuriko Saito, "The Aesthetics of Unscenic Nature," *Journal of Aesthetics and Art Criticism* 56 (1998): 101.

11. For discussions of the ways in which wetlands have been "considered lacking in aesthetic value," see Allen Carlson, "Soiden Ihaileminen: Kosteikkojen Vaikea Kauneus" [Admiring Mirelands: The Difficult Beauty of Wetlands], in Liisa Heikkilä-Palo, ed., *Suo on Kaunis* [*Beauty in the Bog*] (Helsinki: Maahenki, 1999), 173–181; Holmes Rolston, III, "Aesthetics in the Swamps," *Perspectives in Biology and Medicine* 43 (2000): 584–597; and J. Baird Callicott, "Wetland Gloom and Wetland Glory," *Philosophy and Geography* 6 (2003): 33–45.

12. Aldo Leopold, "A Taste for Country" (1953), in *A Sand County Almanac, with Essays on Conservation from Round River* (New York: Oxford University Press, 1966), 179–180. Leopold is referring to Álvar Núñez Cabeza de Vaca (ca. 1490–ca. 1557), a Spanish conquistador whose journey was one of the most remarkable feats of exploration of the Americas. He was the first European to explore what are now Texas and the Southwest of the United States (although it seems that he was not in what is now Kansas). His account of his travels, *La*

relación (*The Report*), was published first in 1542 and then, with some revisions, in 1555.

13. Clive Bell, *Art* (1913; New York: Putnam, 1958), 45.

14. Peirce Lewis, "Facing Up to Ambiguity," *Landscape* 26 (1982): 21.

15. I develop this and related points about the formal beauty of agricultural landscapes in "On Appreciating Agricultural Landscapes," *Journal of Aesthetics and Art Criticism* 43 (1985): 301–312.

16. John Hospers, *Meaning and Truth in the Arts* (Chapel Hill: University of North Carolina Press, 1946), 12–13.

17. D.W. Prall, *Aesthetic Judgment* (New York: Crowell, 1929), 178–227; Hospers, *Meaning and Truth in the Arts*, 11–15.

18. I introduce and develop the distinction between the thin and the thick sense of the aesthetic and the role of life values in aesthetic appreciation in "Environmental Aesthetics and the Dilemma of Aesthetic Education," *Journal of Aesthetic Education* 10 (1976): 69–82, and employ the distinction in a manner different from that in this chapter in "On Aesthetically Appreciating Human Environments," *Philosophy and Geography* 4 (2001): 9–24.

19. The relevant concept of "expression" was initially clarified by George Santayana in *The Sense of Beauty: Being the Outline of Aesthetic Theory* (1896; New York: Collier, 1961).

20. Although functional landscapes are to various degrees designed, it is important to keep in mind that the "designing" is not the artistic designing that is central to the designer landscape approach to the appreciation of human environments, which I criticized in chapter 4.

21. Carlson, "On Appreciating Agricultural Landscapes."

22. Ned Hettinger, "Carlson's Environmental Aesthetics and the Protection of the Environment," *Environmental Ethics* 27 (2005): 69–70.

23. Lewis, "Facing Up to Ambiguity." Lewis's essay is a fine introduction to the ambiguities involved in the appreciation of contemporary agricultural landscapes.

7. WHAT IS THE CORRECT WAY TO AESTHETICALLY APPRECIATE LANDSCAPES?

Substantially different versions of this chapter were presented at the Natturumal (Nature's Voices) Conference, Reykjavik, Iceland, September 1998; the American Society for Aesthetics, Rocky Mountain Division, Santa Fe, New Mexico, July 1995; the American Society for Aesthetics, Pacific Division, Pacific Grove, California, April 1995; and the First International Conference on Environmental Aesthetics, Koli, Finland, June 1994. I thank those present for valuable comments and, especially, Yrjö Sepänmaa, to whom I owe the basic idea of the chapter.

1. Jerome Stolnitz, *Aesthetics and the Philosophy of Art Criticism: A Critical Introduction* (Boston: Houghton Mifflin, 1960).

2. I consider Stolnitz's views on art appreciation in some detail in "Appreciating Art and Appreciating Nature," in Salim Kemal and Ivan Gaskell, eds., *Landscape, Natural Beauty and the Arts* (Cambridge: Cambridge University Press, 1993), 199–227.

3. George Santayana, *The Sense of Beauty: Being the Outline of Aesthetic Theory* (1896; New York: Collier, 1961), 99. The passage is quoted in full in chapter 2.

4. Peirce Lewis, "Facing Up to Ambiguity," *Landscape* 26 (1982): 18–22.

5. Ronald W. Hepburn, "Contemporary Aesthetics and the Neglect of Natural Beauty," in Bernard Williams and Alan Montefiore, eds., *British Analytical Philosophy* (London: Routledge & Kegan Paul, 1966), 305, reprinted in Ronald W. Hepburn, *"Wonder" and Other Essays: Eight Studies in Aesthetics and Neighboring Fields* (Edinburgh: Edinburgh University Press, 1984), 9–35, and Allen Carlson and Arnold Berleant, eds., *The Aesthetics of Natural Environments* (Peterborough, Ont.: Broadview Press, 2004), 43–62. The passage is quoted in full in chapter 3.

6. Santayana, *Sense of Beauty*, 100–101.

7. Clive Bell, *Art* (1913; New York: Putnam, 1958), 45. The passage is quoted in full in chapter 6.

8. Ibid., 27.

9. I discuss these problems in "On the Possibility of Quantifying Scenic Beauty," *Landscape Planning* 4 (1977): 131–172, and "Formal Qualities and the Natural Environment," *Journal of Aesthetic Education* 13 (1979): 99–114.

10. In addition to chapter 2, the basic position is developed in Allen Carlson, "Appreciation and the Natural Environment," *Journal of Aesthetics and Art Criticism* 37 (1979): 267–276; "Nature, Aesthetic Judgment, and Objectivity," *Journal of Aesthetics and Art Criticism* 40 (1981): 15–27; "Nature and Positive Aesthetics," *Environmental Ethics* 6 (1984): 5–34; "Appreciating Art and Appreciating Nature"; "Nature, Aesthetic Appreciation, and Knowledge," *Journal of Aesthetics and Art Criticism* 53 (1995): 393–400; and *Aesthetics and the Environment: The Appreciation of Nature, Art and Architecture* (London: Routledge, 2000). A science-based approach to the aesthetic appreciation of nature is also defended in Holmes Rolston, III, "Does Aesthetic Appreciation of Landscapes Need to Be Science-Based?" *British Journal of Aesthetics* 35 (1995): 374–386; Marcia Eaton, "Fact and Fiction in the Aesthetic Appreciation of Nature," *Journal of Aesthetics and Art Criticism* 56 (1998): 149–156, reprinted in Carlson and Berleant, eds., *Aesthetics of Natural Environments*, 170–181; Patricia Matthews, "Scientific Knowledge and the Aesthetic Appreciation of Nature," *Journal of*

Aesthetics and Art Criticism 60 (2002): 37–48; and Glenn Parsons, "Nature Appreciation, Science, and Positive Aesthetics," *British Journal of Aesthetics* 42 (2002): 279–295.

11. Hepburn, "Contemporary Aesthetics and the Neglect of Natural Beauty," 305.

12. The works of these naturalists and nature writers are so extensive and so well known that it is neither practical nor necessary to reference them. However, the following three collections provide a sample of the writings of most of them, along with numerous others of equal note: William Beebe, ed., *The Book of Naturalists: An Anthology of the Best Natural History* (1944; Princeton, N.J.: Princeton University Press, 1988); Daniel Halpern, ed., *On Nature: Nature, Landscape, and Natural History* (San Francisco: North Point Press, 1987); and Stephen Trimble, ed., *Words from the Land: Encounters with Natural History Writing* (Salt Lake City: Smith, 1988). Beebe's anthology is historically oriented, while the other two feature mainly contemporary work. The collection edited by Halpern has a very useful annotated booklist compiled by the advisory editors as well as an excellent bibliography. Also of interest, in that they are the contributions of working naturalists, are the short pieces gathered in John K. Terres, ed., *Discovery: Great Moments in the Lives of Outstanding Naturalists* (New York: Lippincott, 1961). These four collections feature material reflecting primarily biological and ecological knowledge; for a selection of writings focusing more on geological information, see Frank H. T. Rhodes and Richard O. Stone, eds., *Language of the Earth* (New York: Pergamon Press, 1981).

13. W. G. Hoskins, *The Making of the English Landscape* (London: Hodder & Stoughton, 1955); John Brinckerhoff Jackson, *Landscapes: Selected Writings of J.B. Jackson*, ed. Ervin H. Zube (Amherst: University of Massachusetts Press, 1970); *The Necessity for Ruins, and Other Topics* (Amherst: University of Massachusetts Press, 1980); *Discovering the Vernacular Landscape* (New Haven, Conn.: Yale University Press, 1984); and *A Sense of Place, a Sense of Time* (New Haven, Conn.: Yale University Press, 1994); May Theilgaard Watts, *Reading the Landscape of America* (1957; New York: Collier, 1975). In addition to the works of Hoskins, Jackson, and Watts, the writings of many other individuals, notably cultural geographers, illuminate the landscapes we have created. Many of them appear in the pages of the journal that Jackson founded and edited for many years, *Landscape*, and more recently in the more academic *Landscape Journal*. Examples of books that cover this kind of material are Donald W. Meinig, ed., *The Interpretation of Ordinary Landscapes: Geographical Essays* (New York: Oxford University Press, 1979), and Michael P. Conzen, ed., *The Making of the American Landscape* (Boston: Unwin Hyman, 1990), which has a valuable bibliography.

14. In such a case, we might suspect that the developer is not adequately disinterested and therefore that his or her appreciation is not *aesthetic* apprecia-

tion or, alternatively, that the developer is too disinterested and therefore that he or she cannot appreciate the life values expressed by such landscapes. As I argued in chapter 6, aesthetic experience requires a degree of disinterestedness, but not so much as to make it impossible to appreciate the expressive beauty of the object of appreciation. My point is somewhat reminiscent of Edward Bullough's observations about "over-distancing" and "under-distancing" in his classic study, "'Psychical Distance' as a Factor in Art and as an Aesthetic Principle," *British Journal of Psychology* 5 (1912): 87–98.

15. I make the special role of this kind of knowledge clearer in "On Appreciating Agricultural Landscapes," *Journal of Aesthetics and Art Criticism* 43 (1985): 301–312; "Reconsidering the Aesthetics of Architecture," *Journal of Aesthetic Education* 20 (1986): 21–27; and "Existence, Location, and Function: The Appreciation of Architecture," in Michael Mitias, ed., *Philosophy and Architecture* (Amsterdam: Rodopi, 1994), 141–164.

16. N. Scott Momaday, quoting his grandmother in *The Way to Rainy Mountain* (Albuquerque: University of New Mexico Press, 1969), quoted in United States Department of the Interior, *Devils Tower* (Washington, D.C.: Government Printing Office, 1991), 1.

17. Ibid.

18. I discuss related issues in "Interactions Between Art and Nature: Environmental Art," in Peter J. McCormick, ed., *The Reasons of Art: L'Art a ses raisons* (Ottawa: University of Ottawa Press, 1985), 222–231, and "Is Environmental Art an Aesthetic Affront to Nature?" *Canadian Journal of Philosophy* 16 (1986): 635–650. For a good introduction to environmental art, see Alan Sonfist, ed., *Art in the Land: A Critical Anthology of Environmental Art* (New York: Dutton, 1983).

19. Stephen L. Norton, *Devils Tower: The Story Behind the Scenery* (Las Vegas: KC Publications, 1991), inside front cover.

20. Ibid.

21. Ibid., 20 (my italics).

22. Ibid.

23. Quoted in Donald Crawford, "Nature and Art: Some Dialectical Relationships," *Journal of Aesthetics and Art Criticism* 42 (1983): 56.

24. The quotation is "A picture held us captive. And we could not get outside it" (Ludwig Wittgenstein, *Philosophical Investigations*, trans. G. E. M. Anscombe [Oxford: Blackwell, 1958], sec. 115). The context in which Wittgenstein made the remark concerns the philosophy of language.

25. I develop a somewhat similar line of thought concerning mythological descriptions of landscapes in "Landscape and Literature," in *Aesthetics and the Environment,* 216–240. However, I do not apply the same line to artistic, in particular, literary, descriptions of landscapes.

26. Santayana, *Sense of Beauty*, 100–101.

BIBLIOGRAPHY

Aldrich, Virgil C. *Philosophy of Art*. Englewood Cliffs, N.J.: Prentice-Hall, 1963.

Alison, Archibald. *Essays on the Nature and Principles of Taste*. Dublin: Byrne, 1790.

Andrews, Malcolm. *The Search for the Picturesque: Landscape Aesthetics and Tourism in Britain, 1760–1800*. Stanford, Calif.: Stanford University Press, 1989.

——. "The View from the Road and the Picturesque." In Arnold Berleant and Allen Carlson, eds., *The Aesthetics of Human Environments*, 272–289. Peterborough, Ont.: Broadview Press, 2007.

Appleton, Jay. *The Experience of Landscape*. London: Wiley, 1975.

——. "Landscape Evaluation: The Theoretical Vacuum." *Transactions of the Institute of British Geographers* 66 (1975): 120–123.

——. "Pleasure and the Perception of Habitat: A Conceptual Framework." In Barry Sadler and Allen Carlson, eds., *Environmental Aesthetics: Essays in Interpretation*, 27–45. Victoria, B.C.: Department of Geography, University of Victoria, 1982.

——. *The Symbolism of Habitat: An Interpretation of Landscape in the Arts*. Seattle: University of Washington Press, 1990.

Beardsley, Monroe C. *Aesthetics: Problems in the Philosophy of Criticism*. New York: Harcourt, Brace & World, 1958.

Bedwell, Jim, Larry Blocker, Paul Gobster, Terry Slider, and Tom Atzet. "Beyond the Picturesque: Integrating Aesthetics and Ecology in Forest Service Scenery Management." In Cheryl Wagner, ed., *ASLA 1997: Annual Meeting Proceedings*, 86–90. Washington, D.C.: American Society of Landscape Architects, 1997.

Beebe, William, ed. *The Book of Naturalists: An Anthology of the Best Natural History*. 1944. Princeton, N.J.: Princeton University Press, 1988.

Bell, Clive. *Art*. 1913. New York: Putnam, 1958.

Bell, Simon. *Landscape: Pattern, Perception and Process*. London: Routledge, 1999.

Berleant, Arnold. "Aesthetic Paradigms for an Urban Ecology." *Diogenes* 103 (1978): 1–28.

——. "Aesthetic Participation and the Urban Environment." *Urban Resources* 1 (1984): 37–42.

——. "Aesthetic Perception in Environmental Design." In Jack L. Nasar, ed., *Environmental Aesthetics: Theory, Research, and Applications*, 84–97. Cambridge: Cambridge University Press, 1988.

——. *Aesthetics and Environment: Variations on a Theme*. Aldershot, Eng.: Ashgate, 2005.

——. *The Aesthetics of Environment*. Philadelphia: Temple University Press, 1992.

——. "Architecture and the Aesthetics of Continuity." In Michael Mitias, ed., *Philosophy and Architecture*, 21–30. Amsterdam: Rodopi, 1994.

——. *Art and Engagement*. Philadelphia: Temple University Press, 1990.

——. "The Critical Aesthetics of Disney World." *Journal of Applied Philosophy* 11 (1994): 171–180.

——. "Cultivating an Urban Aesthetic." *Diogenes* 136 (1986): 1–18.

——. "Environmental Aesthetics." In Michael Kelly, ed., *Encyclopedia of Aesthetics*, 2:114–120. New York: Oxford University Press, 1998.

——. *Living in the Landscape: Toward an Aesthetics of Environment*. Lawrence: University Press of Kansas, 1997.

——. *Re-thinking Aesthetics: Rogue Essays on Aesthetics and the Arts*. Aldershot, Eng.: Ashgate, 2004.

Berleant, Arnold, and Allen Carlson, eds. *The Aesthetics of Human Environments*. Peterborough, Ont.: Broadview Press, 2007.

Biese, Alfred. *The Development of the Feeling for Nature in the Middle Ages and Modern Times*. 1905. New York: Burt Franklin, 1964.

Blake, Peter. *God's Own Junkyard: The Planned Deterioration of America's Landscape*. New York: Holt, Rinehart and Winston, 1964.

Bourassa, Steven C. *The Aesthetics of Landscape*. London: Belhaven, 1991.

Brady, Emily. "Aesthetic Character and Aesthetic Integrity in Environmental Conservation." *Environmental Ethics* 24 (2002): 75–91.

——. "Aesthetics, Ethics and the Natural Environment." In Arnold Berleant, ed., *Environment and the Arts: Perspectives on Environmental Aesthetics*, 113–126. Aldershot, Eng.: Ashgate, 2002.

——. *Aesthetics of the Natural Environment*. Edinburgh: Edinburgh University Press, 2003.

——. "Imagination and the Aesthetic Appreciation of Nature." *Journal of Aesthetics and Art Criticism* 56 (1998): 139–147.

——. "Sniffing and Savoring: The Aesthetics of Smells and Tastes." In Andrew Light and Jonathan M. Smith, eds., *The Aesthetics of Everyday Life*, 177–193. New York: Columbia University Press, 2005.

Brottman, Mikita. "The Last Stop of Desire: The Aesthetics of the Shopping Center." In Arnold Berleant and Allen Carlson, eds., *The Aesthetics of Human Environments*, 119–138. Peterborough, Ont.: Broadview Press, 2007.

Budd, Malcolm. "The Aesthetic Appreciation of Nature." *British Journal of Aesthetics* 36 (1996): 207–222.

———. *The Aesthetic Appreciation of Nature: Essays on the Aesthetics of Nature*. Oxford: Oxford University Press, 2002.

———. "Aesthetics of Nature." In Jerrold Levinson, ed., *The Oxford Handbook of Aesthetics*, 117–135. Oxford: Oxford University Press, 2002.

———. "The Aesthetics of Nature." *Proceedings of the Aristotelian Society* 100 (2000): 137–157.

———. "Delight in the Natural World: Kant on the Aesthetic Appreciation of Nature: Part I: Natural Beauty." *British Journal of Aesthetics* 38 (1998): 1–18.

———. "Delight in the Natural World: Kant on the Aesthetic Appreciation of Nature: Part II: Natural Beauty and Morality." *British Journal of Aesthetics* 38 (1998): 117–126.

———. "Delight in the Natural World: Kant on the Aesthetic Appreciation of Nature: Part III: The Sublime in Nature." *British Journal of Aesthetics* 38 (1998): 233–250.

Bullough, Edward. " 'Psychical Distance' as a Factor in Art and as an Aesthetics Principle." *British Journal of Psychology* 5 (1912): 87–98.

Bungay, Stephen. *Beauty and Truth: A Study of Hegel's Aesthetics*. New York: Oxford University Press, 1984.

Burke, Edmund. *A Philosophical Enquiry into the Origin of Our Ideas of the Sublime and the Beautiful*. 1757. Edited by James T. Boulton. London: Routledge & Kegan Paul, 1958.

Callicott, J. Baird. "The Land Aesthetic." In Christopher Key Chapple, ed., *Ecological Prospects: Scientific, Religious, and Aesthetic Perspectives*, 169–183. Albany: State University of New York Press, 1994.

———. "The Land Aesthetic." In J. Baird Callicott, ed., *Companion to A Sand County Almanac: Interpretive and Critical Essays*, 157–171. Madison: University of Wisconsin Press, 1987.

———. "Wetland Gloom and Wetland Glory." *Philosophy and Geography* 6 (2003): 33–45.

Carlson, Allen. "The Aesthetic Appreciation of Architecture Under Different Conceptions of the Environment." *Journal of Aesthetic Education* 40 (2006): 77–88.

———. "The Aesthetic Appreciation of Everyday Architecture." In Michael Mitias, ed., *Architecture and Civilization*, 107–121. Amsterdam: Editions Rodopi, 1999.

———. "Aesthetic Appreciation of Nature." In Edward Craig, ed., *Routledge Encyclopedia of Philosophy*, 6:731–735. London: Routledge, 1998.

——. "Aesthetic Appreciation of the Natural Environment." In Richard G. Botzler and Susan J. Armstrong, eds., *Environmental Ethics: Divergence and Convergence*, 108–114. 2nd ed. Boston: McGraw-Hill, 1998.

——. "Aesthetic Appreciation of the Natural Environment." In Susan L. Feagin and Patrick Maynard, eds., *Aesthetics*, 30–40. Oxford: Oxford University Press, 1997.

——. "Aesthetic Preferences for Sustainable Landscapes: Seeing and Knowing." In Stephen R. J. Sheppard and Howard W. Harshaw, eds., *Forests and Landscapes: Linking Ecology, Sustainability and Aesthetics*, 31–41. New York: CAB International, 2001.

——. "Aesthetics and Engagement." *British Journal of Aesthetics* 33 (1993): 220–227.

——. "Aesthetics and Environment." *British Journal of Aesthetics* 46 (2006): 416–427.

——. *Aesthetics and the Environment: The Appreciation of Nature, Art and Architecture*. London: Routledge, 2000.

——. "Appreciating Art and Appreciating Nature." In Salim Kemal and Ivan Gaskell, eds., *Landscape, Natural Beauty and the Arts*, 199–227. Cambridge: Cambridge University Press, 1993.

——. "Appreciating Godlovitch." *Journal of Aesthetics and Art Criticism* 55 (1997): 55–57.

——. "Appreciation and the Natural Environment." *Journal of Aesthetics and Art Criticism* 37 (1979): 267–276.

——. "Arnold Berleant's Environmental Aesthetics." *Ethics, Place and Environment* 10 (2007): 217–225.

——. "Beyond the Aesthetic." *Journal of Aesthetics and Art Criticism* 52 (1994): 239–241.

——. "Budd and Brady on the Aesthetics of Nature." *Philosophical Quarterly* 55 (2005): 107–114.

——. "Critical Notice of Ziff, *Antiaesthetics: An Appreciation of the Cow with the Subtile Nose*." *Canadian Journal of Philosophy* 17 (1987): 919–933.

——. "Environmental Aesthetics." In David Cooper, ed., *A Companion to Aesthetics*, 142–144. Oxford: Blackwell, 1992.

——. "Environmental Aesthetics." In Edward Craig, ed., *Routledge Encyclopedia of Philosophy Online*. London: Routledge, 2002. Available at www.rep.rout ledge.com/views /home/html.

——. "Environmental Aesthetics." In Berys Gaut and Dominic McIver Lopes, eds., *The Routledge Companion to Aesthetics*, 541–555. 2nd ed. London: Routledge, 2005.

——. "Environmental Aesthetics." In Edward N. Zalta, ed., *The Stanford Encyclopedia of Philosophy*. Stanford, Calif.: Metaphysics Research Lab, Center for the Study of Language and Information, 2007. Available at http://plato.stan ford.edu/entries/environmental-aesthetics.

——. "Environmental Aesthetics and the Dilemma of Aesthetic Education." *Journal of Aesthetic Education* 10 (1976): 69–82.

——. "Existence, Location, and Function: The Appreciation of Architecture." In Michael Mitias, ed., *Philosophy and Architecture*, 141–164. Amsterdam: Rodopi, 1994.

——. "Formal Qualities and the Natural Environment." *Journal of Aesthetic Education* 13 (1979): 99–114.

——. "Hargrove, Positive Aesthetics, and Indifferent Creativity." *Philosophy and Geography* 5 (2002): 224–234.

——. "Interactions Between Art and Nature: Environmental Art." In Peter J. Mc-Cormick, ed., *The Reasons of Art: L'Art a ses raisons*, 222–231. Ottawa: University of Ottawa Press, 1985.

——. "Is Environmental Art an Aesthetic Affront to Nature?" *Canadian Journal of Philosophy* 16 (1986): 635–650.

——. "Landscape and Literature." In *Aesthetics and the Environment: The Appreciation of Nature, Art and Architecture*, 216–240. London: Routledge, 2000.

——. "Landscape Assessment." In Michael Kelly, ed., *Encyclopedia of Aesthetics*, 3:102–105. New York: Oxford University Press, 1998.

——. "Nature, Aesthetic Judgment, and Objectivity." *Journal of Aesthetics and Art Criticism* 40 (1981): 15–27.

——. "Nature, Aesthetic Appreciation, and Knowledge." *Journal of Aesthetics and Art Criticism* 53 (1995): 393–400.

——. "Nature and Positive Aesthetics." *Environmental Ethics* 6 (1984): 5–34.

——. "Nature Appreciation and the Question of Aesthetic Relevance." In Arnold Berleant, ed., *Environment and the Arts: Perspectives on Environmental Aesthetics*, 62–75. Aldershot, Eng.: Ashgate, 2002.

——. "On Appreciating Agricultural Landscapes." *Journal of Aesthetics and Art Criticism* 43 (1985): 301–312.

——. "On Aesthetically Appreciating Human Environments." *Philosophy and Geography* 4 (2001): 9–24.

——. "On the Aesthetic Appreciation of Japanese Gardens." *British Journal of Aesthetics* 37 (1997): 47–56.

——. "On the Possibility of Quantifying Scenic Beauty." *Landscape Planning* 4 (1977): 131–172

——. "On the Theoretical Vacuum in Landscape Assessment." *Landscape Journal* 12 (1993): 51–56.

——. "Recent Landscape Assessment Research." In Michael Kelly, ed., *Encyclopedia of Aesthetics*, 3:102–105. New York: Oxford University Press, 1998.

———. "Reconsidering the Aesthetics of Architecture." *Journal of Aesthetic Education* 20 (1986): 21–27.

———. "The Requirements for an Adequate Aesthetics of Nature." In Seppo Knuuttila, Erkki Sevänen, and Risto Turunen, eds., *Aesthetic Culture: Essays in Honour of Yrjö Sepänmaa on His Sixtieth Birthday, 12 December 2005*, 15–34. Helsinki: Maahenki, 2005.

———. "Saito on the Correct Aesthetic Appreciation of Nature." *Journal of Aesthetic Education* 20 (1986): 85–93.

———. "Scientific Representations of Natural Landscapes and Appropriate Aesthetic Appreciation." *Rivista di estetica* 29 (2005): 41–51.

———. "Soiden Ihaileminen: Kosteikkojen Vaikea Kauneus" [Admiring Mirelands: The Difficult Beauty of Wetlands]. In Liisa Heikkilä-Palo, ed., *Suo on Kaunis* [*Beauty in the Bog*], 173–181. Helsinki: Maahenki, 1999.

———. "Tarkasteluum Kasvattaminen: Mikä on Olennaista Maisemassa?" [Aesthetic Experience: What Is Relevant to Landscape?]. In Yrjö Sepänmaa, Liisa Heikkilä-Palo, and Virpi Kaukio, eds., *Maiseman Kanssa Kasvokkain* [*Face to Face with the Landscape*], 92–107. Helsinki: Maahenki, 2007.

———. "Viljelysmaisemien Esteettinen Arvo Ja Touttavuus" [Productivity and the Aesthetic Value of Agricultural Landscapes]. In Yrjö Sepänmaa and Liisa Heikkilä-Palo, eds., *Pellossa Perihopeat* [*Fields: The Family Silver*], 52–61. Helsinki: Maahenki. 2005.

———. "'We see beauty now where we could not see it before': Rolston's Aesthetics of Nature." In Christopher J. Preston and Wayne Ouderkirk, eds., *Nature, Value, Duty: Life on Earth with Holmes Rolston, III*, 103–124. Dordrecht: Springer, 2006.

———. "What Is the Correct Curriculum for Landscape Appreciation?" *Journal of Aesthetic Education* 35 (2001): 97–112.

———. "Whose Vision? Whose Meanings? Whose Values? Pluralism and Objectivity in Landscape Analysis." In Paul Groth, ed., *Vision, Culture, and Landscape: The Berkeley Symposium on Cultural Landscape Interpretation*, 157–168. Berkeley: Department of Landscape Architecture, University of California, 1990.

Carlson, Allen, and Arnold Berleant, eds. *The Aesthetics of Natural Environments*. Peterborough, Ont.: Broadview Press, 2004.

Carlson, Allen, and Sheila Lintott, eds. *Nature, Aesthetics, and Environmentalism: From Beauty to Duty*. New York: Columbia University Press, 2008.

Carroll, Noël. "On Being Moved by Nature: Between Religion and Natural History." In Salim Kemal and Ivan Gaskell, eds., *Landscape, Natural Beauty and the Arts*, 244–266. Cambridge: Cambridge University Press, 1993.

Cats-Baril, William L., and Linda Gibson. "Evaluating Aesthetics: The Major Issues and a Bibliography." *Landscape Journal* 5 (1986): 93–102.

Collingwood, R. G. *The Idea of Nature*. 1945. New York: Oxford University Press, 1960.

——. *Principles of Art*. 1938. New York: Oxford University Press, 1958.

Conron, John. *American Picturesque*. University Park: Pennsylvania State University Press, 2000.

Conzen, Michael P., ed. *The Making of the American Landscape*. Boston: Unwin Hyman, 1990.

Cooper, Anthony Ashley, third Earl of Shaftesbury. *Characteristics of Men, Manners, Opinions, Times*. 1711. Edited by Lawrence E. Klein. Cambridge: Cambridge University Press, 1999.

Cooper, David E. *A Philosophy of Gardens*. Oxford: Oxford University Press, 2006.

Crandell, Gina. *Nature Pictorialized: "The View" in Landscape History*. Baltimore: Johns Hopkins University Press, 1993.

Crawford, Donald. "The Aesthetics of Nature and the Environment." In Peter Kivy, ed., *The Blackwell Guide to Aesthetics*, 306–324. Oxford: Blackwell, 2003.

——. "Nature and Art: Some Dialectical Relationships." *Journal of Aesthetics and Art Criticism* 62 (1983): 49–58.

——. "Scenery and the Aesthetics of Nature." In Allen Carlson and Arnold Berleant, eds., *The Aesthetics of Natural Environments*, 253–268. Peterborough, Ont.: Broadview Press, 2004.

Daniel, Terry C. "Whither Scenic Beauty? Visual Landscape Quality Assessment in the 21st Century." *Landscape and Urban Planning* 54 (2001): 276–281.

Danto, Arthur. "The Artworld." *Journal of Philosophy* 61 (1964): 571–584.

——. *The Transfiguration of the Commonplace: A Philosophy of Art*. Cambridge, Mass.: Harvard University Press, 1981.

Dewey, John. *Art as Experience*. 1934. New York: Putnam, 1958.

Dickie, George. *Art and the Aesthetic: An Institutional Analysis*. Ithaca, N.Y.: Cornell University Press, 1974.

——. "The Myth of the Aesthetic Attitude." *American Philosophical Quarterly* 1 (1964): 56–65.

——. "A Response to Cohen: The Actuality of Art." In George Dickie and Richard J. Sclafani, eds., *Aesthetics: A Critical Anthology*, 196–200. New York: St. Martin's Press, 1977.

Diffey, Terry J. "Arguing About the Environment." *British Journal of Aesthetics* 40 (2000): 133–148.

Dommasch, Hans. *Prairie Giants*. Saskatoon: Western Producer Prairie Books, 1986.

Ducasse, Curt J. *Art, the Critics, and You*. 1944. Indianapolis: Bobbs-Merrill, 1955.

Eaton, Marcia. *Aesthetics and the Good Life*. Cranbury, N.J.: Associated University Presses, 1989.

———. "The Beauty that Requires Health." In Joan Iverson Nassauer, ed., *Placing Nature: Culture and Landscape Ecology*, 85–106. Washington, D.C.: Island Press, 1997.

———. "Fact and Fiction in the Aesthetic Appreciation of Nature." *Journal of Aesthetics and Art Criticism* 56 (1998): 149–156.

———. "The Role of Aesthetics in Designing Sustainable Landscapes." In Yrjö Sepänmaa, ed., *Real World Design: The Foundations and Practice of Environmental Aesthetics*, 51–63. Helsinki: University of Helsinki, 1997.

Elliot, Robert. "Environmental Degradation, Vandalism and the Aesthetic Object Argument." *Australasian Journal of Philosophy* 67 (1989): 191–204.

———. "Faking Nature." *Inquiry* 25 (1982): 81–93.

———. *Faking Nature: The Ethics of Environmental Restoration*. London: Routledge, 1997.

Elsner, Gary H., and Richard C. Smardon, eds. *The Proceedings of Our National Landscape: A Conference on Applied Techniques for Analysis and Management of the Visual Resource*. Berkeley, Calif.: Pacific Southwest Forest and Range Experimental Station, 1979.

Fisher, John A. "Environmental Aesthetics." In Jerrold Levinson, ed., *The Oxford Handbook of Aesthetics*, 667–678. Oxford: Oxford University Press, 2002.

———. "What the Hills Are Alive With: In Defense of the Sounds of Nature." *Journal of Aesthetics and Art Criticism* 56 (1998): 167–179.

Forman, Richard T. T., and Michel Godron. *Landscape Ecology*. New York: Wiley, 1986.

Foster, Cheryl. "Aesthetic Disillusionment: Environment, Ethics, Art." *Environmental Values* 1 (1992): 205–215

———. "I've Looked at Clouds from Both Sides Now: Can There Be Aesthetic Qualities in Nature?" In Emily Brady and Jerrold Levinson, eds., *Aesthetic Concepts: Essays After Sibley*, 180–198. Oxford: Oxford University Press, 2001.

———. "The Narrative and the Ambient in Environmental Aesthetics." *Journal of Aesthetics and Art Criticism* 56 (1998): 127–137.

Fox, Warwick, ed. *Ethics and the Built Environment*. London: Routledge, 2000.

Fudge, Robert. "Imagination and the Science-Based Aesthetic Appreciation of Unscenic Nature." *Journal of Aesthetics and Art Criticism* 59 (2001): 275–285.

Gilpin, William. *Three Essays: On Picturesque Beauty, On Picturesque Travel, and On Sketching Landscape*. London: Blamire, 1792.

Gobster, Paul. "Aldo Leopold's Ecological Esthetic: Integrating Esthetic and Biodiversity Values." *Journal of Forestry* 93 (1995): 6–10.

Godlovitch, Stan. "Aesthetic Protectionism." *Journal of Applied Philosophy* 6 (1989): 171–180.

———. "Evaluating Nature Aesthetically." *Journal of Aesthetics and Art Criticism* 56 (1998): 113–125.

———. "Icebreakers: Environmentalism and Natural Aesthetics." *Journal of Applied Philosophy* 11 (1994): 15–30.

———. "Offending Against Nature." *Environmental Values* 7 (1998): 131–150.

———. "Theoretical Options for Environmental Aesthetics." *Journal of Aesthetic Education* 31 (1998): 17–27.

———. "Valuing Nature and the Autonomy of Natural Aesthetics." *British Journal of Aesthetics* 38 (1998): 180–197.

Graham, Gordon. "Architecture." In Jerrold Levinson, ed., *The Oxford Handbook of Aesthetics*, 555–571. Oxford: Oxford University Press, 2002.

Groth, Paul, ed. *Vision, Culture, and Landscape: The Berkeley Symposium on Cultural Landscape Interpretation*. Berkeley: Department of Landscape Architecture, University of California, 1990.

Groth, Paul, and Todd W. Bressi, eds. *Understanding Ordinary Landscapes*. New Haven, Conn.: Yale University Press, 1997.

Haapala, Arto, ed. *The City as Cultural Metaphor: Studies in Urban Aesthetics*. Lahti, Finland: International Institute of Applied Aesthetics, 1998.

Halpern, Daniel, ed. *On Nature: Nature, Landscape, and Natural History*. San Francisco: North Point Press, 1987.

Hargrove, Eugene C. "Carlson and the Aesthetic Appreciation of Nature." *Philosophy and Geography* 5 (2002): 213–223.

———. *Foundations of Environmental Ethics*. Englewood Cliffs, N.J.: Prentice-Hall, 1989.

———. "The Historical Foundations of American Environmental Attitudes." *Environmental Ethics* 1 (1979): 209–240.

Hegel, Georg Wilhelm Friedrich. *Hegel's Aesthetics: Lectures on Fine Arts*. 1835. Translated by T. M. Knox. Oxford: Oxford University Press, 1975.

Helphand, Kenneth I. "Landscape Films." *Landscape Journal* 5 (1986): 1–8.

Hepburn, Ronald W. "Aesthetic and Religious: Boundaries, Overlaps, and Intrusions." In Yrjö Sepänmaa, ed., *Real World Design: The Foundations and Practice of Environmental Aesthetics*, 42–48. Helsinki: University of Helsinki, 1997.

———. "Aesthetic Appreciation of Nature." In Harold Osborne, ed., *Aesthetics and the Modern World*, 49–66. London: Thames and Hudson, 1968.

———. "Contemporary Aesthetics and the Neglect of Natural Beauty." In Bernard Williams and Alan Montefiore, eds., *British Analytical Philosophy*, 285–310. London: Routledge & Kegan Paul, 1966.

———. "Landscape and the Metaphysical Imagination." *Environmental Values* 5 (1996): 191–204.

——. "Restoring the Sacred: Sacred as a Concept of Aesthetics." In Pauline von Bonsdorff and Arto Haapala, eds., *Aesthetics in the Human Environment*, 166–185. Lahti, Finland: International Institute of Applied Aesthetics, 1999.

——. "Trivial and Serious in Aesthetic Appreciation of Nature." In Salim Kemal and Ivan Gaskell, eds., *Landscape, Natural Beauty and the Arts*, 65–80. Cambridge: Cambridge University Press, 1993.

——. *"Wonder" and Other Essays: Eight Studies in Aesthetics and Neighboring Fields.* Edinburgh: Edinburgh University Press, 1984.

Hettinger, Ned. "Carlson's Environmental Aesthetics and the Protection of the Environment." *Environmental Ethics* 27 (2005): 57–76.

——. "Objectivity in Environmental Aesthetics and Protection of the Environment." In Allen Carlson and Sheila Lintott, eds., *Nature, Aesthetics, and Environmentalism: From Beauty to Duty*, 413–437. New York: Columbia University Press, 2008.

Heyd, Thomas. "Aesthetic Appreciation and the Many Stories About Nature." *British Journal of Aesthetics* 41 (2001): 125–137.

Hipple, Walter John, Jr. *The Beautiful, the Sublime, and the Picturesque in Eighteenth-Century British Aesthetic Theory.* Carbondale: Southern Illinois University Press, 1957.

Hoskins, W. G. *The Making of the English Landscape.* London: Hodder & Stoughton, 1955.

Hospers, John. *Meaning and Truth in the Arts.* Chapel Hill: University of North Carolina Press, 1946.

——. *Understanding the Arts.* Englewood Cliffs, N.J.: Prentice-Hall, 1982.

Humphrey, Peter. "The Ethics of Earthworks." *Environmental Ethics* 7 (1985): 5–21.

Hunt, John Dixon. *The Afterlife of Gardens.* Philadelphia: University of Pennsylvania Press, 2004.

——. *Greater Perfections: The Practice of Garden Theory.* Philadelphia: University of Pennsylvania Press, 2000.

Hussey, Christopher. *The Picturesque: Studies in a Point of View.* London: Putnam, 1927.

Hutcheson, Francis. *An Inquiry Concerning Beauty, Order, Harmony, Design.* 1725. Glasgow: Robert and Andrew Foulis, 1772.

Jackson, John Brinckerhoff. *Discovering the Vernacular Landscape.* New Haven, Conn.: Yale University Press, 1984.

——. *Landscapes: Selected Writings of J.B. Jackson.* Edited by Ervin H. Zube. Amherst: University of Massachusetts Press, 1970.

——. *The Necessity for Ruins, and Other Topics.* Amherst: University of Massachusetts Press, 1980.

———. *A Sense of Place, a Sense of Time*. New Haven, Conn.: Yale University Press, 1994.

Jackson, Peter. *London Bridge*. London: Cassell, 1971.

James, William. *The Principles of Psychology*. 1890. Cambridge, Mass.: Harvard University Press, 1981.

Jellicoe, Geoffrey, and Susan Jellicoe. *The Landscape of Man: Shaping the Environment from Prehistory to the Present Day*. London: Thames and Hudson, 1987 .

Kant, Immanuel. *Critique of the Power of Judgment*. 1790. Edited by Paul Guyer. Translated by Paul Guyer and Eric Matthews. Cambridge: Cambridge University Press, 2000.

———. *Observations on the Feeling of the Beautiful and Sublime*. 1764. Translated by John T. Goldthwait. Berkeley: University of California Press, 1960.

Kaplan, Rachel, and Stephen Kaplan. *The Experience of Nature: A Psychological Perspective*. Cambridge: Cambridge University Press, 1989.

Kennick, W. E., ed. *Art and Philosophy: Readings in Aesthetics*. New York: St. Martin's Press, 1964.

Klonk, Charlotte. *Science and the Perception of Nature: British Landscape Art in the Late Eighteenth and Early Nineteenth Centuries*. New Haven, Conn.: Yale University Press, 1996.

Knight, Richard Payne. *Analytical Inquiry into the Principles of Taste*. 1805. Westmead, Eng.: Gregg International, 1972.

———. *The Landscape*. London: Bulmer, 1794.

Korsmeyer, Carolyn. "Delightful, Delicious, Disgusting." *Journal of Aesthetics and Art Criticism* 60 (2002): 217–225.

———. "Food and the Taste of Meaning." In Pauline von Bonsdorff and Arto Haapala, eds., *Aesthetics in the Human Environment*, 90–105. Lahti, Finland: International Institute of Applied Aesthetics, 1999.

———. *Making Sense of Taste: Food and Philosophy*. Ithaca, N.Y.: Cornell University Press, 1999.

Kristeller, Paul Oskar. "The Modern System of the Arts: A Study in the History of Aesthetics I." *Journal of the History of Ideas* 12 (1951): 496–527.

———. "The Modern System of the Arts: A Study in the History of Aesthetics II." *Journal of the History of Ideas* 13 (1952): 17–46.

Kuehn, Glenn "How Can Food Be Art?" In Andrew Light and Jonathan M. Smith, eds., *The Aesthetics of Everyday Life*, 194–212. New York: Columbia University Press, 2005.

Leddy, Thomas. "A Defense of Arts-Based Appreciation of Nature." *Environmental Ethics* 27 (2005): 299–315.

———. "Everyday Surface Qualities: Neat, Messy, Clean, Dirty." *Journal of Aesthetics and Art Criticism* 53 (1995): 259–268.

——. "The Nature of Everyday Aesthetics." In Andrew Light and Jonathan M. Smith, eds., *The Aesthetics of Everyday Life*, 3–22. New York: Columbia University Press, 2005.

Leopold, Aldo. *A Sand County Almanac, with Essays on Conservation from Round River.* New York: Oxford University Press, 1966.

Lewis, Peirce. "Facing Up to Ambiguity." *Landscape* 26 (1982): 18–22.

Lewis, Peirce F., David Lowenthal, and Yi-Fu Tuan, eds. *Visual Blight in America.* Washington, D.C.: Association of American Geographers, 1973.

Light, Andrew, and Jonathan M. Smith, eds. *The Aesthetics of Everyday Life.* New York: Columbia University Press, 2004.

Ligo, Larry L. *The Concept of Function in Twentieth-Century Architectural Criticism.* Ann Arbor: University of Michigan Research Press, 1984.

Lintott, Sheila. "Toward Eco-Friendly Aesthetics." *Environmental Ethics* 28 (2006): 57–76.

Litton, R. Burton, Jr.. *Forest Landscape Description and Inventories: A Basis for Land Planning and Design.* Berkeley, Calif.: Pacific Southwest Forest and Range Experimental Station, 1968.

Lovejoy, Arthur. " 'Nature' as Aesthetic Norm." *Modern Language Notes* 42 (1927): 444–450.

Lynch, Tony. "Deep Ecology as an Aesthetic Movement." *Environmental Values* 5 (1996): 147–160.

Macauley, David. "Walking the City." In Arnold Berleant and Allen Carlson, eds., *The Aesthetics of Human Environments*, 100–118. Peterborough, Ont.: Broadview Press, 2007.

Mannison, Don. "A Prolegomenon to a Human Chauvinistic Aesthetic." In Don S. Mannison, Michael A. McRobbie, and Richard Routley, eds., *Environmental Philosophy*, 212–216. Canberra: Department of Philosophy, Australian National University, 1980.

Margolis, Joseph, ed. *Philosophy Looks at the Arts: Contemporary Readings in Aesthetics.* New York: Scribner, 1962.

Marsh, George Perkins. *Man and Nature.* 1864. Cambridge, Mass.: Harvard University Press, 1965.

Matthews, Patricia. "Scientific Knowledge and the Aesthetic Appreciation of Nature." *Journal of Aesthetics and Art Criticism* 60 (2002): 37–48.

Meinig, Donald W., ed. *The Interpretation of Ordinary Landscapes: Geographical Essays.* New York: Oxford University Press, 1979.

Melchionne, Kevin. "Front Yards." In Arnold Berleant, ed., *Environment and the Arts: Perspectives on Environmental Aesthetics*, 103–111. Aldershot, Eng.: Ashgate, 2002.

——. "Living in Glass Houses: Domesticity, Interior Decoration, and Environmental Aesthetics." *Journal of Aesthetics and Art Criticism* 56 (1998): 191–200.

Miller, Mara. *The Garden as Art*. Albany: State University of New York Press, 1993.

Momaday, N. Scott. *The Way to Rainy Mountain*. Albuquerque: University of New Mexico Press, 1969.

Moore, Ronald. "Appreciating Natural Beauty as Natural." *Journal of Aesthetic Education* 33 (1999): 42–59.

——. *Natural Beauty: A Theory of Aesthetics Beyond the Arts*. Peterborough, Ont.: Broadview Press, 2007.

Muir, John. *The Mountains of California*. New York: Century, 1894.

——. *Our National Parks*. Boston: Houghton Mifflin, 1916.

——. *A Thousand-Mile Walk to the Gulf*. Boston: Houghton Mifflin, 1916.

——. *The Wilderness World of John Muir*. Edited by Edwin Way Teale. Boston: Houghton Mifflin, 1954.

Mumford, Lewis. *The Brown Decades: A Study of the Arts in America, 1865–1895*. New York: Harcourt, Brace, 1931.

Nasar, Jack L., ed. *Environmental Aesthetics: Theory, Research, and Applications*. Cambridge: Cambridge University Press, 1988.

Nassauer, Joan Iverson. "Cultural Sustainability: Aligning Aesthetics and Ecology." In Joan Iverson Nassauer, ed., *Placing Nature: Culture and Landscape Ecology*, 65–84. Washington D.C.: Island Press, 1997.

——. "Culture and Landscape Ecology: Insights for Action." In Joan Iverson Nassauer, ed., *Placing Nature: Culture and Landscape Ecology*, 1–11. Washington, D.C.: Island Press, 1997.

——, ed. *Placing Nature: Culture and Landscape Ecology*. Washington, D.C.: Island Press, 1997.

Nicolson, Marjory Hope. *Mountain Gloom and Mountain Glory: The Development of the Aesthetics of the Infinite*. Ithaca, N.Y.: Cornell University Press, 1959.

Norton, Stephen L. *Devils Tower: The Story Behind the Scenery*. Las Vegas: KC Publications, 1991.

Ogden, John T. "From Spatial to Aesthetic Distance in the Eighteenth Century." *Journal of the History of Ideas* 35 (1974): 63–78.

Orians, Gordon H., and Judith H. Heerwagen. "An Ecological and Evolutionary Approach to Landscape Aesthetics." In Edmund C. Penning-Rowsell and David Lowenthal, eds., *Landscape Meanings and Values*, 3–25. London: Allen and Unwin, 1986.

——. "Evolved Responses to Landscapes." In Jerome H. Barkow, Leda Cosmides, and John Tooby, eds., *The Adapted Mind: Evolutionary Psychology and the Generation of Culture*, 555–579. New York: Oxford University Press, 1992.

——. "Humans, Habitats, and Aesthetics." In Stephen R. Kellert and Edward O. Wilson, eds., *The Biophilia Hypothesis*, 138–172. Washington, D.C.: Island Press, 1993.

Osborne, Harold. *Aesthetics and Art Theory: An Historical Introduction.* New York: Dutton, 1980.

——. "The Use of Nature in Art." *British Journal of Aesthetics* 2 (1962): 318–327.

Parsons, Glenn. *Aesthetics and Nature.* London: Continuum, 2008.

——. "Freedom and Objectivity in the Aesthetic Appreciation of Nature." *British Journal of Aesthetics* 46 (2006): 17–37.

——. "Natural Functions and the Aesthetic Appreciation of Inorganic Nature." *British Journal of Aesthetics* 44 (2004): 44–56.

——. "Nature Appreciation, Science, and Positive Aesthetics." *British Journal of Aesthetics* 42 (2002): 279–295.

——. "Theory, Observation, and the Role of Scientific Understanding in the Aesthetic Appreciation of Nature." *Canadian Journal of Philosophy* 36 (2006): 165–186.

Parsons, Glenn, and Allen Carlson. *Functional Beauty.* Oxford: Oxford University Press, 2008.

——. "New Formalism and the Aesthetic Appreciation of Nature." *Journal of Aesthetics and Art Criticism* 62 (2004): 363–376.

Penning-Rowsell, Edmund C., and David Lowenthal, eds. *Landscape Meanings and Values.* London: Allen and Unwin, 1986.

Pollan, Michael. *Second Nature: A Gardener's Education.* New York: Dell, 1991.

Porteous, J. Douglas. *Environmental Aesthetics: Ideas, Politics and Planning.* London: Routledge, 1996.

Prall, D. W. *Aesthetic Judgment.* New York: Crowell, 1929.

Price, Uvedale. *An Essay on the Picturesque.* London: Robson, 1794.

Rees, Ronald. "The Scenery Cult: Changing Landscape Tastes over Three Centuries." *Landscape* 19 (1975): 39–47.

——. "The Taste for Mountain Scenery." *History Today* 25 (1975): 305–312.

Rhodes, Frank H. T., and Richard O. Stone, eds. *Language of the Earth.* New York: Pergamon Press, 1981.

Rolston, Holmes, III. "Aesthetic Experience in Forests." *Journal of Aesthetics and Art Criticism* 56 (1998): 157–166.

——. "Aesthetics in the Swamps." *Perspectives in Biology and Medicine* 43 (2000): 584–597.

——. "Does Aesthetic Appreciation of Nature Need to Be Science Based?" *British Journal of Aesthetics* 35 (1995): 374–386.

——. *Environmental Ethics: Duties to and Values in the Natural World.* Philadelphia: Temple University Press, 1988.

——. "From Beauty to Duty: Aesthetics of Nature and Environmental Ethics." In Arnold Berleant, ed., *Environment and the Arts: Perspectives on Environmental Aesthetics,* 127–141. Aldershot, Eng.: Ashgate, 2002.

Ross, Stephanie. "Environmental Aesthetics." In Donald M. Borchert, ed., *The Encyclopedia of Philosophy*, 3:254–258. 2nd ed. New York: Macmillan, 2006.

——. "Gardens, Earthworks, and Environmental Art." In Salim Kemal and Ivan Gaskell, eds., *Landscape, Natural Beauty and the Arts*, 158–182. Cambridge: Cambridge University Press, 1993.

——. "Landscape Perception: Theory-Laden, Emotionally Resonant, Politically Correct." *Environmental Ethics* 27 (2005): 245–263.

——. *What Gardens Mean*. Chicago: University of Chicago Press, 1998.

Saarinen, Thomas F., David Seamon, and James L. Sell, eds. *Environmental Perception and Behavior: An Inventory and Prospect*. Chicago: Department of Geography, University of Chicago, 1984.

Sadler, Barry, and Allen Carlson, eds. *Environmental Aesthetics: Essays in Interpretation*. Victoria, B.C.: Department of Geography, University of Victoria, 1982.

Sagoff, Mark. "On Preserving the Natural Environment." *Yale Law Journal* 84 (1974): 205–267.

Saito, Yuriko. "The Aesthetics of Unscenic Nature." *Journal of Aesthetics and Art Criticism* 56 (1998): 101–111.

——. "Appreciating Nature on Its Own Terms." *Environmental Ethics* 20 (1998): 135–149.

——. "Ecological Design: Promises and Challenges." *Environmental Ethics* 24 (2002): 243–261.

——. "Environmental Directions for Aesthetics and the Arts." In Arnold Berleant, ed., *Environment and the Arts: Perspectives on Environmental Aesthetics*, 171–185. Aldershot, Eng.: Ashgate, 2002.

——. *Everyday Aesthetics*. Oxford: Oxford University Press, 2008.

——. "Everyday Aesthetics." *Philosophy and Literature* 25 (2001): 87–95.

——. "Is There a Correct Aesthetic Appreciation of Nature?" *Journal of Aesthetic Education* 18 (1984): 35–46.

——. "The Japanese Appreciation of Nature." *British Journal of Aesthetics* 25 (1985): 239–251.

——. "The Japanese Love of Nature: A Paradox." *Landscape* 31 (1991): 1–8.

——. "The Role of Aesthetics in Civic Environmentalism." In Arnold Berleant and Allen Carlson, eds., *The Aesthetics of Human Environments*, 203–218. Peterborough, Ont.: Broadview Press, 2007.

Santayana, George. *The Sense of Beauty: Being the Outline of Aesthetic Theory*. 1896. New York: Collier, 1961.

Savile, Anthony. *The Test of Time: An Essay in Philosophical Aesthetics*. Oxford: Oxford University Press, 1982.

Schopenhauer, Arthur. *The World as Will and Representation*. 1844. 2 vols. Translated by E. F. J. Payne. New York: Dover, 1966.

Scott, David, and Alden P. Armagnac. "London Bridge Comes to America." *Popular Science*, September 1968, 68–71.

Scruton, Roger. *The Aesthetics of Architecture*. Princeton, N.J.: Princeton University Press, 1979.

Sell, James L., Jonathan G. Taylor, and Ervin H. Zube. "Landscape Perception: Research, Application and Theory." *Landscape Planning* 9 (1982): 1–33.

——. "Toward a Theoretical Framework for Landscape Perception." In Thomas E. Saarinen, David Seamon, and James L. Sell, eds., *Environmental Perception and Behavior: An Inventory and Prospect*, 61–83. Chicago: Department of Geography, University of Chicago, 1984.

Sepänmaa, Yrjö. *The Beauty of Environment: A General Model for Environmental Aesthetics*. 2nd ed. Denton, Tex.: Environmental Ethics Books, 1993.

——. "Environmental Aesthetics." In Robert Paehlke, ed., *Conservation and Environmentalism: An Encyclopedia*, 221–223. New York: Garland, 1995.

Shafer, Elwood L., Jr., and James Mietz. *It Seems Possible to Quantify Scenic Beauty in Photographs*. Upper Darby, Pa.: Northeastern Forest Experiment Station, 1970.

Shepard, Paul. *Man in the Landscape: A Historic View of the Esthetics of Nature*. New York: Knopf, 1967.

——. *The Tender Carnivore and the Sacred Game*. New York: Scribner, 1973.

Sheppard, Stephen R. J., and Howard W. Harshaw, eds. *Forests and Landscapes: Linking Ecology, Sustainability, and Aesthetics*. New York: CAB International, 2001.

Sibley, Frank. "Aesthetic Concepts." *Philosophical Review* 68 (1959): 421–450.

Sitney, P. Adams. "Landscape in the Cinema: The Rhythms of the World and the Camera." In Salim Kemal and Ivan Gaskell, eds., *Landscape, Natural Beauty and the Arts*, 103–126. Cambridge: Cambridge University Press, 1993.

Smith, Ralph A., and Christiana M. Smith. "Aesthetics and Environmental Education." *Journal of Aesthetic Education* 4 (1970): 125–140.

Sonfist, Alan, ed. *Art in the Land: A Critical Anthology of Environmental Art*. New York: Dutton, 1983.

Sparshott, Francis E. "Figuring the Ground: Notes on Some Theoretical Problems of the Aesthetic Environment." *Journal of Aesthetic Education* 6 (1972): 11–23.

Stecker, Robert. "The Correct and the Appropriate in the Appreciation of Nature." *British Journal of Aesthetics* 37 (1997): 393–402.

——. "Reflections on Architecture: Buildings as Artworks, Aesthetic Objects, and Artificial Environments." In Michael Mitias, ed., *Architecture and Civilization*, 81–93. Amsterdam: Rodopi, 1999.

Stolnitz, Jerome. *Aesthetics and the Philosophy of Art Criticism: A Critical Introduction*. Boston: Houghton Mifflin, 1960.

——. "On the Origins of 'Aesthetic Disinterestedness.'" *Journal of Aesthetics and Art Criticism* 20 (1961): 131–143.

Sullivan, Louis. "The Tall Office Building Artistically Considered." 1918. In *Kindergarten Chats and Other Writings*, 202–213. New York: Dover, 1979.

Terres, John K., ed. *Discovery: Great Moments in the Lives of Outstanding Naturalists*. New York: Lippincott, 1961.

Terrie, Philip G. "John Muir on Mount Ritter: A New Wilderness Aesthetic." *Pacific Historian* 31 (1987): 135–144.

Thompson, Janna. "Aesthetics and the Value of Nature." *Environmental Ethics* 17 (1995): 291–305.

Thoreau, Henry David. *The Works of Thoreau*. Edited by Henry Seidel Canby. Boston: Houghton Mifflin, 1937.

Townsend, Dabney. "The Picturesque." *Journal of Aesthetics and Art Criticism* 55 (1997): 365–376.

Trimble, Stephen, ed. *Words from the Land: Encounters with Natural History Writing*. Salt Lake City: Smith, 1988.

Tuan, Yi-Fu. *Passing Strange and Wonderful: Aesthetics, Nature, and Culture*. Washington, D.C.: Island Press, 1993.

——. *Space and Place: The Perspective of Experience*. Minneapolis: University of Minnesota Press, 1977.

——. *Topophilia: A Study of Environmental Perception, Attitudes, and Values*. Englewood Cliffs, N.J.: Prentice-Hall, 1974.

Tunnard, Christopher, and Boris Pushkarev. *Man-Made America: Chaos or Control? An Inquiry into Selected Problems of Design in the Urbanized Landscape*. New Haven, Conn.: Yale University Press, 1963.

United States Department of Agriculture, Forest Service. *National Forest Landscape Management*. Vol. 1. Washington, D.C.: Government Printing Office, 1972.

United States Department of the Interior. *Devils Tower*. Washington, D.C.: Government Printing Office, 1991.

von Bonsdorff, Pauline. "Urban Richness and the Art of Building." In Arnold Berleant and Allen Carlson, eds., *The Aesthetics of Human Environments*, 57–68. Peterborough, Ont.: Broadview Press, 2007.

von Bonsdorff, Pauline, and Arto Haapala, eds. *Aesthetics in the Human Environment*. Lahti, Finland: International Institute of Applied Aesthetics, 1999.

Walton, Kendall. "Categories of Art." *Philosophical Review* 79 (1970): 334–367.

Watts, May Theilgaard. *Reading the Landscape of America*. 1957. New York: Collier, 1975.

Welsch, Wolfgang. "Sport Viewed Aesthetically, and Even as Art?" In Andrew Light and Jonathan M. Smith, eds., *The Aesthetics of Everyday Life*, 135–155. New York: Columbia University Press, 2005.

Winters, Edward. "Architecture." In Berys Gaut and Dominic McIver Lopes, eds., *The Routledge Companion to Aesthetics*, 655–668. 2nd ed. London: Routledge, 2005.

Wittgenstein, Ludwig . *Philosophical Investigations*. Translated by G.E.M. Anscombe. Oxford: Blackwell, 1958.

Wright, Frank Lloyd. "In the Cause of Architecture." 1908. In *Frank Lloyd Wright on Architecture: Selected Writings, 1894–1940*, 29–81. Edited by Frederick Gutheim. New York: Duell, Sloan and Pearce, 1941.

Zangwill, Nick. "Formal Natural Beauty." *Proceedings of the Aristotelian Society* 101 (2001): 209–224.

——. "In Defence of Extreme Formalism About Inorganic Nature: Reply to Parsons." *British Journal of Aesthetics* 45 (2005): 185–191.

——. *The Metaphysics of Beauty*. Ithaca, N.Y.: Cornell University Press, 2001.

Ziff, Paul. *Antiaesthetics: An Appreciation of the Cow with the Subtile Nose*. Dordrecht: Reidel, 1984.

——. "Anything Viewed." In Esa Saarinen, Risto Hilpinen, Ilkka Niiniluoto, and Merrill B. Provence Hintikka, eds., *Essays in Honour of Jaakko Hintikka on the Occasion of His Fiftieth Birthday on January 12, 1979*, 285–293. Dordrecht: Reidel, 1979.

——. "Reasons in Art Criticism." In *Philosophical Turnings: Essays in Conceptual Appreciation*, 47–74. Ithaca, N.Y.: Cornell University Press, 1966.

Zube, Ervin H. "Themes in Landscape Assessment Theory." *Landscape Journal* 3 (1984): 104–110.

Zube, Ervin H., James L. Sell, and Jonathan G. Taylor. "Landscape Perception: Research, Application and Theory." *Landscape Planning* 9 (1982): 1–33.

Leopold, Aldo, 93, 97–98, 113, 145n.23; and ecological aesthetic, 19

Lewis, Peirce, 103, 107

life values of objects: in agricultural landscapes, 99–103; and expressive beauty, 98–99; in human environments, 66–67; and objectivity, 152n.27; and sustainability, 101–103

London Bridge: in Lake Havasu City, 69–70, 71; in London, 69, 70

Lopez, Berry, 113

Lorrain, Claude, 27

Lovejoy, Arthur, 7

Making of the English Landscape, The (Hoskins), 115

Mannison, Don, 39–40. *See also* Human Chauvinistic Aesthetic

Marsh, George Perkins, 5–6

Mateo Tepee, 118–120; 121, 122, 123, 124. *See also* Devils Tower

Michelangelo, 117

Mickey Mouse, 115

Mont-Saint-Victoire, 120, 122, 124

Muir, John, 6, 35, 113, 146n.25

musical compositions, 66

mystery model of aesthetics (Godlovitch), 13, 18, 40

mythology: and environmental aesthetics, 12, 15, 137n.59; and landscape appreciation, 118–120, 125–127, 159n.25

Nassauer, Joan, 56–57

natural disasters, Muir on beauty of, 6

natural environment, interlocking ecosystems in, 58

Natural Environmental Model: as adequate aesthetics of nature, 38, 50–51; and applied aesthetics, 35; common sense and scientific knowledge in, 33–36; and functional fit, 59; and human environments, 79; for nature appreciation, 11–12, 31–34, 103, 113; objectivity in, 35–36; and positive aesthetics, 19, 35; ramifications of, 34–37; as rejection of art-based approaches, 36. *See also* scientific cognitivism

natural objects, 24–26. *See also* life values of objects

natural sciences: influence of, on nature appreciation in nineteenth century, 5; and Natural Environmental Model, 11–12, 18–19, 34, 36; and nature appreciation, 11–12, 79, 103, 112–113

nature appreciation: Aesthetics of Engagement in, 30–31; anthropocentrism in, 18, 28, 35–36; Anything Viewed Doctrine of, 9, 39–40, 94, 104; artistic approaches to, 8–9, 24–28, 29; As Nature Constraint for, 9, 12, 40–42, 56, 86, 104, 110, 127, 147n.11; boundaries and foci in, 31–33; cognitive models of, 11–12, 14–15, 135n.44; in early twentieth century, 7; freedom approach to, 12, 44, 47–48, 148n.22; and functional fit, 58–59; Human Chauvinistic Aesthetic in, 29, 30–31, 32, 34, 39–40; Natural Environmental Model for, 11–12, 31–34; as nature, 11–12, 29, 40–42, 104, 144n.13, 147n.11; nonaesthetic approach to, 8–9, 29, 39–40, 144n.13; noncognitive models of, 11, 12–14, 15–16, 46, 48, 135n.44; in North America, 5–6; Objectivity Desideratum for,